INSTINCTIVE SHOOTING

INSTINCTIVE SHOOTING

THE MAKING OF A MASTER GUNNER

BY **BUZ FAWCETT**

EDITED BY **MARC C. PATOILE**

ILLUSTRATED BY **RUSSELL LAWS**

FOREWORD BY **JAY CASSELL**

Skyhorse Publishing

Skyhorse Publishing books may be purchased in bulk at special discounts for sales promotion, corporate gifts, fund-raising, or educational purposes. Special editions can also be created to specifications. For details, contact the Special Sales Department, Skyhorse Publishing, 307 West 36th Street, 11th Floor, New York, NY 10018 or info@skyhorsepublishing.com.

Skyhorse® and Skyhorse Publishing® are registered trademarks of Skyhorse Publishing, Inc.®, a Delaware corporation.

Visit our website at www.skyhorsepublishing.com.

10 9 8 7 6 5 4 3 2 1

Library of Congress Cataloging-in-Publication Data is available on file.

Cover design by Tom Lau
Cover image credit: Russell Laws

Print ISBN: 978-1-5107-4273-4
Ebook ISBN: 978-1-5107-4277-2

Printed in China

CONTENTS »

FOREWORD »

BY JAY CASSELL

Not long ago, I had the opportunity to go on a preserve hunt in upstate New York. It was a cold day, in the 30s, with gusty winds. I was hunting with a friend, Michael, and a dog handler who had two English spaniels with him. The plan was to run one dog for perhaps an hour, then switch them out so dog No. 1 could rest and dog No. 2 would get to work off his energy. I was carrying my little Browning 20-gauge—a gun I can shoot well with . . . or not.

We were hunting selectively cut sorghum fields, with some rows cut almost to the ground and others left standing at about fifteen inches. The terrain was rolling, with patches of ice and snow making the walking a challenge. Two days earlier, a party of twelve hunters had worked these fields, going mostly for pheasants. Almost four hundred birds had been put out; one hundred eighty were shot. And while many of the birds had flown back toward their netted pens— the safe zone—there were still plenty of ringnecks out in the fields. There were also chukars all over the place.

To make a long story short, I hit almost every pheasant I shot at—though I did miss one that got up practically under my feet. And I missed every chukar I shot at—which was probably half a dozen.

I hit some kind of a mental wall with the fast, erratically flying little birds, and it drove me crazy.

The next day, back at home, I went to my bookshelf and picked up a copy of *Instinctive Shooting* and reread it. Written by Buz Fawcett, who knows a thing or two about shotgun shooting—especially with side-by-sides—the book espouses that you need to envision the shot before you take it. You shouldn't even be aware of the barrel. I hadn't been doing that—nor had I been pointing the gun the way I should have. Nor had my footing been consistent. The worse part was that I let my ego get in the way—I wanted to shoot well in front of my colleague Michael. All told, I did as many things wrong as I could have. I wasn't fluid, my process of shooting was inconsistent, and I missed birds I should have knocked down. As Buz notes, "The instinctive shot begins when the master eye first perceives the target. Not, as some believe, when the gun is mounted. By then, the shot is almost over." Isn't that the truth!

Buz's book brought me back to reality, made me think about what I should have done. It brought my confidence back. So whether you need a refresher, or if you are just starting out shotgunning and want to get off on the right foot, *Instinctive Shooting* is a good place to start—it's right up there with other solid shotgunning books by the likes Churchill, Jennings, and McDaniels. Especially if you like side-by-sides, this book is for you.

Jay Cassell has hunted all over North America. He has written for Field & Stream, Sports Afield, Outdoor Life, Petersen's Hunting, Time, *and many other publications and has published numerous books. He lives in Katonah, New York.*

INTRODUCTION »

Take Heart. It Happened to Me, Too

When I was a kid, I was a great shot. Really! By the time I was fourteen or so, I had won a number of High Gun awards at local trap clubs. On Sundays, while other youngsters were receiving the benefits of catechism and the Gospel, I was learning the lore of the gun.

My dad was so proud that he awarded me my grandfather's Model 1912 Winchester. It was the same firearm that Captain Billy had used as captain of the 1924 Olympic trap team.

Captain Billy Fawcett was the Founder of Fawcett Publications, which published *Whiz Bang*, a racy pocket-sized publication designed to fit the pocket of a WWI doughboy's tunic. The company went on to publish such notable magazines as *True, The Man's Magazine* and *Mechanics Illustrated*, to name but two of many.

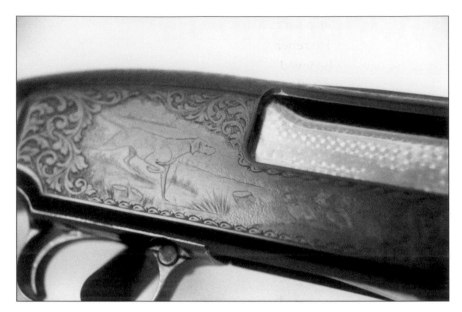

My grandfather's singles trap gun was a lovely Winchester Model 1912. It originally was a field gun, but over the years it had gradually been transformed into a trap model.

That Model 12 was, and still is, a lovely firearm. It had been manufactured in 1919 and tastefully engraved, apparently as a field gun. Later, its 30-inch barrel had been crowned by a Simmons ventilated rib. In deference to my size, Captain Billy's stock had been removed by my father and a truncated Model 12 stock was installed. In spite of the fact that it kicked the whey out of me every time I used it, I shot it successfully until my shooting was visited by what I called the "Dark Ages." My brilliance with a shotgun didn't last.

In the beginning, Dad had told me, "Here, point this at the target and pull the trigger." In those earliest of days, I was using a sort of single shot 16-gauge, similar to those that every well-meaning father gives to an offspring in the hopes that, by some miracle, the youngster will overcome the deficiencies of design that the father had struggled with when *his* father gave him a gun just like it. I couldn't overcome it, and the results were predictable.

In an attempt to change those results, Dad dug around in his gun cabinet and came up with a lovely .410 Ithaca side-by-side. We went forth with some sort of a little ground trap and tiny targets called mosquitoes. He repeated his famous instructions, "Here, point and shoot." Since I believed everything he told me, I did as instructed and, before long, the little targets were exploding with satisfying regularity. I simply pointed at the target and pulled the trigger.

When I graduated to trap, I again inherited Captain Billy's Model 12. It didn't fit me very well. But, my God, how that gun kicked. It took me 'til Thursday or Friday each week, before the bruising achieved an ugly yellow-green, which I came to consider as preparation for Sunday's weekly beating.

Years later, I look back with wonderment at the vicious pounding I gladly took. Especially in light of my recent discovery that Captain Billy's Model 12 had a 2 9/16-inch chamber. Oh, I know, all Model 12, 12-gauges are supposed to have 2 3/4-inch chambers (easily verified by *The Winchester Model Twelve* by George Madis), but this one, made in 1919, had the shorter chambers to accommodate the old, roll-crimp shells.

Gradually, I overcame some of the weekly bruising by padding both myself and the gun. At the time, I figured looking like the victim of child abuse was simply the price one paid to achieve championship caliber.

I haven't shot that gun in decades. Self-inflicted pain isn't one of my vices. But recently, I took it in to have it refurbished as a family heirloom.

"Did you know this has a short chamber?" the gunsmith asked. My jaw fell open.

"You're kidding!"

"Nope, look it here." He'd removed the barrel and dropped a chamber gauge into it. "Musta kicked like hell," he observed.

Musta indeed. Instead of the nominal eight to ten thousand pounds of chamber pressure, I was being whacked by a hell of a lot more than that. But the relative abuse the gun rendered had little to do with the evil times of the "Dark Ages" that had begun to dawn on me.

The "Dark Ages" began when my dream of a lifetime was realized. I was hired as associate editor of *Sports Afield* magazine in New York. The rare benefit of this position was that I was invited for shooting at various get-togethers held by manufacturers for members of the outdoor media. Unfortunately, at the same time, I was fulfilling the duties of an associate editor—editing, lots of editing. And the "Dark Ages" crept into my life like fungus invading a host.

You see, the problem with editing is this: you are also required to read all of the copy that you are editing. Sure, every now and then an article about shooting shotguns would crop up. Unfortunately, few of them bore any resemblance to my father's sage instructions of, "Just point and shoot." And, so I read. And, little by little, the garbage that those writers were touting seeped in. Sustained Lead was very popular back then. Shortly, it was followed by Swing Through and its henchman, Pull Away. My final fall from grace into the "Dark Ages" came when I saw an infamous chart published by someone on leads. You probably remember it too. It has a series of ducks flying, together with a "calculation" of the exact amount of lead necessary to hit them when they are flying at so many miles per hour. I realized immediately that trying to calculate which technique to use on what kind of target, flying at some speed or another, made successfully shooting a shotgun damned near impossible. And, my shooting began to suffer—a lot.

Luckily, there was one event that helped to bring my shooting career out of the "Dark Ages." I met Ad Topperwein. Ad was a legendary demonstration shooter (or what we used to call a "trick shot"). I met Ad at a function for outdoor writers and was amazed at his ability with a firearm. This led me to Herb Parsons, who was another demonstration shooter for Winchester. Luckily, Herb had made a motion picture that featured his son, twelve-year-old Fred. Herb's motion picture simply tantalized me. Herb was a Tennessean who shot for Winchester for many years, and he was just not doing what the sage tomes were hyping in the pages of *Sports Afield*: "Keep your head down, swing, and follow through." He was doing something altogether different.

By the time I moved on to *Guns & Ammo* in Hollywood, California, as a short-termed Editor, I had lost all semblance of proficiency with a shotgun. Finally, I quit shotgunning altogether. The only good aspect was that the short-chambered Model 12 was no longer kicking the whey out of me, since I wasn't shooting at all.

These "Dark Ages" stayed with me through my eventual move to Minnesota, where I was working as a writing instructor. But since shooting, in my family, is genetic, some shooting began to creep back into my life, first with muzzleloaders and then with a smattering of pumps, semiautos, and finally over-and-unders. By this time, my shooting had improved but a little. And, then the crash occurred, which took me to the bottom of the pit of darkness. In an effort to overcome my malaise, I sought help from Mike Schmidt, then manager of the Minneapolis Gun Club, where my grandfather, Captain Billy, had held some sway a long time before.

At the time, my guns were a Browning 12-gauge with a straight stock and a 20-gauge with the same configuration. I was buoyed by a slight improvement in my results, so I had sought out Mike to see if I could continue this slight upward swing.

Mike watched me for a couple of minutes. "Buz," he said, with a well-meaning tone in his voice, "you should really learn how to shoot."

I was devastated. I felt like an alcoholic must feel when finally confronted with the sorry state of his life at the bottom, just moments before that first call to Alcoholics Anonymous. Only for shooters, there was no AA. At least, not one I knew of or could afford. And certainly not one that would attempt to teach me anything but the same techniques I was already using, and failing with.

The Turning Point

Northern Wisconsin is replete with grouse. I had missed aplenty of grouse shots, but since there was no one around when I hunted them, I felt no sense of shame. My only feeling was a quiet satisfaction with the lovely turning of the leaves and the rocketing birds.

Suddenly, behind me, there was a particularly load roar of wings. In the covert I was hunting, the cover wasn't dense, it was absolute. To my right, high, was a blur of movement; brown body, rocketing from aspen glow to dark pine gloom. A second roar, there was the bark of a shotgun. What happened? The gun hung limply in my arms. I opened it. A single shell arced through the stillness and fell, muffled by the damp leaves. A rapid ruffle of wing beats drew me to a secluded glen in the pines nearby. There, fluttering a final tattoo, lay the most mystical of all creatures in the upland gunner's life—a mature adult grouse—the drummer-of-the-woods; the solitary, shy, elusive male who had survived many seasons of predatory pressure. A moment of elation, a moment of sadness, and the wonderment of it all. But, how? What had happened? In that instant, I knew I had found a calling—to replicate that perfect shot.

The Road to Glory

Well, not exactly. In the best-told stories, after that glorious moment of revelation the hero, face filled with resolve and a shine of enlightenment, rises from the mire and steadily climbs the heights, while a heavenly choir sings hosannas.

In the first place, while I had a hint as to the destination, I had no idea how to get there. I knew I wanted to replicate that miraculous shot. But I wasn't quite sure exactly what *that* shot was or where it came from. I only knew I wanted to feel it again—that wonderful feeling of wonderment and glory. But how?

Struggling to find out, at least, what I had experienced, I bought books, films (in those days, 16mm), and eventually, as they became available, tapes. I found that what I was looking for was apparently an elusive thing called "Instinctive Shooting." There were all manner of practitioners: Ad, of course, and Herb; but there were others. Annie Oakley had taught women for a time in England. Robert Churchill, an Englishman, advocated a technique which looked suspiciously like that which Annie taught in England before her return to America. Churchill, however, seemed to replace the free-flowing style of Ms. Oakley with the more stilted moves of the military. Over on this side of the pond, an itinerant shooting instructor, Lucky McDaniel, took to the roads of the United States, and, for a few bucks here and there, taught children and adults how to shoot washers and aspirin tablets, among other things, out of the air with a BB gun. His grand finale was to throw a BB in the air and have a kid he had just taught to hold a gun an hour before, shoot it with another BB from the rifle.

But even more of my discoveries came from some related activities. Archery was a big contributor. Howard Hill was my hero as a kid. I would sit mesmerized in a darkened theater watching the archery master perform seemingly impossible tasks with the bow and arrow. I read everything I could on tennis, baseball, handball, and, in fact, any activity where someone was required to hit something on the move.

Gradually, I learned it wasn't the *hitting* the object that was the problem. It was how one first *looks* at the object *before* the strike. How does a *predator* look at its intended prey?

Later, I started teaching shotgunning classes based upon this method of instinctive shooting, which I had melded from a variety of sources and coupled with my own experience of what worked and what didn't work with modern side-by-side shotguns. I began to become a predator, instead of the prey of Captain Billy's Model 12. But, discovering how a predator *really* looks at prey wasn't without its own failures.

I can remember an awful moment when, after I'd been teaching for a couple of years, two of my graduates asked me to go dove hunting. Well, I had used my new technique extensively on targets but, at that time, I had little experience with instinctive shotgunning on game. The first day was a disaster. Walking into the dove field with my students, I hit the very first bird, and not a single one thereafter. Again, devastation!

That night on the phone with my wife, I whined, "It's no good, it won't work—I can't hit a damned thing. All this work and I haven't learned a damn thing."

"Okay," she said without the slightest hesitation, "get out there and do what you'd tell one of your students to do in that situation, or else sell the damn guns and get a real job."

That night, I revisualized the entire day. This revisualization is a process which eventually became a method in my school and, later, also became part of most every college and professional sports coaching program as well, at least in some way or another. Anyway, visualization was new to me at the time and something I discovered by chance. Just as I was falling asleep, I replayed the hunt over and over again. It became quite clear that I was more interested in appearing to my graduates as a dazzling shot—worthy of the shooting instructor that I'd become in my own mind—than I was in simply following the technique as it then existed. My ego was interfering with my predator.

The following day I went nearly one-for-one, expending twelve shells for ten birds. It became clear—in instinctive shooting, it's the process that's important—not the result. More simply put, the technique is everything. It is the lion's anticipation of the charge, the bird dog's intensity on point, and the cat's laser-like focus before the leap. Breaking the target or hitting the bird is simply quiet applause signaling success. It is the anticlimax signaling the end of the game.

Once you are certain of hitting each and every target, *how* you hit them (rather than how many you hit) becomes the fascination.

Sherlock Holmes put it best: "Ah-ha, Watson. The game's afoot."

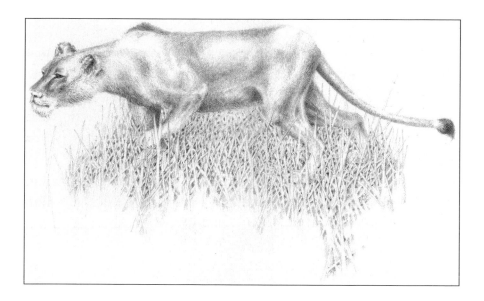

THE PREDATOR

The Early Years

As a youngster, I was fascinated by the food-gathering tools of early people. I hesitate to call them "primitive people," because they were on the cutting edge of technology, *during the times in which they lived*.

The first high-tech scientist made *the most* significant discovery. He found that instead of grabbing those pesky small lizards with his bare hands, he could catch them more easily by stunning them first with a stick. He had made a valuable contribution to the future of mankind. He was the very first to find that he became a more efficient hunter by **EXTENDING THE REACH OF HIS ARMS**.

Unlike his fellow predators, early man was comparatively slow afoot. Prey was limited to man's running speed, and even then, man doesn't bend well enough to grasp at a gallop. So whacking with a branch was a significant discovery.

The sharpened branch was a natural evolution and hitting gave way to piercing. But somewhere in there, amidst the biffing and jabbing, the real advancement took place. In an instant, the first guided missile scientist was created. Somebody threw a rock.

Rock throwing worked well, but it wasn't until the first guidance officer was created that man took his first significant steps toward instinctive shooting.

On this auspicious day, a brilliant experimenter learned that if you first *point* at a lizard, the rock can be hurled with eerie accuracy. From then on, pointing was in.

The sharpened stick was then hurled by hand. Its speed was eventually increased through the use of an atlatl, a throwing stick. The speed was trebled by the bow. Bows and arrows were, and still are, absolutely deadly in the hands of an experienced instinctive archer.

Take a moment to reflect that there is almost no difference between the stance of

One animal, Homo sapiens, *is slow and has a relatively short tongue. But it has learned to launch its food-gathering tools with deadly accuracy.*

the instinctive archer and the more common shotgunning stance. Indeed the stance we know as the "rifleman's stance," the one most commonly used by shotgunners, can be traced directly back to archery.

As a youngster, I wasn't allowed to use the various examples of early food-gathering tools found around my father's study— he was an amateur anthropologist and archeologist. But it didn't take much imagination when the originals were close at hand for an inventive youngster to create his own tools. And thereby an enigma was created. When left to my own devices, alone in the woods and fields around our home, I was absolutely deadly with spear or bow or even slingshot. (Though, frankly, I never mastered the traditional sling of Goliath fame.) But when my father finally agreed to watch my feats of accuracy, the abilities fled from my spears and bows and slingshots. It was a devastating blow I couldn't hit a thing.

It was almost as if there was two of me: one who prowled the outback in search of prey, and one who attempted to communicate theses feats to my father.

It wasn't until many years later, while developing the technique which I currently teach, and the subject of this book, that I was able to resolve the enigma.

And lest you think I'm lapsing into some kind of mysticism, let me assure you, you've probably experienced the same sensation.

If you're a hunter, and I assume you've done some hunting, you've probably experienced a wild flush. A pheasant or grouse lets you pass, then explodes into violent flight. Your head turns. You see the bird. Suddenly, it's as if you're underwater. Everything shifts into slow motion. People in a high-speed car crash often experience the same sensation. Even though you seem mired in sand and move slowly, you do move. Every flap of the bird's wings is frozen in time. It's a pheasant. Its red facial feathers are vivid, like scales on a fish. From somewhere comes a shot. It's dim and far off. Someone else shot your bird. It is falling. It hits the ground. You come out of slow motion. About here you realize a shell has been fired. The empty is in *your* shotgun. You shot. Or at least some part of you did. Your hunting partners rush in, filled with congratulations.

"Damnedest shot I ever saw," one shouts, pounding you on the back. "Whoa, we got a 'trick shot' on our hands," another murmurs looking at you with new respect. But in your mind's most secret place, that mental room where all truth lives, you admit what you'll never say. You didn't have a damned thing to do with that shot. It was as though someone else took over your gun and shot the bird.

Well, someone else did!

The Other Part of Our Brain

Do you remember, as a youngster in school, a teacher telling you that you use only 10 percent of your brain? Geniuses use up to 5 percent more.

Did those statistics bother you? They did me. Nature just doesn't work like that. Nature figured out how to make every living thing, plants and animals, on this planet interdependent. Then when it got around to me, it made a 100 percent brain and gave me the use of a meager 10 percent. Was there something I was missing? Could the original usage have been lost to antiquity like the appendix?

I thought about the disparity for a long time. If we only use a small percent, why didn't nature create a smaller head? But no, there we are with 90 percent mashed potatoes, and 10 percent brain. Hummmm.

I wish I could say, "Then in a flash it came to me." But it didn't. In fact, I was probably using that huge part of my brain long before I was aware of its existence.

From the time I was a child I recognized that I was able to shoot a bow, throw a rock, or launch a spear better if I didn't think about it first. It sure was true with baseball. If I had to think about how to throw the ball, it never made for a strike. And, I remember my Dad saying about shooting, "Just point and shoot. Don't think."

Actually, I had been teaching shooting professionally for several years, and getting about the same results that other instructors do, when I suddenly realized what had been right on the tip of mind since I was a child.

IT IS THE BIG PART OF OUR BRAIN THAT IS IN CHARGE OF USING THE FOOD-GATHERING TOOLS.

And then the other part of that awesome realization: **WE HAVE LITTLE OR NO CONTROL OVER THAT PART OF OUR BRAIN.**

But wait a minute. If we are able to use *it*, there must be some control. Actually, the reverse may be true.

IT IS ABLE TO USE US.

We'll probably all agree that for most of *Homo sapiens's* span on this planet, humans have been hunter/gatherers. Only for the last tick of our 200,000-year time clock (give or take a hundred thousand) have we farmed and been relatively stable in our homelands.

Throughout most of our history, before we were accountants, writers, lawyers, doctors, or the like, we were hunters. Much of our cultural life was directed by primal drives: the drive to protect the genetic base, the drive to protect the home turf, the drive to procreate, and the drive to stave off hunger. Of all our drives—those instincts which come programmed into our DNA—the most vital is the last, the primal drive to stave off hunger. Its most obvious partner is the attack response.

Without our ability to attack and kill prey animals, the other primal drives were of little importance. Before we could raise our children in the safety of our home cave we had to eat.

And so it is my belief that the largest part of the brain of *Homo sapiens*, the modern human, is and always has been, devoted to the ability to kill prey animals with some sort of launched, swung, or thrown tool.

Finding, tracking, even setting up the ambush is part of what we have come to call the conscious mind. The other part we refer to as the *sub*-conscious mind. Meaning that the *sub*-conscious part is somehow beneath or less important than the conscious mind.

I believe that demeans a part of our brain that has sustained us for hundreds of thousands of years. It isn't *less than* the part we are aware of; it is simply different.

Homo sapiens

It takes very little stretch of the imagination to see *Homo sapiens* as a predator. This is especially true when we take a look at the techniques man uses when he displays his talents as a predator.

Take, for instance, this business of pointing I mentioned earlier. All predators point. At least all air-breathing, *ambushing* predators point. Furred, feathered, skinned, or scaled, all ambushing predators point in some manner. The point is nothing but the pause before the attack. During that moment, however brief, the eyes of the predator fix on a tiny part of the prey animal, that part which will receive the attack. The eyes of the predator, generally forward looking, triangulate on the target and estimate range. If the prey is moving, they also measure speed, angle, height above the ground, and size—all are needed information. With all data in, the attack is launched. There is no time for thought. The predator streaks toward its prey, adjusting as the prey dodges. If the attack is successful, the result is dinner. If not, the result is hunger. Some predators launch themselves. Some launch a part of their body, as in the tongue of a lizard or toad. Even if an animal is relatively slow and has a short tongue, it has learned to launch its tools with deadly effect.

There is one ingredient *Homo sapiens* shares with every other predator—the *eyes* of the predator. No matter how hard the cheetah drives toward the prey, no matter how much the lioness turns or changes direction, no matter how steep the falcon's dive, the eyes of the predator move in a straight line toward the prey. They never leave the preselected prey animal; they never leave the preselected spot on that animal. Show me a lioness that jumps over a bush during the attack, and you've seen a lioness who's just lost her lunch.

Man, like the chameleon, is slow. But like the chameleon, man can launch a device to catch prey animals.

The Predator

You already know I feel the large part of our brain is responsible for the attack response. Consider the calculations involved in hitting a clay target.

Let's say we're going to launch a 108mm clay target off a 90-foot tower. It will travel 60 mph out of the trap. Forty yards away, it will have decelerated to 30 mph and have dropped twenty feet. We will throw it at an angle of 167 degrees away from you. Your assignment will be to determine the vector of seven-eighths of an ounce of shot from a 12-gauge shotgun at a velocity of 1270 fps through a barrel with .010-inch restriction.

I don't know about you, but that target would be melted in the sun by the time I calculated the correct answer. Even if we had a computer, the target would be on the ground before we could type in the data for calculation.

Yet, the large part of your brain can figure out the answer in thousandths of a second, even if the target size is changed, and it's thrown in a different spot every time, at different speeds. The brain can do this, **AS LONG AS THE CONSCIOUS MIND DOESN'T INTERFERE.**

To keep from calling it the "Large Part of Your Brain" every time, I have nicknamed it simply "The Predator."

While we don't seem to have any direct control over the Predator, we are able to train it—program it. We do this the same way a batter learns to hit the ball or a quarterback his tight end. Indeed, these are sports I've come to call "hunter-killer sports."

Early man found the same thing to be true. The more he practiced with his hunting tools, the better he got. These practice sessions led to competitions and the competitions to games: games in which the participants practice the attack response and, in many cases, protection of the home turf.

In racquet sports, the participant kills a small prey animal over and over with a club. In badminton, they even put feathers on the prey and call it a "bird" or shuttlecock. The pitcher throws a projectile at a target. The catcher's glove simulates prey. The batter tries to kill it. The game is a series of mixed metaphors, but nevertheless, games like these please us because they allow us to practice and give vent to our most basic instincts—our primal drives.

This recognition of the Predator, as the controller of food-gathering tools and weapons, isn't unique. Far-Eastern cultures have grappled with this concept for centuries. Indeed, I believe anyone who teaches activities of this nature for very long will eventually realize there is another element in the puzzle: an element distinct and different from the conscious mind.

The Predator does not see time the same way our conscious mind does. In the attack, time as we know it seems compressed. That is, things seem to slow down.

Consider the ping-pong player. This is one of the hunter-killer sports, and it clearly creates the ability for time compression amongst its top players.

Someone watching an Olympic match will see serves and volleys traveling at blinding speed. The players seem to move with impossible quickness and return shots the viewer had trouble even seeing. Yet when asked about a particularly difficult ball return, players often respond, "Oh, it wasn't *that* fast."

Recently, one of our graduates, who also plays tennis, remarked about the difficulty in hitting a particularly formidable opponent's serve. "Finally, I had to use time compression," she said, "in order to return her serve." When asked, the student admitted she focused on the edge of the ball to slow it to a manageable speed. This is the skill of the Predator.

2

WHAT IS INSTINCTIVE SHOOTING?

There is a lot of talk going around now about instinctive shooting with a shotgun. Back when I came across these words, they were barely mentioned in a handful of obscure readings. I experienced it before I had the words to describe it. We all have.

Instinctive shooting is loosely described as everything from shooting a BB gun without sights to shooting from the hip. Since no two people ever seem to agree wholly on exactly what instinctive shooting is, I will define it as it applies to this book and our shooting school.

Annie Oakley was a staunch supporter of instinctive shooting. In an early quote, Annie is reported to have said, "Shooting a shotgun is no more difficult than pointing your finger." Annie taught in England for the princely sum of one pound per lesson in 1887 while the Wild West show made appearances in the British Isles. She returned to this country and eventually taught at Pinehurst, North Carolina, until the time of her death. Annie's deadly accuracy was combined with a shooting style of grace and beauty—a combination not seen again until, I believe, the Wingshooting Workshop followed on this same path toward instinctive shooting. But Annie never got her technique into writing.

Robert Churchill espoused an instinctive style in England during the early 1900s. In reading his book, I believe that he ran into the same problems I did in my early years—it's a whole lot easier to shoot instinctively than it is to teach it.

Churchill came up with some pretty neat stuff, however. His shooting stances were a real contribution, but I sincerely believe they were based on Annie's teachings. Unfortunately, Churchill took Annie's squared-away stance out and blended in a bit of the military protocols—always a danger in instinctive shotgunning.

Churchill's patterning for fit is a contribution as well. But Robert Churchill wasn't the only instinctive supporter to make his way into print. Lucky McDaniel copyrighted a book in 1980 on instinctive shooting. McDaniel is better known for his teaching technique that first taught students, using BB guns, to shoot taped steel washers out of the air and eventually worked down to aspirin tablets and, finally, shooting another BB with a BB.

Down through the ages, most trick shots—Annie Oakley, Herb Parsons and the like—have used instinctive shooting to amaze and astonish. To the uninitiated, instinctive shooting does indeed seem to border on the miraculous. But it's more than fodder for trick shooters.

An instinctive shotgun shooter has the ability to hit a moving object *without establishing a perceived relationship between the barrel and the target.*

Now that's a pretty big statement. Because in most current descriptions of instinctive shotgunning, the writer continues with the definition: "The shooter is only dimly aware of the barrel in the lower part of his/her vision." In fact, when performed properly, *the shooter has no perception of the barrel.* If the shooter is looking at, or is even "dimly aware" of, the barrel or bead, he/she is concentrating on the wrong thing, and will miss. So let's proceed a step further. If the shooter *is establishing a relationship between the barrel and the target* by: (1) swinging the barrel along the flight path of the target and firing as he passes through the target; (2) intersecting the barrel onto the target and firing as he pulls away along the apparent flight path of the target; and (3) establishing a sustained lead ahead of the target. If these are the methods, *then the shooter is simply aiming* by *our* definition.

Frankly, it has been my experience that the conscious mind is not very adept at shooting moving targets. It is too analytical, nonspatial, and slow.

In the first two of the three commonly taught methods mentioned above (Swing Through and Pull Away), the shooter depends on the lag in mechanical lock time and muscular reaction to hit the target. The shooter is actually attempting to move the shotgun at a speed faster than the target. But nobody tells the shooter how much faster. And it wouldn't work even if he were told what speeds. At least, it would not work all of the time. The third commonly taught method (Sustained Lead) demands that the shooter first estimate the range, speed, angle, acceleration or deceleration, and size of the target. He must then guess at the proper lead and shoot while trying to keep the barrel moving at the target's speed. All of these methods are wrongfully focused upon aiming—aiming to swing faster than the target, aiming to pull away from the target, or aiming consistently in front of the target.

This reliance upon aiming of shotguns is even more obvious when we consider the firearm choice of most modern shotgunners: pumps, semiautomatics, and over-and-unders. These firearms offer the shooter—and you see this term commonly used by most modern gun writers—"a narrow sighting plane." Believe me, if you are shooting instinctively and are POINTING the shotgun correctly, **A SHOTGUN DOES NOT HAVE A SIGHTING PLANE.**

The most brilliantly designed and most easily pointed shotgun is the classic side-by-side. In the hands of an expert, the side-by-side can do everything the "narrow sighting plane" shotguns can do, plus the one thing side-by-sides do best: point naturally.

The most brilliantly designed and most easily pointed shotgun is the classic side-by-side.

When an expert uses a side-by-side, missing a target becomes the exception. When the expert does miss, he or she knows exactly where the charge of shot went, and why.

There are two exercises I would like you to do to help illustrate this instinctive technique.

First, however, we'll need to determine which eye is your master eye.

3

EYES—THE MOST COMMON PROBLEM

Testing for Eye Dominance—Does It Work?

If I were to pick the most common problem for shooters who come to our school, the Wingshooting Workshop, it would be eye dominance.

There are two common ways in which lay people can test for eye dominance.

If you are right-handed, point at a distant, small magpie's nest in a far tree. Now, close your left eye. If the finger is still on the nest, you are right-eye dominant—maybe.

1. If you are right-handed, point at a distant small object with the right hand. Close the left eye. If the point stays on the object, the right eye is dominant.

2. Hold your hands at your waist. Cross the thumbs and forefingers so they leave a small hole. Raise the hole up, with your arms fully extended, and look through it at the distant small object with both eyes open. Now close the left eye. If you can still see the small object your right eye is dominant.

SAME SIDE DOMINANCE. Here, Chuck Gossett demonstrates how the hole-in-the-hand-test works. He makes a hole through his fingers. He raises the hole and looks at the camera lens. The camera saw the right eye and, therefore, understood the right eye was dominant.

The problem with both of these simple tests, as well as those performed by eye professionals, is that one should be adding something to that declaration:

"You appear to be right-eye dominant, AT THIS MOMENT."

Amazingly, in our school, we have identified what appears to be FOUR different eye dominances for *Homo sapiens* the hunter.

They are:

1. Same-side dominance (i.e., right-handed, right-eye dominant).
2. Cross-dominance (i.e., right-handed, left-eye dominant).
3. Ambi-dominance (i.e., right-handed with eye dominance shifting alternately from right to left and left to right).
4. Hemispheric dominance (i.e., right-eye dominant when the target or prey is in the right hemisphere, left-eye dominant when the target or prey is in the left hemisphere).

The blind dominant eye or phantom eye really isn't a separate form of dominance. It's probably an anomaly, but an extremely elusive one and it points the way to a universal solution.

We once had a professional eye-person in the school who, when ambi-dominance and hemispheric dominance were revealed during the course of the school declared, "Nonsense, I've never heard of such a thing." Several hours later, I asked, "Remember that thing you never heard of (ambi-dominance)? Well, you have it." He came to agree.

Paul S., another graduate of the Wingshooting Workshop, who makes his living as an eye professional, made a prophetic statement: "We don't see with our eyes, we see with our brains."

We See with Our Minds

Think about it. We don't see with our eyes. We see with our brains. If that doesn't sound profound, let me demonstrate. With both eyes open, hold two fingers together, about an inch in front of your open, master eye. Notice how the fingers have become transparent; you seem to be looking through them. Now you and I both know you can't see through your fingers. But your brain is making an adjustment

Here's a simple demonstration of our brains at work. With both eyes open, look at another person's right eye. Now slowly insert two of your fingers between your right eye and his. Keep your fingers an inch or so from your own eye. Notice how your fingers seem to have become transparent.

for the blockage. This little trick is going to be very important when it comes to shooting high overhead shots.

Just the other day, I noticed an article about a nationally recognized shooting instructor. In it he was quoted as saying, "You *must* shoot with both eyes open. If you close one eye, you lose 50 percent of your vision."

I'm here to tell you it simply isn't true. A recent workshop graduate is a lawyer who has litigated numerous actions involving the loss of an eye. The best evidence from his experts now shows that a person only suffers a 15 percent loss when one eye is completely lost.

And, indeed, a person who is blind in one eye, or even missing an eye, can shoot as well as a person with two eyes. The brain has several different ways of establishing depth perception, even when one eye is lost or not open.

To carry that even further, because of the eye anomalies and because we see with our brains not our eyes, *a person with two eyes may still not be able to shoot well with both eyes open.* Because most instructors insist that shooters shoot with both eyes open, I believe they're relegating some 30 to 40 percent of shooters to mediocre shooting or even making them worse shooters if they follow this advice.

Only this last year, I had a student who had just been to a large, well-known shooting school hosted by an equally well-known ammo company. The instructors conferred about him and called him in and, with sincerest apologies, informed him he should probably take up another sport. They said his shooting would always be poor. Luckily he didn't believe them.

Within minutes of his shooting at the Wingshooting Workshop, I could see that his particular anomaly cropped up—he had ambi-dominance. It was serious to enough to cause real problems. But once recognized, it could be dealt with. Today, he is a 95 percent shooter.

Let's take a closer look at each of the forms of dominance.

1. **SAME-SIDE DOMINANCE** This can be right-handed, right-eye dominance, or left-handed, left-eye dominant. These are the lucky ones, as it is the easiest form of dominance for shooters. These shooters learn to hit targets with relative ease. Yet, this can cause its own kind of problem, since they seldom seek professional help because they are naturally lucky with good hand-eye coordination in general.

Some will think it strange that I include same-side dominance with eye anomalies. But it is a form of dominance, so in order to recognize it you should consider it as one of the anomalies. Same-side dominance may simply be one of the only eye anomalies that are useful to instinctive shooters.

SAME-SIDE DOMINANCES. When they point at a distant object with a firearm that falls within their parameters of fit, the barrels go to that object without fail every single time.

2. **CROSS-DOMINANCE** Cross-dominance is quite common. My own brothers and father were plagued with it. Their solution was, as right-handed individuals, to shoot left-handed. This is an easy fix if the individual in question is cross-dominant *all the time*. If that's the case, shooting from the other side is one solution. Unfortunately for newcomers, left-handed guns are harder and more expensive to come by, along with everything else for lefties. For a left-hander with cross-dominance, they get the unexpected benefit of getting something cheaper for once in their life: a right-handed shotgun.

Cross-dominance is quite easy to spot. Let's say a right-handed person points with the right hand at a distant small object, like a ball. To someone standing behind the pointer, the hand will appear to

be pointing off to the left. That's because the stronger left eye pulls the right finger over to it. This is assuming the pointer is looking only at the ball and not at the hand.

Gun aimers are not vexed by this to the same extent as gun pointers, since aimers have shotgun beads as reference points to the target. But aiming is a flawed technique and usually drops most shooters off at 60 to 70 percent, so this is not a fix for the cross-dominant shooter to take up aiming.

CROSS-DOMINANCES. When they point at a distant object, with a firearm that falls within their parameters of fit, the left eye will always pull the firearm off to the left, 18 inches. No question.

When a cross-dominant, right-handed, instinctive shooter shoots at a target crossing right to left at around twenty yards,

Chuck Gossett demonstrates what happens in cross-dominances, seen from the target's side. Chuck is closing his right eye. Notice how far off on his left the eye is pulling the barrels.

the shot will pass eighteen inches in front of the target— again, because the dominant left eye is pulling the pointing finger over to it. Naturally, the gun barrels go with the finger. As a result, the barrels end up pointing to the left of the target. Usually this still results in a hit. When shooting at the target crossing left to right, the shooter is eighteen inches behind the target. Usually this results in a miss. This often plagues the cross-dominant shooters in something like sporting clays and they often struggle to find the real reason behind their inconsistencies.

3. **AMBI-DOMINANCE** is the saddest of all the eye dominances; it continually holds out hope that the phenomenon has ended, for those shooters who are unaware they have it and think it is just a bad streak. As long as the shooter is same-side dominant, shooting usually progresses normally and they are lucky. When cross-dominance suddenly appears, all hopes of hitting targets disappear, but more so on one side or the other. In many people, this is the answer to "I have some good days and bad days" phenomena. But ambi-dominance creates all kinds of hell for the shooter to self-diagnose, as the dominance shifts from eye to eye, and it is not consistent.

A right-handed person, when right-eye dominant, has no trouble shooting targets passing from right to left. When a dominance shift occurs, the shot passes eighteen inches to the left as the left eye pulls the hand over in front of it. Generally, a shooter cannot see his own shot string so this is difficult for the shooter to tell what is happening. However, a person standing directly behind usually can. An instinctive shooter can be trained to almost always know where the barrel was pointing at the time of the shot. The exception to this is when there's been a dominance shift. The student whose shots pass eighteen inches to the left, when asked by the instructor, "Were you pointing at the target?" answers, "Yes." He's telling the truth. He really *was* pointing at where his Predator THOUGHT THE TARGET WAS.

1. A short story to illustrate. (All these next comments are about targets passing from right to left for right-handed shooters). Point at a distant small dot with the right hand. Gradually, close the right eye. Allow the pointing finger to move with the new visual information. Suddenly open the right eye. The finger will be pointing to the left of the target dot.

   VITAL POINT! VITAL POINT! EVERYBODY READ THIS!

   When the Predator is confused, it usually shoots high. Let me say that again; it is so important! When the Predator is confronted with something new, self-doubt, something it hasn't seen before, or is otherwise confused, it will generally shoot high. A change in eye dominance can trigger confusion in the Predator.

2. Dominance shift for right-handed shooters can cause shot to pass eighteen inches in front of, or to the left in a ten- to twenty-yard shot. The amount of the miss depends on the size of the shooter, width of eyes, and length of arms. While the amount of miss in inches appears irrelevant and small to the shooter, it usually appears to the coach as eighteen inches. This is important to the coach, since there are other causes for misses to the left of a target crossing right to left.

3. A shot pattern that constantly passes to the left can also be caused by something completely out to the instinctive shooter's

control, such as stock that is too long or has an incorrect cast. These we call MECHANICALS. We'll deal with these when we get to the chapter on gun fit. A miss to the left can also be caused by a soft anchor—that is, a mounted gun that is not held tightly against the lower jaw. The finger will pull the barrels to the right in an attempt to point at the leading edge, creating an angle. A tiny angle at the shooter means a larger one at the target. A half-inch gap at the anchor point can cause a six-inch or more gap at the target. This usually results in a badly broken target or a miss.

4. THE SOLUTION FOR THE AMBI-DOMINANT SHOO-TER. Placing a piece of transparent or semi-transparent tape over the off-side eye may switch dominance back to the handed eye and *keep it there.* For the right-handed shooter, this means taping over the left eye. Sometimes when the shooter is learning to shoot instinctively, the entire shooting glass on the off-side must be covered to keep the individual from peeking around the tape. The drive to see with both eyes is powerful. Once the Predator learns to tolerate it, the tape can gradually be reduced in size till a simple spot remains.

Using a dot of tape over the off-side eye is a time-honored fix for target shooters. But for instinctive shooters and hunters it poses a pair of problems: it can be dangerous walking around in the field with a piece of tape over one eye and it doesn't always work. (See eye winking later in the chapter for a solution with fewer problems.)

4. **DEALING WITH HEMISPHERIC DOMINANCE.** Luckily, hemispheric dominance is quite rare. I've only seen it twice, and then only in gun aimers (i.e., Swing Through, Sustained Lead, or Pull Away shooters). These individuals tend to shoot in the rifleman's stance with the off-leg forward and gun leg back. Because the stance is open, these people also lift the gun elbow to create a false pocket. Shooting from this cramped position, these gun aimers also tend to

move the firearm with the hands, arms, and shoulders, since the bent legs preclude keeping the body behind the gun, save for 45 degrees either side of center.

Hemispheric dominance can be seen when, as the targets moves from one hemisphere to the other, the gun barrel takes a decided jump as the other eye takes over and directs the shotgun.

With the hemispheric, right-handed shooter, the right eye is dominant as long as the target is in the right hemisphere. On a right to left crosser, as the barrels cross the center line of vision, the left eye becomes dominant and the barrels take a decided jump to the left to accommodate the change.

So far, the solution to all of these remains the same—the eye wink.

THE EYE WINK

Instinctive shooters move the entire body, and it is always kept positioned behind the gun exactly the same way, with the vertical and horizontal angles always the same. Since the shotgun only moves forward in relation to the body, hemispheric dominance seldom, if ever, crops up.

Hemispheric dominance must not be confused with a frequent aiming fault. In attempting to focus first on the barrel's bead and then with the target, the barrel will swing in a series of short jerks. As the eye sees the target, the target pulls the barrel along with it. But as the eye is refocused on the bead, the barrel stops, since the target is no longer pulling it. Refocusing on the target causes the barrel to jump ahead again to catch up with the target. This process is repeated over and over. The barrel moves ahead in a short series of stops and starts.

This should never happen to instinctive shooters, since they cannot see the barrel.

True, hemispheric dominance is different than this, since the jump occurs only once.

I first noticed hemispheric dominance when watching a Swing Through shooter practice-point. Instead of assuming a proper ready position, the individual simply stood facing the kill-zone and swung the arm to practice-point the target. I noticed that each time the target moved from the pointer's right hemisphere to the left, the hand jumped eighteen inches to the left.

With a gentle correction of the stance to tracking, the jump disappeared. The individual agreed to experiment. When adopting the original stance, with only the hand and arm pointing, the jump reappeared. When the pointer closed the left eye, the phenomenon vanished again.

The best way to control hemispheric dominance is with proper technique, which we'll deal with in the chapters on the ready position and mount.

5. **THE BLIND DOMINANT EYE OR PHANTOM EYE.** When Mick B. arrived at the Wingshooting Workshop, he had been shooting most of his life—badly. A hunting accident in his youth had left him blind in his right eye. His hunting companion swung on a bird, rode it, and finally shot, missing the bird but hitting Mick.

He was nearing sixty years old when he arrived at our school. Just two weeks before, the blind right eye had been removed. Immediately, a near-blinding light sensitivity vanished. For years the left eye, the one with vision, had been protected by dark, almost black, sunglasses, with limited success. Within days of removing the blind eye, the sensitivity diminished. We'd observed a similar phenomenon when trying to place a patch over a cross-dominant eye. The un-patched eye's pupil would dilate and get larger in sympathy with its patched partner. Naturally this would create light sensitivity in the uncovered eye. Depth perception decreased as well. You may remember from photography, as the aperture of your camera's lens gets larger, depth-of-field decreases. As the aperture of the lens is reduced (made smaller), the depth-of-field increases. The same is true for our eyes. Instinctive shooters always try to keep the pupils of their eyes as small as possible to keep depth-of-field as deep as possible. Naturally that means dark glasses are out. More about this later.

DEPTH-OF-FIELD. Depth is critical to instinctive shooters. In this photo and the following one, I've shown how the iris of the eye affects depth-of-field, and therefore your ability to focus on objects. In the first photograph, I used a large opening in the lens, and focused on the yellow, 20-gauge shell, which is second in line from the front. Notice all of the other shells are out of focus.

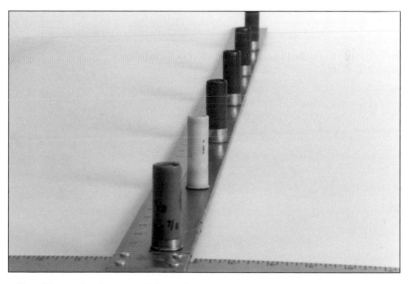

Now, I have simply stopped down the camera lens and used a longer exposure time. The 20-gauge shell is in focus, but so are all the other shells (all 12-gauges). Dark glasses fool your eyes into thinking there is not as much light as there really is. As a result, the iris of your eye opens and depth-of-field is reduced, as in the previous photo.

But Mick's problems were more complicated than light sensitivity. His ophthalmologist should have made *that* connection early in Mick's life.

Though right-handed, Mick had always shot left-handed. He had always been a gun aimer—he sighted along the barrel and pulled the trigger. Occasionally, he would hit a bird, but not with any kind of frequency.

After we'd worked on the fundamentals of instinctive shooting, we repaired to a target field where I'd set up for left to right crossers, the easier targets for southpaws.

I replaced Mick's dark glasses with his clear lenses and I added yellow clip-ons to keep's Mick's remaining pupil small and to absorb ultraviolet.

Imagine how astonished I was to see the shot pattern pass eighteen inches ahead of the first target. The second, third, fourth, and fifth were all missed in the exact same spot—not nineteen inches, not seventeen inches—eighteen inches.

"Mick," I said with disbelief and an aura around my words, "Close your right eye."

"I don't have a right eye," he said.

"I meant, slap your right eyelids together."

He did, and the next target was nothing but a puff of dark smoke. So was the next. But the third shot charge passed eighteen inches ahead of the target.

"Your right eye was open."

"How in the hell can I tell?" he snapped. "It all looks the same to me whether the lids are open or closed, and I can't feel my eyelid very well either."

The simple solution was to tape the lids closed. We did, and Mick began to learn instinctive shooting at an astonishing rate. He'd spent a lifetime shooting, but his brain finally could see the target where it really was. Remember, we see with our minds, not our eyes. His mind still saw everything as if he still had the two eyes of his youth.

We also discovered, even though Mick had been shooting left-handed all his life, his brain was still strongly right-eye dominant. His brain, and as it turns out, the brains of many others with able sight, simply will not accept a change of dominance unless the lids of the dominant eye are shut.

Amazingly, Mick hit five shots in a row with my right-handed gun, shooting right-handed and leaving the lids of the blind dominant right eye open. He probably would have kept on hitting. But he said aloud, "I shouldn't be able to do this." The Predator was listening. He began to miss.

As we were to discover, it isn't that easy to close the lids on a brain that strongly wants to see with both eyes open. This is especially vital for instinctive shooters since we do not have the barrel as a reference point.

This then is the source of our term "Blind Dominant Eye."

We use the same term when it crops up in people with two perfectly able eyes, but whose brains refuse to accept a dominance change without touching the lids of the dominant eye together (i.e., winking the lid closed).

For instance, John is right-handed but he is also ambi-dominant—his dominance shifts from eye to eye. He is also afflicted with a blind dominant eye. So John must close the left eye to be able to shoot right-handed. True, since his dominance will be in the right eye, part of the time, he will hit targets part of the time. But suddenly, he will begin to miss and nothing will get him back on. With equal suddenness, his accuracy returns and hope soars, only to be dashed again later on when the left eye takes over—again.

So John must close one eye. It's easier to teach him to close the left eye, since he's right-handed. But, when to close it? Close it too soon and depth perception may be affected. Close it too late and John will actually have to back up the barrels on right-to-left crossing targets.

So, we choose the safety as our eye-closing device. Since all the guns in the Wingshooting Workshop are side-by-sides and all have automatic safeties, we teach that pushing the safety off always happens at exactly the same time—at the beginning of the mount. In the gun's first inch of travel forward during the mount, the safety is released and the off-side eye (in John's case, the left eye), winks shut.

This momentary eye closing when the safety is pushed off must be built into every single mount for the shooter dealing with anything other than same-side dominance. The shooter has no way of knowing when a dominance change will occur, and since closing the eye actually sharpens the target, it can't hurt a thing. And it is the only thing that helps many shooters dealing with these dominance problems.

The Brain's Rangefinder

Earlier I mentioned that the brain, the Predator, has ways of range estimation with just a single eye.

Back to Tom M., the lawyer dealing with vision cases, who explained that vision researchers have found human brains can use familiar objects to estimate distance. Even more incredibly, the Predator can vibrate the pupil of the good eye back and forth fast enough so the brain can use the two, ever-so-slightly different pictures, to estimate range. This confirmed what I was able to observe an instance like this myself.

A student began to nod while he was practicing eye closure and pointing. As I watched, he always began nodding. We'd throw a target, he'd point at it, and immediately he'd begin nodding.

"Did you know you're nodding?"

"What do you mean?" he asked.

"When your eye closes, you nod your head up and down."

"No I don't."

"Okay, get over there and point at my right eye."

He did.

"Now close your left eye."

He did and immediately began to nod.

"You're nodding."

"I am not," he replied, getting just a bit testy.

I wish I had brought a video camera. I showed him in a mirror and he finally believed me.

"Oh my God, I see it," he said, "but I can't feel a thing."

"That's because it isn't *you* doing it." His subconscious part of the brain (Predator) was moving the pupil up and down by nodding his head to gain depth perception. I've never seen that phenomenon since, but the human brain is full of tricks. Who knows what the next one will be.

Selecting Glasses

Just a note here on selecting shooting glasses—instinctive shooting depends on eye brain function more than any other style of shooting. The end result is this—when the instinctive technique is mastered, the shooter simply feels that she is looking and pointing at the target. There are no barrels—just the shooter and the target. But all parts of the technique must be in place, together with a fitted gun, shells, shirt, hat, footwear, earplugs, and, of course, shooting glasses. Get the best—medium yellow (the shade is #15 yellow in a photographic filter). Get the best shooting glasses you can afford—you want them to be optically correct. Over the years, even with all of the colors on the market these days, I believe that this medium color has turned out to be the best for hunters as well as shooters. And I live in Idaho, where the sun is bright, so I understand the temptation to want darker shooting glasses. You'll find your shooting will suffer.

Be careful to select a pair of shooting glasses that can be adjusted vertically. Most shooting glasses are constructed for shooters who cheek the shotgun, chin down, eyes forward looking down the barrel. The shooter looks out through the upper part of the glasses. They must be kept high on the face so the lower part of the lens doesn't bump the stock. As instinctive shooters, we need shooting glasses that fit us like normal corrective glasses do, so we are looking out through the relative center of the lenses (not the top, like aiming shooters do). I like the Decot Hi-Lo International glasses, which can be so centered on any shooter's face. I have also used Bausch and Lomb Ray Ban yellow shooting glasses most of my life, as did my dad after WWII. Unfortunately, as of this writing, Ray Ban is no longer making shooting glasses. There may be others that fit your face; try them on while shooting and get the best lenses you can afford.

These days it's easy; you can have them make 3mm polycarbonate lenses in #15 yellow, which can be inserted into a wide variety of frames and can be made in corrective lenses as well as normal lenses for those who don't need the correction. They can even lighten or darken the yellow of the finished lenses on request while you wait at many vision centers.

However, you want to remember these glasses are also meant to be protective, not just for fashion. We had a graphic demonstration of shooting-glass quality recently at our school. Scott arrived at the school, with a pair of yellow (a requirement we have in the Work-shop, as we believe it makes that big of a difference), wraparound (definitely not a requirement and not what I prefer), inexpensive (usually a bad idea) shooting glasses. This wraparound thin style is in vogue these days for everything from lounging at the beach to motorcycling and skiing.

During mount practice, he proceeded normally while in the class-room. But as we began to shoot crossers, I noticed his barrel wavering and falling behind, ever so slightly. Since he was progressing within parameters, I wasn't concerned until the second day, when, even though his mount was near perfect, and his eye anomaly conquered, he wasn't progressing as expected. And, the wavering was still there about twenty feet out from the trap.

"Is the leading edge sharp?" I asked.

"Yeah," he said, "I guess so."

"Look at one without the glasses on."

He did.

"That's better," he explained as he watched the bird without shooting.

"Scott, I'm going to try something."

In my supplies for students are shooting glasses with high-quality lenses, by the same manufacturer as the wraparounds, which often contain lenses as low quality as you can get.

"Scott, try these," I said holding out the metal-framed, brow-banned glasses with the shooter's style circle above the nose pieces.

"WOW!" he exclaimed immediately. "That's awesome."

He creamed the next shot and 99 percent of the shots thereafter.

I know that there are now optically correct wraparounds at a significantly increased price. Just make sure they are optically correct. They can only put a certain level of correction in these wraparound lenses, because they have an inherent amount of distortion due to the lens curvature.

The color is important as well. We've selected medium yellow for several reasons. The color, while at first appearing very bright, causes the eyes to react to light the way nature intended, by reducing the eyes' irises to their smallest diopter. Like a camera's lens, small opening, great depth-of field. Because the opening is small, I believe it also helps keep stray ultraviolet light out, which comes in from behind all glasses except side-shaded glacier glasses. With dark glasses, the eyes are fooled into thinking there's less light than there really is. The irises open up. Depth perception is reduced. Stray UV can more readily enter the eye. In my past life, I was a photographer for *National Geographic* magazine, so believe me, I have thought about lenses and glasses for the better part of my life, and I apologize if many shooters might find my diatribe on shooting glasses a bit boring. Trust me—simply put, you'll be a better shooter with the yellow glasses I am recommending here.

Yellow also has other advantages. Any black and white photographer will tell you the yellow K1 (#8) and K2 (#15) filters were used to (1) increase contrast and (2) absorb ultraviolet.

When you first put on your #15 medium-yellow-colored shooting glasses on, you'll say, "Whoa, that's bright."

What you're feeling are the muscles of your eyes pulling the irises down to unusually small diopters. Stick with the glasses for a few minutes and gradually this feeling will disappear. You will begin seeing detail you never noticed before.

Do we use yellow all the time? Yes. Remember, instinctive shooters are basically hunters who shoot clays, not vice versa. Therefore, it's imperative that the equipment we use in practice and clay target work is the same equipment we take into the field. I have closets full of equipment and clothing that looked practical (or cool) when I bought them, but turned out to be figments of a marketer's imagination. Interchangeable lenses for every possible lighting condition. Good on paper, no good in the field. Yellow will simply improve your shooting, under all conditions. There, sorry, enough said about getting yourself some high-quality yellow shooting glasses.

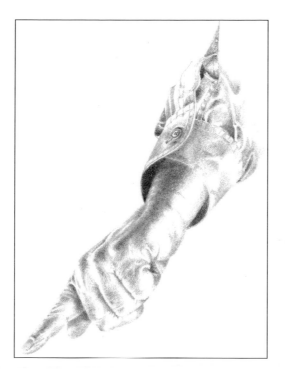

4

POINTING—THE KEY TO GOOD SHOTGUNNING

Learning to Point

Most shotgunners or would-be shotgunners wrongly believe that having a shotgun in hand is critical to learning how to *point* a shotgun. Nothing could be further from the truth. Learning to point is only incidental to learning to shoot.

Most of us, in learning a pointing-related activity, try to learn the activity and pointing at the same time. Usually, it takes longer to learn both simultaneously than it does both one at a time.

First, I like to teach you how to point. Then adding a shotgun and learning to shoot is a relative cinch. I am sorry if this sounds too basic, but we cannot underestimate the need for learning to point in order to have any success with instinctive shooting.

Remember, instinctively shooting a shotgun is closely related to throwing a ball, rock, or football. Shooting a shotgun instinctively is akin to shooting a slingshot, bow and arrow, hurling a spear by hand

The key to learning to shoot instinctively is learning how to point. Whether you're throwing a ball, releasing a narrow, throwing a spear, or hitting a ball, the fundamentals remain the same. You've got to look at the target, not at the launcher or hitting device.

or aided by an atlatl. The key to all of this is pointing. We use our minds to "kill" a target or game bird. Shotguns are only incidental launching devices to get the shot where we pointed it.

Exercises

Before reading the rest of this chapter, please put down the book for a few moments to do these exercises. The explanations are for right-handed people. If you are left-handed, just reverse the instructions.

To practice these, you must first place a tiny "target" on a distant wall, or pick a distant spot outside. It must be small. In a room, you might spot an existing nail hole. Barring this simple solution, you can punch a piece of tape with a paper punch and put the resulting dot on a distant wall. Use a contrasting color of tape, as you want to be able to focus on the dot, not the larger tape. A small round sticker would be even better, or punch a nail hole, if your spouse won't mind.

The best way to practice your pointing skills is to put a focus point on a distant wall. This single factor, a focus point, will remain constant throughout the rest of your shooting life.

EXERCISE ONE. Stand erect facing the dot. Now, with your right arm, point at the dot. Bring the arm down. Now point at the dot again but do not bring your hand up any higher than your shoulder and do not in any way look at your hand; look only at the dot. Again, pointing at the dot without looking at your hand, close your left, or off-eye, then lower your head until you are sighting along your finger. Notice that the finger was pointing exactly at the dot. Not close, but exactly. If, when you sight down the finger you find the finger pointing off to the left (to the right with left-handers) and this occurs often, you probably have a dominance problem. By that, I mean the off-side eye is pulling the finger under it rather than under your dominant-side eye.

Exercise One: From across the room, with your head high, your hand no higher than your shoulder, first point at the dot. Now close your left eye, lean down to your pointing finger, and sight along it. The finger will be precisely on the dot, if no eye anomalies are present.

If you are right-handed and you constantly point to the left of the dot when you sight down the right finger after pointing, then you're left-eye dominant. At least you are some of the time. Try this same exercise with the left hand. If the left pointing finger is consistently on the target when you sight down the finger with the *left* eye, then there is a dominance problem. If it only happens sometimes—part of the time it works with the right forefinger and part of the time with the left forefinger—then you are ambi-dominant and you must treat the situation as if you are cross-dominant.

Close the off-side eye. Try the exercise again. If you are consistently on target, then you have solved the problem. Ambi-dominance may be solved with an occluded patch (Scotch brand tape) over the off-eye. But the tape goes on your shooting glasses, not your eyeball.

Closing the eye also works, but it must be closed at exactly the same time, every time, as the gun is mounted. Failure to patch the off-side eye or close it will result in a miss when you are dominant in the off-side eye. If you are simply cross-dominant, you can tape the eye, close the eye, or shoot on the other side (which isn't as difficult as you'd think). In the Wingshooting Workshop, we routinely switch people from one side to the other. It only takes about a day. Indeed, an accomplished wingshot (what we call a Master Gunner) should be able to shoot effectively either left- or right-handed.

This is a bit radical, but often, people who are ambi-dominant or cross-dominant have difficulty remembering to close the off-side eye at the instant the safety is released. This, because there is no barrel or beads to simulate an aiming situation where closing one, is more normal. So, we have begun placing two or three cotton balls on the upper eyelid of the closed, offending eye, then holding the eye shut with Vetrap™.

We first pull the eyelid down, then place the cotton balls on the lid. Vetrap is wrapped around the head and under the left ear. The tape only sticks to itself, not to the subject. This may all sound a bit odd, but it is a valuable training tool. As a result, we have solved a lot of eye dominance issues that some shooters have struggled with for years.

SUMMATION OF EXERCISE ONE. If you look at a tiny part of a distant object (really focus), then point at it with the dominant side hand, it will always point at the target as long as you do not look at the hand.

EXERCISE TWO. Now we will take Exercise One a step further. With the off-side (left) hand, point at the target—only bring the left hand over, low, and in front of your right shoulder. Now close the left eye and sight along the left finger with your dominant right eye. It too will be pointed directly at the target.

SUMMATION OF EXERCISE TWO. If you point either finger at a small focal point of a distant target, that finger will always align itself with the dominant eye. *Always*. If that finger is carrying a pair

Exercise Two: Point at the dot with the left hand. And, again, close the left eye, and lean down to the pointing finger. It, too, will be pointing directly at the dot, if no eye anomalies are present.

of shotgun barrels on either side of it, the barrels will always point at the focal point. *Always.*

Not once working with the hundreds and hundreds of students who have been through the Wingshooting Workshop has that demonstration failed to work. *Not once.* But there's more.

Each time you did the exercises you fully extended your arm and extended your forefinger. Now I didn't tell you to extend your arm and finger. That is cellular knowledge. That ability was programmed into your DNA at the instant a sperm fertilized an egg that eventually became you. If you don't believe me, ask someone who hasn't read this book, a friend or even a casual bystander, to first face, then focus, then point at a distant object.

Watch what happens.

Think about it. You have just seen our inheritance, the bequest received from our forbearers through hundreds of thousands of years of genetic programming.

EXERCISE THREE. Here's another exercise/demonstration. For this one, it might help to have someone read the directions to you as you perform them. Point your off-side hand (i.e., your left hand if you are a right-handed shooter) at the target dot. Bring your right hand up behind the left, also pointing at the target. Do not look at either hand. Smoothly, pull both hands together back toward your chin while concentrating on the target. Do not let the hands touch each other. As soon as you reach your chin, reverse and smoothly move both hands, pointing, back toward the target. Again reverse until you have achieved a smooth sawing back and forth movement. All the time you are focusing and pointing at the target. Nice, right? It feels good. While continuing the smooth forward and backward motion, slowly lower the rear hand slightly. Notice how difficult the movements become. Raise the rear hand, so it is again in line with the front. See how the movements smooth out. The hands move smoothly only when in alignment.

Exercise Three: First, point at the dot with your off-side hand. Second, bring up the master hand behind the first, both pointing at the dot. Third, bring them back toward your mouth, and immediately return to the dot. Keep in slow motion until you have created a pleasant sawing motion back and forth.

Now, as you're moving slowly back and forth, move the rear hand slightly below the front. See how difficult it becomes. Return the rear to behind the front, and the graceful movement back and forth resumes. In other words, in alignment, the motion is smooth, out of alignment, the movement is awkward. This demonstrates why we need to eliminate consideration of pistol grips, or even semi pistol grips, from our side-by-sides.

SUMMATION OF EXERCISE THREE. To be able to successfully point at a target with the finger after having first mounted a shotgun, both hands must be in alignment, held on the same plane. This is probably because through time we have learned to adapt our hands to straight tools. We learned eons ago that straight objects fly more efficiently than curved ones (except boomerangs, which work on different and far more complex principles). Thus we adapted our hands to work most efficiently with straight tools.

EXERCISE FOUR. Here's an interesting little exercise discovered by one of our students, Ben B. Face the target dot. Bend the right or left arm at the elbow and point at the target with the finger. Your forearm and finger now are only waist high. While focusing on the target, move the finger slowly to the right. Notice how it seems to resist leaving the target. Move it to the left, very slowly. It's like there's a physical resistance to any movement away from the target—bungee cords stretched on both sides trying to pull your finger back to center.

SUMMATION OF EXERCISE FOUR. The Predator has a powerful desire to keep the pointed finger on the target when the target is still. The finger resists being moved off the target. When the target is moving, the same thing is true. However, as we will soon find, the Predator is also able to learn. It will take advantage of anything it can to successfully hit (or kill) the target. It will do so as long as *you* don't interfere—as long as *you* don't try to direct the fingers by looking at them.

While these exercises are interesting and I believe that we have inherited some powerful knowledge through genetic engineering, there stills remains the difficult process of figuring out how to put this information to use. First, we have to take what we've learned and apply it to a practical activity—hitting a moving target.

Again it was Ben B. (a natural researcher) who found proof that focusing on a small portion of the target is the best practice. Interestingly enough it was the African lioness who gave us the breakthrough we were looking for.

In a back issue of *National Geographic* magazine, Ben discovered a series of photos of an African lioness on the attack. She was coming toward the camera from a distance. It was perfectly obvious from the photos that she was not looking at the area encompassed by the photograph. She was not even looking at the wildebeest in the foreground. What she was looking at—focused on, with pinpoint intensity—was the tip of the wildebeest's nose. She hit rough ground halfway through her charge. Even upside down, after her fall, she maintained total focus on the tip of the wildebeest's nose.

Once I realized that the trait of pointing was not only an inherited one, but one we shared with other predators, a single fact became obvious: there was a need to spend more time investigating this ability in our fellow predators to determine: How do *they* point?

How can *we* use *their* genetically-engineered knowledge in our quest for perfect shotgunning? The answer came through careful dissection of their attack procedures, breaking them down into basic elements, then interpreting and reassembling those elements into a viable shooting technique. Pointing is the key to successful shotgunning.

5

A SHOTGUN THAT FITS YOU

What Is It? How Do You Get One?

You hear a lot of advice about gun fit in the popular magazines—most of it ill advised. In general, what little that is in print doesn't apply to instinctive shooters and, certainly, not to practitioners of the technique taught at the Wingshooting Workshop.

In a recent magazine, one writer had this advice about gun fitting: "You should ensure at the outset that you have a gun that fits. By that I mean when you throw it up, it should feel good."

Wow! "When you throw it up. . . ." This sounds like a serious case of the flu. And, "it should feel good?" What? As in warm, soft, and fuzzy?

Here's another bit of advice you see all too often about gun fit: "Close your eyes and mount the gun. When you open them, you should be looking down the barrel." Or a variation of the same: "The beads should align themselves." Another article says that for a pattern which is high, "the front bead should appear to be sitting on top of the center bead."

Let me assure you of this: if an instinctive shooter sees the barrel, let alone the bead, that shooter is going to miss. Indeed, the beads have been removed from the barrels of our Wingshooting Workshop's fitted guns. In made-to-order guns, we advise that you order them without a bead if you want to become a Master Gunner of instinctive shooting.

In the warm embrace of soft lights, soft leathers, rich woods, and the pungent smell of Rangoon oil, gun solvents, and furniture polish, a wayward gunroom salesman awards you his ultimate trust by offering, "Go ahead, close the gun, mount it and point it right between my eyes." A trusting counsel, he must be looking out for your best interest, you think. This is most impressive and calls for your ultimate trust of him as well. After all, he trusts you to point a powerful firearm at his head. A bond is formed. You now trust him, and he knows it. He rejects several guns for you, until he finally declares, "Aha! That one fits like a glove." Not surprisingly, "that one" is also the most expensive. What you *may* find surprising is that after buying "that one," your shooting has not improved.

The truth is that none of these sales pitches, whether in print or in a showroom, is of much use to an instinctive shooter. Sure, those pearls of folklore wisdom may get you closer to a good fit than simply picking one out of a rack or, worse yet, choosing out of a catalog.

In some cases, "close" may be what you get even when fitted with an expensive try gun. The problem with a try gun is that it usually belongs to someone else. Therefore, you are still at the mercy of someone else, together with their advice *and* their shooting technique—which may not be yours, and certainly is not ours. Their advice and technique factors heavily into how they will "fit" the gun. A try gun should always be in the hands of the person who will make a stock. Otherwise some of the important information may not be imparted to the customer—vital information such as stock thickness (which affects cast), stock depth, distance from heel to toe (which affects drop), thickness at wrist, shape of the butt, and the like.

Because the Wingshooting Workshop's technique is unique, we mount and fit our shotguns differently than others do. If you fully understand gun fit and how to accomplish it, then you are no longer at the mercy of others.

Often, a good off-the-peg gun, one that you admire, will get you close to a good fit as well. So if you are going to pay to have a gun fitting or a gun fit to you, making sure that you get a gun at the end of the process that fits is always up to you. "Close" will never do. In gun fit, exact is all that counts.

There are other variables as well. As you age or gain weight or lose it, your body's relationship with the firearm in question will change as well. If you fully understand why a gun fits, you will recognize the changing scheme of things and can gradually change the gun to conform to any changes in body dimensions.

Most shooters conform their bodies to the shotgun, rather than vice versa. So if you are going to pay for a gun that fits, make sure it actually fits and is not just "close."

For all of these reasons, I advise most students and graduates of our Wingshooting Workshop to make that first entry-level, side-by-side shotgun purchase of good design but modest in price. You will be doing some things to it that might make you hesitate if you started with a more expensive firearm. Once you've been through the process, you'll have confidence and may select a more expensive shotgun the next time around. Then, you can do the same with more expensive purchases having the sure and certain knowledge that the outcome will always be perfection.

There are four basic stock dimensions that we concern ourselves with in fitting any shotgun. The primary dimensions are length-of-pull, cast, drop at heel, and pitch. We'll also be concerned with the shape of the butt, stock thickness, and dimensions of the grip or wrist, which may also affect the basic dimensions but are separate animals. Balance is important to consider, as well. You may be asking, "Why did you leave out drop at comb or, more accurately stated, "drop at nose of comb"? Due to the manner in which our students learn to mount the shotgun, cutting the comb usually isn't necessary. As the drop at the heel goes up or down, so does the drop at the nose of the comb. If, at some time in the future, you are having a stock made for you, then drop at the nose of the comb is important. But you'll already have that measurement from your entry-level shotgun which, in effect, takes the place of a try gun in our system.

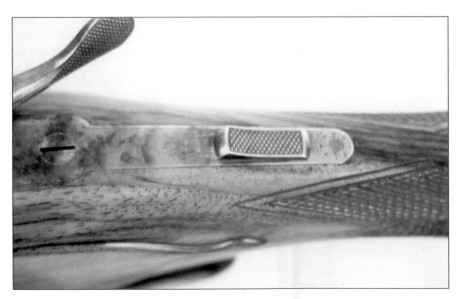

There are only two bolts or pins that attach the stock to the action body in a good side-by-side. You can see the slotted one, which is under the top lever. The other comes up from below and threads in just behind the safety.

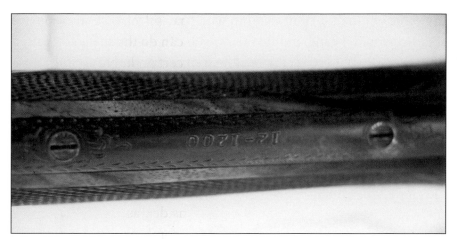

The two slotted fasteners in the tang of the trigger guard are simply wood screws that hold the tang in place.

Fitting by reshaping the stock is done quite easily with most, but not all, side-by-sides. The stocks of these guns are attached with a bolt (also called a pin), which extends from the upper tang, under the top lever, down through the stock to the trigger plate. A second bolt extends from the trigger plate upward to the upper tang, just at the rear of the safety. That's it, just two pins—unless you want to include that there are wood screws that attach the trigger guard to the underside of the stock.

Most of the vertically formatted guns, pumps, semiautos, and over-and-unders have stock bolts that, while they allow some adjustment for a shooter in the open stance, don't even come close for a shooter in a fully closed stance, such as the stance we use in the Wing-shooting Workshop. Bending a stock

Most vertical formatted shotguns, pumps, semiautos, and over-and-unders have large stock bolts which attach the stock to the action. These preclude bending the stock as much as we need it in the closed, instinctive shooting stance we use.

up to the one-half inch of cast-off, which many Workshop graduates require, would mean bending the stock bolt on a vertically formatted gun. From that point on, it would be impossible to remove the stock. This is one of the many reasons why we find vertically formatted guns to be inferior to the side-by-sides for instinctive shooters.

I like my shotguns balanced half an inch ahead of the hinge pin in a walk-up gun (i.e., hunting over dogs). Notice how the weight of the shot is placed directly above the hinge pin, which is the center of balance.

First, we will address this business of balance. If a gun isn't balanced, it won't feel right, no matter how well it fits. Balance is not a stock dimension, but it is vital when dealing with the stock. Balance may be altered through weighting or un-weighting the stock. A good stock maker can place the balance pretty much anywhere you want it. For instance, I like my balance to be half an inch ahead of the center of the hinge pin when the firearm is empty in my walk-up guns. This puts a slight positive weight in my lead hand. Loaded, the weight of the shot is directly above the hinge pin, so the weight of the shells won't affect the balance. The remainder of the shells is behind the pin and thus subtly moves the balance toward the pin, depending on the weight of shell you're using—high brass, low brass, no brass, or whatever. Later in this chapter, balance will be discussed in greater detail.

Now that balance is out of the way, let's take a close look at each of the dimensions, see what each does, and consider how each affects shooting performance—how each dimension allows the firearm to become a servant of the mind.

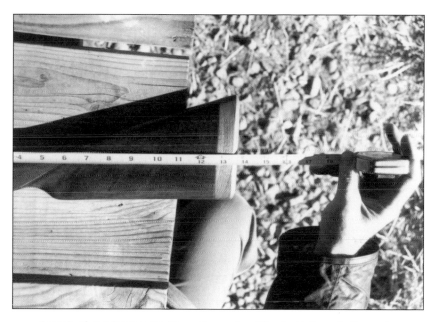

Length-of-pull is measured from the center of the front rigger to the center and crown of the butt.

LENGTH-OF-PULL

Length-of-pull or "LOP," as it is often abbreviated, is an interesting dimension. It is not an "absolute" dimension and can vary quite a bit, while still serving the shooter well. LOP is sometimes also referred to as stock length. It is actually a measurement taken from the center of the front trigger (or, if only one trigger, then from that single trigger) to the center and crown of the butt of the stock. The measurement is properly taken from the front trigger, not the middle of the two triggers, so make sure anyone who is working on a gun for you is measuring it from the front trigger. Some confusion exists over this point. To add to the confusion, in some illustrations, you'll see two other measurements taken from the trigger to butt: (1) trigger to heel and (2) trigger to toe (as opposed to the center and crown of the butt, which we were speaking of when measuring LOP). These two additional dimensions reveal pitch, which we can measure differently, and more simply. For all of these reasons, make sure any LOP measurement is confirmed with a definition, as set forth above (center of the front trigger to the center and crown of the butt of the stock).

First, I want to define some terms we use in the Wingshooting Workshop, as they affect LOP issues. We have two sides—the "gun-side" and the "off-side." The gun-side is the side on which you mount the firearm. Therefore, in a right-handed shooter, the gun-side is the right side. We could add that the gun elbow is the right elbow, the gun leg is the right leg, and the gun shoulder is the right shoulder. You get the idea. The left side is referred to as the "off-side." If left-handed, you would reverse these terms.

Second, let's take a look at LOP, as it is usually affected by the rifleman's stance. Here, the shooter is leaning forward into the off-side leg (i.e., the left leg, for a right-handed shooter) and the leg is slightly bent. The gun's butt is against the shoulder, the gun-elbow up, the cheek is down on the comb, and the shooter's eyes

Swing shooters use a modified rifleman's or boxer's stance. Left leg slightly forward and bent, right leg back, leaning into the shotgun. The right shoulder is slightly back.

In the rifleman's stance, notice how if the muzzles are pointed at the target, the butt is pointed directly at the ball joint of the shoulder. Every time that gun recoils, it will slam muscle, tendons, and flesh between the shotgun's butt and the bone on the inside.

are looking down the plane of the barrel. Notice, in this right-handed shooter, the right shoulder is slightly back in the American rifleman's stance, and is even further back in the British rifleman's stance. Now step away from these riflemen and tell me what you see. Nothing unusual stands out, right? They look normal. But let me point out that while the muzzles may be pointing at the target, the butt is pointing directly at the ball joint of the shoulder. Remember for every action, there will be an immediate and opposite reaction—recoil, which is a backward force in reaction to the blast of the shot. In a shotgunner, this stance means that you are about to receive the full recoil of a 12-gauge shotgun on the ball joint of your shoulder—pinching skin, muscle, and nerves between walnut and bone. This sensation is usually as pleasant as hitting your thumb with a hammer.

In the Wingshooting Workshop, we call the rifleman's stance the "open stance." Some refer to it as a "boxer's stance," as boxers lead

We fit the shotgun in a stance called "goofy foot." This is half of a walking step. We are basically hunters. We are always in a walking step, facing the game. To deepen the pocket, notice how Chuck has crossed his arms, which brings the gun shoulder forward.

with the jab (and they also get knocked on their heels by their opponent's jab. Not a pleasant thought for our shotgunner).

To measure the firearm for LOP in the Wingshooting Workshop, we use a closed stance, not an open stance. Some would call this a hunter's stance, and it is one we have lovingly termed "goofy foot." It doesn't look goofy, but it is the opposite of what most shooters have been taught, so they initially think of it as being a "goofy" request to step forward with what is normally their "back foot" to make it the one slightly in front.

The "goofy foot" is half of a walking step forward (for right-handed shooters, this means your right foot is forward), with the weight resting on the right leg and the left heel raised and un-weighted. The shoulders are squared away to the target dot. You'll learn more about goofy foot in the chapter on the ready position. It's enough to know that in the Wingshooting Workshop, goofy foot represents a fully closed shooting stance or position—it is your natural walking position. Imagine trying to walk like a rifleman all day long. You would have to skip like a schoolgirl. What we are teaching is a natural walking position, with your shoulders square to the potential target (i.e., you are walking upright and following your pointing dog).

Besides ease of walking, this position has other advantages. In a closed shooting stance, the shotgun can be mounted well inside the ball joint, with the toe of the stock in the pocket (that hollow just inside the ball joint and over toward the neck). The comb of the stock is about opposite the top of the shoulder. The shoulder

The shotgun's toe fits in the pocket inside the ball joint, close to the neck. This gets the barrels almost in line with the master eye. The lower jaw is pointed at the target, which allows the stock to snug in even closer to the neck.

itself is shrugged forward, wrapping itself around the outside of the stock, deepening the pocket. Lowering the gun elbow will help lock the stock against the anchor point (which is generally where your teeth meet), when the chin is pointed at the target. That's also why the shape of the butt must be flat with rounded edges for our shotgunners, not a concave-shaped butt, as riflemen do (as they are shooting off the shoulder).

So, how long should the LOP be? We have a rule-of-thumb guideline that'll get you started. It's also something of a catch-22; it's hard to get your final LOP until you know how to shoot with this technique. Yet, it's more difficult to learn the technique without the proper LOP.

So what to do? In general, we shoot shotguns with a LOP from half an inch to one inch shorter than what is considered "normal." For instance, I am six feet tall. I wear a 34/35-inch sleeve on my dress shirts (which Americans call a "long" sleeve). When I used to shoot a shotgun based upon the swing techniques (swing-through and pull-away) in the traditional American rifleman's stance, I shot a shotgun with a 14 ½-inch LOP. With the Wingshooting Workshop method, my shotguns are a 14-inch LOP.

There are several reasons why we do this: We set up the shotgun so it fits our squared shooting stance on a warm day, in June, wearing nothing but a dress shirt. Since recoil on the shoulder is not a factor for us (as we don't mount to the shoulder ball), we needn't use thick recoil pads or recoil absorbing vests. We set the shotgun up so in the mounted position there are two fingers of distance between the thumb's rear joint and the nose. You can easily extend that distance to three fingers without affecting the way the firearm points. That extra finger-length, of course, represents the thickness of clothing on colder days.

In the mounted position, there are two fingers of distance between the nose and the first knuckle of the thumb. This allows for additional clothing before the shoulder is pushed back where it can again be slammed by the stock. In reality, we can go back to as much as three fingers (shown here) before the shoulder joint again begins to align with the stock.

But there's more to it than that. As the shotgun is mounted, thrust forward, and cammed up by lowering the gun elbow, the shoulder follows the butt forward, stopping as the stock contacts its anchor point. This of course means as days get colder and you layer on more clothing, the shoulder simply stops sooner. Thus the mount is self-compensating for clothing, another big plus for this technique over the ones using a static shoulder. So the gun fits the shooter in any weather, without having to change pads, etc.

Let's mention another extremely important point here: the thumb, arched on the ball of the safety, is what sets the final fit of the shotgun. Because this point is so critical, we like to make that location rock

The thumb on the safety begins to set the fit of the entire shotgun. The ball on the safety is jammed under the thumbnail on the inside. Sure it's an irritant. But it helps keep you from forgetting the safety as the mount begins.

solid. When using a safety which is concave, the thumb can be located toward the front or the rear. I know of one shooter who pushes against the very back edge of the safety. The thumb needs to be located in a single precise spot which is the same every time, whether gloves are worn or not. This is why I prefer shotguns with a half ball in the middle of the safety. This ball is always in the same spot. It can also be jammed under the fingernail at the inward corner. It's an irritant, true. But that irritant also helps us remember to turn off the safety during the mount (which anyone learning a new shotgunning technique can tell you he has forgotten at one time or another). So enough about LOP. Let's move on to the next basic dimension.

CAST

Cast is the lateral angle of the stock, and it is measured from the center line of the barrels. Think of it as the swish of a trout's tail. Cast can be difficult to measure, unless you have an appropriate jig to hold the firearm steady, while you locate the center line of the barrel as it relates to the center line of the stock. For this measurement, a fancy gadget helps.

But, you can also accurately measure it with fishing line. First, put a piece of masking tape on the comb of the stock, with one edge running down the center of the comb. This line represents the center line of the stock. Second, loop a piece of thin, monofilament fishing line over the bead and above the muzzles. If the bead is removed, tape the string to the under rib, or put a pair of matchsticks or dowels in the muzzles. Place the loop around the sticks and keep tension on

To measure cast, first begin by placing a piece of tape down the center line of the stock from heel to toe or down the center of the comb or both.

Now tie a piece of fine monofilament line to the bead at the muzzle. If there is none, have a helper hold the line in the center of the top rib at the muzzles.

the line. Third, keep the line taut and draw it down the center line of the rib and past the butt of the stock. Now, hold a ruler on the tape at the butt from the tape's center line to the line of the monofilament. The distance to the right or left of the stock's center line is the cast. If the tape line is to the right of the line, the stock is cast off; to the left, its cast on. The amount, say 1/4 inch, that is common is the cast in inches.

Another method (one which I use in the school) is to lay the shotgun down on a long and straight piece of patterning paper that is longer than the gun. I use 30-inch butcher paper. Center the rib up one edge of the paper. If you suspect the shotgun has right cast, keep the majority of the paper to the left as the gun is upside down and you are facing the butt. A piece of tape with its edge down the center of the butt will indicate cast. Simply put a dot on the paper under the tape's edge. The distance from the paper's edge to the dot is the cast.

There is another more expensive solution to measuring cast. Paul Hodgins of Logan, Utah, is making a very good gauge which measures cast as well as drop at the heel. Drop at the heel, as opposed to drop at the comb, is usually all we need if we are working with an off-the-rack or non-custom gun. By raising and lowering the heel, we move the pattern up and down. By moving the cast back and forth, we move the pattern from side to side. A good gauge for measuring cast can be important in transmitting the correct dimensions to your stock bender or stock maker, but in a pinch the other (simple and inexpensive) methods set forth earlier will provide you with reasonably accurate results.

As for adjusting the amount of cast to the shooter, Robert Churchill came up with a spiffy formula, which we'll explain in greater detail when we get into patterning. For right now, it's enough to know that when a shotgun is patterned at sixteen yards, the center of the pattern will move one inch for each 1/16 inch of stock movement IN THE SAME DIRECTION. This is exactly the same way the rear sight of a rifle or pistol works. If you have ever sighted-in a rifle, this will sound familiar to you.

Imagine this: If you mount a straight-stocked shotgun in the pocket as close to the neck as possible, and focus and point at a distant object while pulling the stock against your anchor-point (lower jaw), it's reasonable to assume the barrels will be pointing off to the left if you're right-handed. It would look something like this to someone standing above and behind you.

If the shotgun has the correct amount of cast for your body size, the stock will travel from the pocket over to your anchor point, then change direction to the right, until it aligns with your extended finger, which is being directed by the master eye. If everything fits, the barrels will point EVERY SINGLE TIME to where the finger is pointing, which is at the target. And it will all happen without looking at the barrels or (even worse) the bead.

There's nothing mysterious about cast. Imagine that you've mounted the firearm. The toe of the stock is in the pocket of your shoulder. Now, you're a right-handed shooter, the stock is over, and it's resting against your lower jaw when your chin is pointed at the target. Wow! Look how far off to the left the barrels are pointing. Okay, so that's why we use cast. The stock first has to travel from the pocket over to the jaw, then change direction so the barrels can align themselves with the pointing finger out there between the barrels. Of course, the pointing finger is aligning itself with the master eye. If you have the cast correct, the barrels are now pointing exactly where you're looking so there's no need to peer down the barrel. Hitting the target now can become automatic to where you are looking—as long as the drop is also correct.

DROP

Drop is the vertical movement of the stock (here you might think of a whale's tail), which in turn moves the strike of the pattern higher and lower on the patterning paper. Drop is measured in relation to the plane of the barrels. If you don't have a proper drop measuring tool, a simple measurement can be obtained by laying the shotgun upside down on a table with the bead hanging over the edge, so the barrels lie flat. If your shotgun has two beads, take the middle one off Actually, our shotgunners take any and all of the beads off, as they are an unnecessary distraction. Now, let's measure the distance from the heel down to the table. That's the drop at the heel. If you take the measurement at the nose of the comb, that is the term sometimes wrongly called the drop at the comb. The true drop at comb is where your anchor point contacts the comb.

In an experiment to fully understand the effects of cast and drop, I once sacrificed a solid plastic stock on an old Remington 1100. By putting the stock between a pair of trees, I bent the stock way off to the right (in relation to the shooter) and began patterning. After each shot on a large piece of patterning paper at 20 yards, I bent the stock back toward center about 1/4 inch at a time. The results confirmed our theory. The patterns marched back to center, which would have been my correct cast-off (I'm right-handed), then continued on to

You can measure the gun upside down, or by stretching monofilament line along the top rib and taking the measurement from the heel to the line.

the left of the target-point as the stock was returned to straight. I had the same results when I lowered the heel of the stock, then raised it one-quarter inch at a time. And remember Churchill's formula: one-quarter inch equates to four inches of movement on the paper. The stock of this old Remington finally cracked in my experiments, but I had graphic proof of what cast and drop do when employed correctly.

What is the proper amount of drop? While it's obvious you want the pattern centered up on the target laterally, that isn't necessarily the case when you consider positioning the pattern vertically.

Most field guns are set up so that when shot from a rifleman's stance, the pattern will hit the target point 50 percent above the target, 50 percent below. The downside to this benchmark is that on a going-away and rising shot, the shooter has to cover the rising target in order to hit it. That's just another way of saying, "Shoot at something you can't see." The barrel is covering the target at the moment the shot is taken. Trap shooters set their stocks so the pattern will always be above the barrel. They can point under the target and hit with the full pattern. That's okay for them since they consistently shoot the same rising shot at the same range. Always counting on a rising shot won't work for us (as we intend to hunt with the same guns we shoot clays with), or at least we didn't think it would work in the beginning, before we learned even more about how clever the Predator really can be.

I can only tell you what I like and how I set up my school guns. Graduates of our Wingshooting Workshop have seen the merit in this theory as well and have followed suit. I prefer a gun to shoot a full pattern high in my own guns and two-thirds high, one-third low in the school guns. Either way, we can look at the target, point slightly below it, and fire without having to take our focus from the bird. Whether you take my extreme or the two-thirds high of my students, the target will always be in the center of the pattern, because the Predator will always allow for lead without conscious thought on your part. *You* always seem to be pointing right at the target.

Once I had a doubter exclaim, "Yeah, that's fine, but that'll screw up a dropping target." In theory, the 50/50 pattern might be better for the dropping target than our 66/33 pattern. Actually, it doesn't screw up a dropping target. We thought the doubter might be right, before we knew fully about the Predator. The conscious mind will rationalize almost anything. In reality, the Predator doesn't care— not about range, not about rising or dropping, not fast or slow, and not about angle. As long as you don't interfere, the Predator will make the calculation and kill the target. There are some things, like fit, that make the Predator's job easier, and that's where the 66/33 (or even the full pattern high, as I opt for) has advantages over the 50/50 model for field shooters and nearly all sporting clays activities.

PITCH

Pitch is the angle created by the plane of the butt and the plane of the barrel. If you rested your shotgun on its butt, barrels up, and if the barrels were perpendicular to the surface of the table (90 degrees), the gun would be said to have zero pitch. If the gun were leaning forward toward the trigger-guard side, it is said to have downpitch or positive pitch. The opposite orientation would be up or negative pitch. Some people measure this angle in degrees, which is great if both you and the stock maker have an accurate tool for measuring.

However, there is an easy way, which works on any gun you might be looking at anywhere in the world. Push a table up against a wall. Make sure the angle created by the two is 90 degrees. Then put your shotgun's butt on the table, muzzles up, and slowly slide the gun toward the wall. Keep the butt flat down on the table. When the action contacts the wall, the muzzles should be leaning slightly away from the wall (downpitch) depending on what kind of butt is on the stock. In the Workshop, we measure all of our guns the same way, at twenty-six inches up the barrel from the chambers. And to keep it simple, we only have two pitches, again,

With one and one half inches of downpitch measured twenty-six inches up the barrel, the school guns with smooth, polished wooden butts kick down one-half inch on recoil. Actually, that amount of downkick was when we were using ammunition with much higher chamber pressures. Currently, the downkick is somewhat less, with lower chamber pressure ammunition, but it really doesn't matter since the shooter is controlling follow-though, which is precipitated by recoil and muzzle jump.

because we mount our firearms differently than in other techniques.

One of the telltale signs of our guns is the shape of the butt—we want ours to be flat. They are designed to be mounted with only the toe inserted into the pocket of the shoulder and the inside of the stock as close to the neck as possible. That's right—a good portion of the butt extends above the shoulder. That's because we shoot with our heads high, chins thrust forward, pointing at the target. In this position, the comb of the stock aligns itself with the shooter's lower jaw. Remember, we are pure pointers, not aimers. The Predator is going to direct the muzzles, not our conscious mind. If we see the barrels, the Predator is shut off and misses. Like a batter, you must keep your eye on the ball, not on the bat. A pure pointer could illustrate the point and even shoot perfectly well with the *chin* on *top* of the stock (comb), but never with the *cheek* on top. When you see an instructor who is teaching one of the swing techniques, but who, on occasion, wows the class with a demonstration of "hip shooting," you're on the receiving end of a con job. The instructor is showing you instinctive shooting, but is still really teaching you a swing technique.

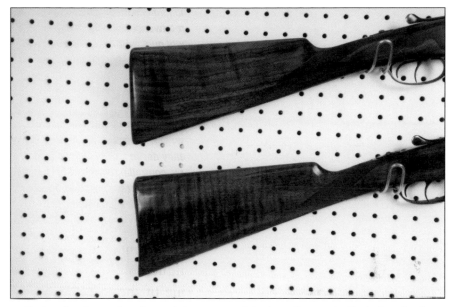

Notice also that we've changed the contour of the butt. Shotgun butts designed to be shot off the shoulder are often convex. This makes the toe of the stock somewhat sharp. To facilitate downkick, we flatten the butt. This also helps the stock slide smoothly from the armpit to the pocket and back again.

For the swing shooters, the butt is crescent shaped (some even have a concave metal plate on the butt). This crescent shape is so the firearm can be placed on the shoulder, and the head dropped to the comb in the aiming stance, without the gun slipping off the end of the shoulder. In this position, pitch determines where the shotgun points, up or down. Just imagine the angle of the butt tipping back and forth. As the toe moves back toward the shooter, it forces the barrels higher and higher. As a result, there are almost an infinite number of pitches for every barrel length. Pitches vary widely among manufacturers of guns. With one gun manufacturer, you even get a complicated chart that's almost undecipherable by customer and salesman alike.

In our technique, pitch controls muzzle jump and thus controls the kick direction at the butt. Put another way, pitch can help control the dismount. Since the dismount is part of our follow-through, pitch is extremely important. Downward kick of the gun is as important

« *This plywood shotgun with an articulated butt is shown with an unnatural amount of downpitch. Zero pitch would be if the plane of the butt and the barrel equal 90 degrees: straight up and down.*

You can easily see an exaggerated amount of downpitch makes the butt kick up. A stock that's unwittingly cut at 90 degrees to the comb, in order to shorten and add a recoil pad for a small or young shooter, can deliver a vicious uppercut. This, undoubtedly, has created countless non-shooters who immediately give up the sport as stupidly painful. ≽

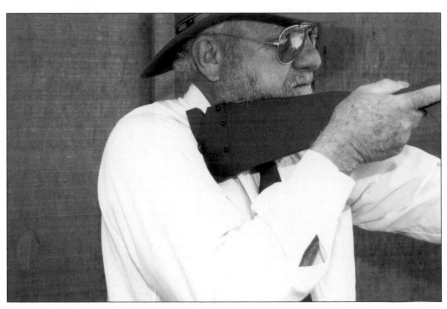

to our gun dismount as a smooth swing is important to the Swing Through, Pull Away, or Sustained Lead shooters.

To give you a graphic demonstration of pitch and how it works, please refer to the photographs. In the photographs, you'll see a simulated gun with an exaggerated butt. In the first photograph, the butt is attached with the heel of the stock, exaggeratedly long. If we set the firearm on a table, the muzzles would lean far out over the trigger guard. This would be a very unusable form of downpitch or positive pitch (from now on we'll

Up-pitch is obviously the reverse of downpitch. The shotgun is now leaning away from the vertical.

just call it downpitch). If we put the firearm *on someone's shoulder* you can see the firearm would point at the ground. Recoil would cause the firearm to move upward and to the shooter's rear. The same unfortunate situation develops when an uninformed gunsmith cuts a stock off at 90 degrees when installing a pad. The resulting five inches or so of downpitch causes the gun to point low and recoil viciously upward. This cruel mistake is often furthered when this type of gun ends up in the hands of a diminutive shooter who has been informed that "the pad will cushion the recoil; just lay your cheek on the comb and

The shotgun with exaggerated up-pitch will kick down on recoil.

To deliver the proper amount of down-kick on recoil, which is one-half inch, the shotgun with a smooth butt should lean away from the vertical one and a half inches. An accomplished shooter can alter this dimension by leaning slightly forward (increasing the up-pitch) to make the butt recoil downward more swiftly, or lean slightly backward (increasing the downpitch) to insure the firearm stays put on recoil.

look down the barrel." The first few shots are very likely to create another non-shooter, as the stock delivers a vicious uppercut to the person's face and slides up the top of the shoulder from recoil.

Now, let's take the replaceable butt and attach it to the stock with an exaggerated toe. Put it on the table and you can see the firearm leans away from the trigger guard and toward the comb side of the stock. This is an exaggerated form of up-pitch. Placed on the shooter's shoulder you can see it will cause the shotgun to point upward. You can see the tendency will be for the shotgun to kick downward on recoil. But, on a shoulder-mounted shotgun, up-pitch makes a shotgun point up.

For us it's different: with only the toe of the butt stock anchoring momentarily in the pocket of the shoulder, UP-PITCH MAKES A SHOTGUN BUTT KICK DOWN AND DOWNPITCH MAKES A SHOTGUN BUTT KICK UP. I'll explain this more fully in a moment.

By altering the pitch, we control what the stock will do on recoil. And, since the shotgun is a rigid piece of equipment, we are also controlling what happens at the other end of the firearm, the muzzles.

Here's another piece of information that'll help you understand the dynamics of recoil. When the primer is hit by the firing pin, it directs a blast of hot gas into the main charge, which begins to burn. While it feels like an explosion to us, it is in reality a controlled burn that accelerates as pressure increases. Finally, the case mouth opens, and the ejecta (the shot and the wad) travel down the barrel. As it does so, the ejecta exert friction on the barrel walls. The resulting force is forward and down. This is because the barrels are hinged at the front end of the action. As the ejecta exit the barrel, the firearm recoils backward and the muzzles jump up. Naturally, the butt goes down.

If we held our shotguns like other shooters, with our lead hand holding onto the wooden forend just ahead of the hinge pin, the problem is even more exaggerated. The lead hand becomes a pivot around which the shotgun can rotate. This is a situation that has caused thousands of shooters to drill holes in the shotgun muzzles, like leaf-cutter bees—in an attempt to reduce muzzle jump.

But we don't hold our shotguns like other shooters. We hold the barrels well ahead of the forend. Indeed, in a well-fitted shotgun, the heel of the lead hand is just under the nose of the splinter forend. This

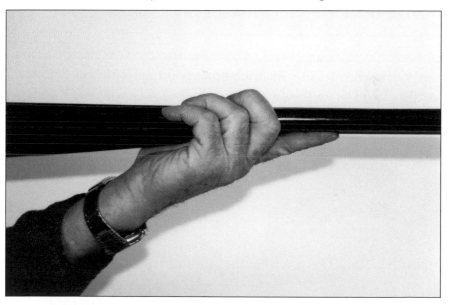

By adjusting the pitch and placing the lead hand in exactly the same place every time, in our case with the heel of the hand just touching the nose of the forend, the amount of muzzle jump and kick down was carefully controlled. This process, muzzle jump and down-kick, is what begins the follow through which takes us back to the dog.

means both hands working together can keep the shotgun angles, IN RELATION TO THE BODY, constant. Rotating the shotgun muzzles up or down is a no-no. But, you don't have to deface your side-by-side to control muzzle jump—and holes in the muzzle are unnecessary in our method in any event.

We'll get to the way we mount the shotgun in a later chapter devoted to the subject. We'll briefly mention mount here, only as it pertains to pitch. We use a shooting position which is half of a walking step. We don't need to change anything from walking position to shooting position. Nothing is forced into position. The head is upright, the body is upright, and the muscles are relaxed. In other words, while walking, we are *in* our shooting position, always ready to shoot. Remember, WE ARE HUNTERS WHO SHOOT CLAYS, NOT CLAY SHOOTERS WHO HUNT. There is a vast difference, since we expect to hit 100 percent (whether they be birds or clay targets) and are satisfied with nothing less than perfection. For these reasons, we must support the firearm with bone, which doesn't get tired and relax the muscles until the instant before the shot.

Because we shoot from a walking stance, we must also shoot with the gun shoulder forward in its normal walking position. Because we shoot in an upright walking stance, the stock must be mounted

higher on our shoulders for the comb to reach our anchor point—the lower jaw.

The toe of the stock is placed in the pocket of the shoulder. Put your off-side hand up to your gun shoulder. Feel the ball

To find the pocket, stand with your shoulders at 90 degrees to your feet. Now reach up to the ball joint of your shoulder. As you roll the shoulder forward, you'll feel the pocket deepen. The side of the stock is touching the neck, and the toe is below the collar bone.

joint of the shoulder? Now, bring your hand inside the ball joint, and under the collar bone toward your ribs. Inside the ball joint and your ribs is the pocket. Roll your shoulder forward and you'll feel the pocket deepen, a natural receptacle for the toe of the stock. I've been at this a long time and now am able to move the gun up and sideways until the stock is almost brushing my neck. I do this by dropping the gun elbow.

In this relaxed shooting position, we want our stock to move downward one-half inch on recoil. This is because we have three different dismounts, depending on what the target(s) are doing:

1. full dismount
2. demi-dismount
3. no-dismount, dismount

At this point, we should say something about recoil, since it's vital to a smooth dismount and follow through. Today, most readily available shotgun shells have between 8,000 and 10,000 pounds of chamber pressure. This is because there must be enough leftover energy to operate the common gas-operated mechanism of a semi-automatic shotgun.

Since we only use shotguns with double triggers (which by definition are never semiautomatics), we can reduce that chamber pressure to between 5,000 and 6,000 pounds. Also, because we always center the target in the pattern, we can reduce the amount of shot to the bare minimum to achieve the highest ballistically-perfect shot pattern (you only need one that is about as thick as a nickel and eighteen inches across). The resulting velocities will be from 1,200 to 1,300 feet per second (fps). Now don't get woofed by the concept of double triggers. Once you learn to use them, which will take about fifteen minutes, you can get off the fastest second-shot in gundom.

Thirty years ago, I decided to use the same anchor point for instinctive shooting a shotgun that I did when instinctive shooting my bow. With my head high and chin pointing at the target, the stock would inscribe a line from the corner of my mouth to the angle

Russ Laws illustrates the anchor point that we use. The bow is drawn until the index finger can be placed in the corner of the mouth. The release, then, is straight back, through the angle of the mandible.

of the mandible (that point where the jaw changes direction from downward to forward).

From that shooting position, I wanted my shotgun to recoil downward one-half inch upon the first shot. Why? Since we don't swing the shotgun, our follow-through is not to continue swinging the barrels along the flight path of a target that has already disappeared. Rather, we use recoil or downkick (which is a function of muzzle jump) to continue on a smooth circuitous path that takes us back to where we started. In hunting, this "starting point" takes us back to the pointing dog. In target shooting, we return back to the trap. This way, we can choose whether to continue a full dismount or, if looking for a faster second shot, we can choose the demi-dismount. The demi-dismount is simply the one-half inch downkick and then a re-mounting. Or, we can choose the no-dismount, which is a dismount in which you simply hang onto the gun and point for an instantaneous second shot. Remember, our shells have one-half the typical chamber pressure and one-half the recoil, so we can control the downkick, if we choose. Think of it as shooting a 20-gauge load in a 12-gauge shotgun. Or, a 28-gauge load in a 20-gauge shotgun.

Actually, that one-half inch of down-kick was achieved with heavier recoiling shells that we once used in our schools. We have found that even lighter recoil shells are advantageous. With our seven-eighths and three-quarter-ounce 12-gauge shells, that down-kick is slightly less than when the 90-degree position is utilized. When doing a demonstration, I can alter the degree of pitch by angling my body forward or back slightly to achieve more or less downkick (depending upon the need.)

Happily, we use only two pitches, regardless of barrel length. If the shotgun has a smooth wooden butt, we use one and a half inches of downpitch at twenty-six inches. If the shotgun has a half-inch recoil pad (it is there to protect the shotgun, not you), then we use zero to one-half inch downpitch at twenty-six inches. Why?

The wooden butt more readily slips on recoil, but even a slick recoil pad tends to conform to the shoulder on recoil and thus resists slipping downward somewhat. But we want the butt to recoil downward one-half inch. Experimentation has shown us that the above-referenced dimensions will give us one-half inch downkick when the firearm is mounted in the proper stance from the correct position. By

the way, it should be stated that a recoil pad is a handicap to a proper mount of the gun. Therefore, the pad itself must be specially prepared to slide smoothly during the mount and dismount. We don't want the pad to drag on clothing the way most pads do these days. It is easy to make the recoil pad slippery (which we will detail in a later chapter). But even a slippery

If the shotgun has a recoil pad, which we use to protect the shotgun, not the shooter, then it has from zero to one-half inch of downpitch at twenty-six inches measured up the barrel.

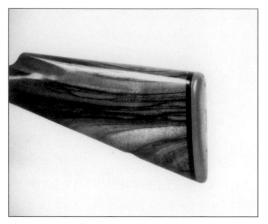

If a recoil pad is used, then it must be made slippery to facilitate the one-half inch of downkick on recoil.

pad conforms slightly to the shoulder upon recoil and, therefore, it requires a different pitch than a bare butt end would.

We want to take a moment here to talk about barrel lengths, since they are closely allied to gun fit. We do not select barrel lengths for the ultimate use to which the gun will be put. In other words, in our method, you'll use the same shotgun in the woodcock tangles or quail edges as you would to hunt ducks or geese. For us, accuracy always overcomes firepower. For us, barrel length and gauge is dependent on the size of our bodies and length of our arms. Gun swingers worry about hitting brush while swinging. We keep the shotgun in the ready position until the kill. It then moves straight forward and back. In the mounted position, the firearm's muzzles may travel an inch or less before the dismount occurs. Also, since we are not swingers or aimers, we do not need a heavy barrel to overcome our natural tendency to stop as the aimed shot is taken, as none of this is part of our method.

We do, however, have parameters for barrel length. A six-foot man could easily shoot barrel lengths from twenty-seven inches to thirty inches without compromising the

In my opinion, the shotgun and shooter should be well matched. A six-foot-three man with 25-inch barrels does not make as attractive a picture as he would with, say, 28- or 29-inch barrels.

overall appearance. The shotgun should look as if it belongs in your hands. A six-foot-four man with a 26-inch barreled 28-gauge looks a little silly, and would tend to over-control the firearm—and simply has too much upper-body strength for so little weight. A five-foot tall woman would have the reverse problem with 30-inch barrels. It would simply look strange—especially with the short stock that we favor, and it might feel funny, since the balance would probably be atrocious, unless severely corrected by a gunsmith. In her hands, the resulting gun would require

No matter how lovely the lady, a five-foot woman does not make as lovely a picture with 30-inch barrels, as she would with shorter barrels, which will also be balanced with the necessary shorter length of stock that she will require.

a great deal of upper body strength and would be hard to handle. The same gun in the hands of a strong man of six foot two might look right, have a bit longer stock, and therefore the balance-point would not be hard to correct, if necessary to correct at all.

When the guns are reversed, the 30-inch barreled L.C. Smith in Steven Theodore Roosevelt's hands and the 25-inch barreled Ugartechea in his wife, Tammy's, the picture falls into place.

BALANCE

Back to balance one final time, as we now have a gun that fits. Balance is a term bandied about frequently, yet few define it, and even fewer adjust the balance to suit their own desires. Side-by-side manufacturers carefully set up their products so that loading the shotgun will not greatly alter balance.

To check the balance, lay your side-by-side on a table so that the trigger guard and stock hang over the edge. Now, carefully lay a cartridge on the top, so its rim is in line with the end of the breech (as if the gun were loaded but now you can see the cartridge on top). Notice how the shot is positioned over the hinge pin. The hinge pin is the formal center of balance in a side-by-side. But, the balance seldom falls directly *on* the hinge pin. With the shot sitting above the hinge pin, the balance is not drastically affected when the shotgun is loaded.

For strictly walk-up guns (used when hunting over dogs), gunners generally prefer a shotgun with the balance ahead of the hinge pin. This gives them a slight positive balance in the lead hand to keep the barrels from lifting overmuch on rising birds. For strictly driven guns (used when birds are driven toward the guns by beaters,

Balance can, and should be, a matter of choice. Manufacturers attempt to place the center of balance in a side-by-side on the hinge pin. But the balance is seldom actually "on" it.

Many who shoot driven birds, passing or generally high targets, prefer to have the balance fall behind the hinge pin. This way the stock is helping to raise the barrels during a long day's shoot.

or used on dove and duck hunts), gunners generally prefer them to be weighted behind the hinge pin, so that the stock is helping the gunner raise the barrels during a long day's shooting. You can have the balance adjusted to accommodate the type of shooting you intend to do most, or you can just have it balanced in the middle of the two positions.

But, adjusted how much? I can only tell you what I prefer and balance my shotguns accordingly. As I said before, my favorite walk-up shotguns balance one-half inch ahead of the hinge pin. This is the least tiring to carry. It feels good in the hand and on the shoulder.

But many of the school guns are balanced up to one and a half inches ahead. This is because lower-priced firearms are not subjected to quite as much expensive draw-filing during manufacturing. Draw-filing by hand lightens barrels and affects balance. It is not unusual to see pricey firearms with 30-inch barrels weighing six and a half pounds and delicately balanced one-half inch ahead or behind the hinge pin. These manufacturers aren't concerned about the added cost of draw-filling during manufacturing. Of course, all of this can be adjusted by a gunsmith, but it often isn't cost effective on inexpensive shotguns to spend a lot of money correcting balance issues.

You must be very careful to constantly check balance if you are going to be changing chokes, if you are adding tubes (neither of which is something we recommend, nor do we find a need for it in our method), or if you are installing a recoil pad. You must insure your ministrations have no vile affects on the center of your affection.

As you can see, fit of the gun is critically important, especially if you are going to shoot instinctively. It is even more critical for the beginning student of the instinctive method. Once you have perfected the method, you can shoot pretty much anything, even switching between taking shots with right- or left-handed shotguns—not that you'd want to, but if you needed to demonstrate a shot or prove a point. The only dimension that affects me much is an overlong shotgun. At over six feet tall, I can demonstrate shooting with school guns having stocks as short as twelve inches. They pose no problem for me to shoot. Our technique, with its forward-rolling

Shooters shooting our technique can easily shoot a stock that's somewhat too short. In the mount, the shoulder continues to follow the butt forward, until the cheek hits the anchor point. This is always the same distance behind the rear hand. This takes a bit of experience, but I do it all the time when demonstrating with a shorter student's shotgun. What's difficult is shooting a gun that is too long. Once the shoulder is pushed back, out of its 90-degree position, the butt is pointed more into the joint of the shoulder.

shoulder, will almost automatically compensate for a too short stock. A too long stock will push my gun shoulder back, and recoil begins to land on the ball joint of the shoulder. This hurts.

As much as one-eighth inch too long of a LOP is immediately obvious. A too short stock will hit targets for me, but the trigger guard may painfully bang my middle finger. If I had to keep this up (as in the case of a borrowed gun), I'd pad the glove of my middle finger with a section of cut-off shotgun shell or a piece of padding (such as the foot and shoe padding available at a drug store).

SHOTGUN SHOOTING SHOULDN'T HURT. IF IT DOES, YOU'RE EITHER SHOOTING A TECHNIQUE THAT'S NO GOOD, YOUR GUN DOESN'T FIT, OR BOTH.

Patterning for Fit

As I stated previously, patterning for fit is something of a catch-22. You can't pattern effectively until you have a stock with the correct cast and length-of-pull and you have developed a mount that's consistent. If you try to pattern before you learn to shoot consistently, the fit will change *after* you learn to shoot (including the length of pull).

This is where a shooting school comes in. It is much easier to learn our method with a shotgun that's too short than it is with a shotgun of the correct length. Our school guns are adjustable Ugartecheas. We begin students with shotguns anywhere from one-quarter to one-half inch (or in some cases even three-quarters of an inch) too short. In the beginning, shooting a new technique that's so radically different from what they believe to be true causes shooters to tense up. By the second day of classes, that same shooter is relaxing more and the stock can be gradually lengthened. The desired length is usually achieved by the third day. Oh sure, the downside of a gun that is too short is that a shooter may occasionally get smacked across the knuckle with the gun. But we can anticipate this circumstance and provide them the school's padded gloves and teach a low elbow, so there is simply no pain involved in this brief learning process. Moving out to the correct LOP from a shorter one is something like removing training wheels from a kid's bike; it's easier to do it in stages than to remove the wheels all at once. And the shorter LOP is very helpful to the novice instinctive shooter, just like the training wheels are to the kid.

So it's best to come back to patterning for fit, after you've learned to shoot the technique, because patterning is best achieved with the correct length-of-pull. Here's how the patterning is done.

If you can borrow a suitable pattern board at a range or gun club that is fine, so long as you follow the other parts of the process below. Otherwise, we'll show you how to set up a large target frame at sixteen

The school's target frame is made of pipe with hooks on the top. These are to hang a simple wooden frame onto and using 40-inch butcher paper stapled to the wooden frame. A focus point is placed in the lower third of the paper.

yards. There are lots of great designs out there these days. Our simple design consisted of a pipe with a wooden frame, to which we staple patterning paper. For backing, we used common field fence, such as sheep wire or hog wire (it has different names in different parts of the country). It's fencing fabric with 4-inch or 5-inch squares. You could use a plywood backing, but it gets shot up pretty quickly.

We prefer to have the patterning board set above eye level. There is another practical consideration if you are going to the expense of constructing your own patterning board, and that is the direction of the wind. We have pipe sections sunk into the ground, into which the patterning-board legs fit. So we can change the direction so that no matter which direction the wind blows from, it is always blowing the patterning paper onto the board.

Now, with the paper mounted on the patterning frame, place a small half-inch dot in the center of the paper's lower third. Remember, you want a pattern that's two-thirds to three-fourths of a pattern, high. Now, step off sixteen yards. That's sixteen yards from your eyes to the paper, not from the muzzles, toes, or tips of your fingers.

You will use only the right barrel for right-handed shooters, and you'll fire exactly ten shots. Simply mount, as you've learned, making sure all the fundamentals are in place. If you must wink an eye, do so on the safety release (so that we don't drop back into some bad habit of attempting to aim). Point your chin at the target and mount, point, and shoot. Do not look at the target between shots. Doing so may cause you to compensate for a pattern that's forming to the left of the target. You want to find out where the shotgun points instinctively, when you are not visually *controlling* where it points.

This is why looking down the beads by yourself in a mirror, or even together with a Cheshire-smiling salesman in a gunroom, is of little value. In instinctive shooting it is not where the barrels appear to be pointing, it's where the patterns are hitting that counts. Your Predator can control or adapt to where it points, but we want to know where it naturally points without your subconscious control of a badly fitting gun.

Once you've found the "average" center, measure sideways to a vertical line drawn up from the target point.

When you've fired your ten shots, which are to be *pointed* and not aimed shots, they should be one on top of the other. If you are right-handed, they will be off to the left of center and if the drop is correct, about three-fourths of a pattern high.

Robert Churchill came up with some sage advice on how to interpret what you now have on the pattern paper. What I do is to place my hands on either side of the apparent patterns. Discount any fliers or shots that are obviously out of place, which is why you shoot ten shots, so you have an average. You want an *average* center. Halfway between your two hands, make a dot. This is the average center of the pattern.

Churchill's rule goes like this:

"For each one inch of correction on the paper, move the stock one-sixteenth inch in the same direction."

From the average center, measure the distance to a vertical line drawn upward from your target dot (notice I didn't use the term *aiming* point).

Let's say the distance from the average center of your patterns to the vertical line is five inches. But you don't want your gun shooting five inches to the left at sixteen yards. So you'll have to move your patterns to the right five inches.

This means you'll have to have the stock bent five-sixteenths farther to the right. I say *farther* because most side-by-sides will have some cast-off (or cast to the right), already built in. For right-handed shooters, that's great. For left-handed shooters, the same stock would have to bent from the right, past the center, and over to the left. Even that is no big deal for a good stock bender. But now you're beginning to see why a shooting school is so important.

Here's another point: Wood is only wood. When heated, its fibers can slip one against the other. My point is that they can also slip back. When I bought my Parker Reproduction, the first thing I did was to pattern it. It was two full patterns high. We shortened it to my length of pull and bent it down as much as possible. It was still shooting a full pattern and a half high. After the comb was lowered, we began the process of bending in cast. In my case, I use seven-sixteenths inch at the heel, nine-sixteenths inch at the toe. It was perfectly bent to my measurements. But, within two weeks, the stock had straightened out. We bent it again. Again, it straightened out, going from cast off to slightly *cast on*. Finally, reluctantly, I had a bit of fiberglass injected into the stock. It held. But the whole process took one heck of a long time.

The point of all this is, you don't have to give up on a gun. Several times, I'd about had it with the Parker Reproduction, but it was so beautiful, I simply had to make it shoot like my other guns. It took two years and several thousand dollars to accomplish the fit. Hopefully, you seldom come across a problem with fit like this.

There's another kind of patterning. And that is an aimed pair of shots. Side-by-sides are regulated to shoot *point-of-aim* (notice I've changed from the term point to *aim*) at forty yards. To test for regulation of the barrels, we actually aim the shotgun like a rifle. Use one piece of paper with a small dot in the center, and fire one aimed shot out of one barrel at the dot. I do it at sixteen yards. With another piece of paper, fire a second shot at the dot with the other barrel. Now place the two aiming dots one on top of the other. The two patterns should be one beside the other. At sixteen yards, the patterns are still converging. But you can see they'll be one atop the other at forty yards. Over-unders do the same thing but they do it top to bottom. If it's a new gun and your tests indicate it isn't regulated, return it to the dealer so it can be returned to the factory.

We've never had this problem with Ugartecheas, but the school guns have their chokes regulated from the breech end before they're ever shot. This ensures that even though in some cases the chokes aren't looking where they're supposed to, as long as the long axis of the barrels are correct, adjusting the chokes usually takes care of the problem.

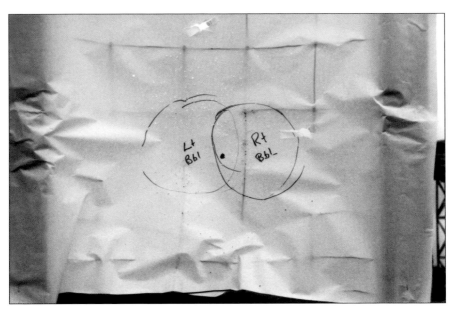

This target is a bit of a fake. I wanted to show what a pair of "aimed" shots look like on the same piece of paper. This is about where they landed. Interestingly, my Predator refused to allow "pointed" shots to land anywhere but one on top of the other.

If it's an older gun and there is no factory, it will have to go to a gunsmith who specializes in side-by-side barrels. If a shotgun looks like it hasn't been used much, and the price is very right, be suspicious. Be sure you have the right to return the piece if it doesn't check out with your gunsmith and the patterning paper. A shotgun that isn't regulated will show it up right away. You may hit with one barrel but not the other.

But with a shotgun that has been shooting well for you for a long while and suddenly isn't, recheck your fundamentals (see chapters on mounting). Then check for a change of eye dominance. If everything else checks out, go to the patterning paper.

6

CARRYING IS THE FIRST PART OF SHOOTING

How to Carry Your Break Open Shotgun

At the Wingshooting Workshop we practice total muzzle control. This means always being able to see the muzzle. But there's more to it than that. Total muzzle control also means "always being ready to shoot." And to this end, there is a single precept: THE BARREL IS NEVER OUT OF ALIGNMENT WITH THE MASTER EYE. Proper barrel/eye alignment is achieved from the moment the shotgun is put together until it is returned to its fitted case at the end of the day. Proper carries are the key to keeping the barrels aligned with the eye. The shotgun may be beneath the master eye, as in the ready position, or slightly off to one side, as in the broken-open-over-the-shoulder-position. But the barrels are always in alignment with, and point in the same direction as, the master eye.

Barrels to the rear violate the first rule of total muzzle control. You must always be able to see your muzzles and the barrels must always be in alignment with the master eye. At the very least this is very rude to the person behind you.

The proper carries advocated in the Wingshooting Workshop are as follows, in order of importance:

1. Broken open over the gun shoulder (the shoulder on which you mount your gun), barrels forward.
2. Broken open over the forearm on the gun side.
3. Closed, first two fingers of the gun hand gripping the toe of the stock, barrels straight up. The action is gripped by the outside by the forearm and on the inside by the upper arm.

4. Closed, gun hand at the grip of the stock below the belt, barrels lean lightly against the gun shoulder.

Right and left shoulder arms are out for the sportsman. This is a muscle carry. Eventually the arm becomes tired. The barrels behind are lowered to get bone support and the muzzles are pointed head high. Even in the proper muzzles-high mode, the barrels are not in alignment with the master eye. A swift shot is all but impossible.

There are several things to keep in mind when carrying a firearm:

1. As soon as the action is closed, the barrels are up. No exceptions. On side-by-side shotguns, the safeties are not true hammer (tumbler) or firing pin blockers. Most side-by-side shotgun safeties simply block the triggers. That means the tumblers are free to fall against the firing pins if the sears fail in some way. An inadvertent low discharge threatens dogs and other shooters. With the barrels high, an inadvertent discharge will fly harmlessly into the air. But the safest way to carry a side-by-side is to have it broken open.

2. The trigger finger never enters the trigger guard until the moment before the trigger is pulled.
3. The safety is never released until the shotgun is on its way forward in the mount.

How to Use the Carry Positions

Broken open over the gun shoulder

This is my favorite position in the field when hunting. I have total bone support for the shotgun and the gun hand controls the barrels. We have a high-speed dismount (we say you are "dismounting" from a carry position to the ready position, and all shots start from the ready position, even if just for a moment) from this broken-open-over-the-shoulder position in which the barrels slide down the shoulder and arm. However it may be a bit too complicated to safely teach out of a book. It is blindingly fast, but unless you're under expert supervision while you properly learn how to complete this high speed dismount safely, it could be dangerous if not perfected.

We'll focus on the safer dismount from this broken, over-the-

shoulder position which is still very fast and easy. Under normal situations, simply reach up to the barrels at the breech end, lift the shotgun off your shoulder, and bring the gun hand up to the wrist of the stock. Your thumb should

Technically, this carry is part of the rapid dismount from the shoulder. It is actually a holding position if the dog has not locked up on a bird and is still moving. It's not very comfortable but it conforms to our rules: muzzles up; barrels in line with the master eye. The gun hand is kept below the belt with the barrels leaning lightly against the shoulder.

Right and left shoulder arms are out for the sportsman. In this muscle carry, the arm becomes tired. The barrels behind are lowered to get bone support, and the muzzles are pointed head high. Even in the proper muzzles-high mode, the barrels are not in alignment with the master eye, and a swift shot is all but impossible.

In the first step of the rapid dismount (practice this for a long time with the firearm unloaded, before attempting a field), you reach across with the offside hand and grasp the barrels with the thumb against the nose of the forend. The gun hand releases the barrels and moves sideways until it is in line with the shoulder and at the same height. The offside hand tips the gun off the shoulder and it slides, muzzles forward, barrels in line with the master eye, to the inner elbow.

Do not allow the trigger guard to slide down in front of the arm. This will surely allow the firearm to slam shut, damaging the action.

Pull the gun forward with the offside hand still on top of the barrels. Pull until the trigger guard slides past the gun hand. The thumb is on the inside of the top lever to protect the action. The toe of the stock is still on top of the elbow.

With full pressure against the top lever, grasping the stock at the wrist, lift smoothly with the elbow. The idea is to raise the stock to the barrels. Never raise the barrels to the stock. With the action closed the stock is moved to the armpit, the thumb of the gun hand goes to the trigger guard while the trigger finger supports the gun under the wood beside the trigger plate.

be on the inside of the top lever. Put full pressure on the top lever and lift the stock to the barrels. The barrels remain pointing about a foot ahead of your feet. Now you can ease the cross bolts into position. Trust me, it takes a lot longer to *tell* you how to do it than it does to just *do* it. If you do close the firearm, it's best to go immediately to one of the closed-gun positions discussed later.

Let's say you haven't shot and you are following a pointing dog; the focus of your eyes is protected, since you're watching the dog. When your dog goes on point, you begin to focus on the brush or whatever cover the dog is honoring. You're pretty sure the bird is hiding in there, and your focus is *still* protected. This is important because when the bird *does* appear, your focus will be ripped from the brush to the tip of the bird's beak.

Broken open, over the gun arm

While the students use the over-the-shoulder carry a lot in school, I do not use it a lot. The difference is that I'm carrying two shell bags

If the dog is on point, simply reverse the hand to its normal location in the ready position.

If the dog is still moving, but birdy, move the offside hand up to the chin while lowering the gun hand below the waist. The gun hand should be holding the wrist of the stock. Do not allow the fingers near the triggers. Then drop the offside hand, so it doesn't block your view. The barrels can now lean gently against the gun shoulder.

When the dog does go on point, simply pull back with the gun hand and catch the stock with the armpit. Immediately the gun hand under palms the stock, finger on the ball of the safety, trigger finger under the stock, away from the triggers. I usually like to keep my offside hand away from the barrels, as Chuck is doing here. This way my vision is not blocked and a shot can be all but instantaneous.

during the first two days of school and one bag on the third day. Most of the time in the school, I carry the shotgun broken open, over the forearm of the gun arm. While this would appear to be a muscle intensive position, in truth, it is not.

Traditionally, the hand warmer or slash pockets found on many leisure or sporting coats arose as hand warmer pockets for someone carrying a firearm. With the shotgun broken open

over the forearm, the hand can be thrust into the slash pocket. Now the coat bears the full weight of the shotgun. This many not be a very good carry for the hunting field in cold weather since the hand, possibly with a glove on it, is incased in fabric (making it difficult to remove quickly). But, on the range, it is fine and can be very comfortable.

I carry the gun over my forearm, but grasp the edge of the shell bag with my hand. I can fully relax the arm and let the bag carry the weight. Keep the trigger guard *behind* the arm. We've had some shotguns do nosedives into the dirt when a student gets the trigger guard *ahead* of the arm. Since our shotguns do not have pistol grips, and with most of the weight ahead of the arm, there's nothing to keep the gun from slipping out, unless the trigger guard is behind the arm.

For graduates, this is the most common field carry. The shotgun is broken open, muzzles forward, barrels in line with the master eye. From this carry, using our rapid dismount, a gunner can bag a bird or break a target quickly and smoothly.

Always place your carry straps for shell bags or game bags across the body (e.g., how women protect their purses in crowded subways) by strapping them over the head and one shoulder. Never allow anything to simply hang off the gun shoulder, where it might interfere with the shoulder pocket and thus interfere with a proper mount. It's also a good idea to keep the shell bag ahead of your gun hip. If it gets behind you or at the side, it can swing backward when you go up for a high overhead and throw you off balance.

Closed, vertical carry

So far, all the carries I've described have required the gun elbow to be bent. After a while your arm can get stiff in a bent position and you might like to get it straightened out. The closed, vertical carry is the answer. It is also extremely fast to get into action. Like the others, it provides bone support and doesn't block vision when in rough terrain or while trying to flush a hiding bird.

In the closed, vertical carry position, the firearm is loaded and closed, with the safety on. The first two fingers of the gun hand go around the toe, trigger finger on top, the rest of the fingers are underneath. The forearm is around the outside of the stock. The barrels are cradled against the inner elbow, and rise up along outside of the biceps. By pressing in with the forearm, the firearm is locked against the upper arm. It is quite secure, and though off to one side, it is in the same plane as the master eye. The dismount is extremely swift.

While in this carry position, the offside hand comes across and up to the barrels. The barrels are grasped so the heel of the hand just touches the nose of the forend. Now, lift with the gun hand and the stock will slide upward into the armpit in the coiled position, fingers just touching the chest. The gun hand slides forward to the wrist, "small" or the "hand" of the stock. At the same time, your gun hand rotates slightly under the wrist of the stock, bringing your thumb into contact with the safety, trigger finger alongside the trigger guard and supporting the gun. This is the final movement in achieving the ready position.

And, as you will see in the next chapter, the shot always begins with the critical ready position, however brief.

7

THE ALL-IMPORTANT
READY POSITION

During my rounds of the Shooting Grounds, back when we were open to the public, I one day stopped at a field to watch a group of shooters practicing for the upcoming hunting season. Most seemed to be shooting about 60 percent, save one poor chap. He was terrible. His technique worked against him, exacerbated by a truly horrible ready position. After shooting at his allotted number of targets, he came back and asked, "I can't hit a damned thing. Can you give me a hand here?"

"Are you a hunter?" I asked, knowing full well what his answer would be. But his answer surprised me.

"Yeah. Always get my limit of pheasants too. But I'm no good on these damned clays."

"I'm sorry. I can see that. Tell me, about how many shots does it take to get your limit?" Knowing the limit was three roosters, I was curious as to the number of shots it took him to bring these three birds to bag.

"No more than six 'er seven," he said, showing a certain pride.

"You get your three birds with only six or seven shots?" I asked, as I was unable to hide my astonishment in the face of the shooting demonstration he'd just displayed, which was far less than 50 percent.

"No, six 'er seven magazines," as he gazed down at his gun.

You've heard the phrase, "My jaw fell open in amazement?" Well, I'm sure this was the case. I simply stood there and gaped at his semi-automatic shotgun, which held five shots. He was expending thirty to thirty-five shots for his three-bird limit.

In the first place, this is an example of a shameful waste of wild-life. There is no way of knowing how many birds died every time this man went out. A pheasant is a tough customer and often gets away wounded. He takes a hard hit, and head shots are best, to bring him down and keep him down.

Hoping my disgust didn't show, I said, "Well, we'll get you shooting better. First, though, I want to change the way you carry your shotgun and your ready position."

"Wha'da'ya mean?"

I showed him that by carrying the shotgun in his loose approximation of port arms, the muzzle had to make a wild swing first from his left shoulder to his right, and then downward as the butt was raised to his shoulder. "The muzzle is moving too much from this port arms carry to your ready position," I explained. "You want as little muzzle movement as possible, and then only in relation to the target. The muzzle and target always work as one—then, only from a ready position that facilitates as little movement as possible."

I showed him a carry and the resultant ready position we instinctive shooters use.

"I can't do that," he replied to my rather lengthy explanation.

"Oh, why not?"

" 'Cuz that's not how I carry my shotgun," he said and hurried off to find his companions.

Later, I saw him demonstrating to his buddies the few things that I had shown him. They seemed to find it amusing, and invented numerous parodies to the technique while enjoying beers in the parking lot after shooting was over. There are a few guys who just can't be helped. For all the rest who aren't closed-minded, there is promise.

I offered this illustration because I would like to have your undivided attention. I know you'd never behave like this guy. The proof is that you're reading this book. No, I want your undivided attention, not because I fear you are closed-minded, but because this is the most important chapter in the book and I am afraid that you will not take the next point seriously enough.

The ready position is everything. THE READY POSITION IS EVERYTHING. **THE READY POSITION IS EVERYTHING.** *THE READY POSITION IS EVERYTHING.* Can I emphasize this point any further?

Do not schlep through this chapter. Whether you succeed or fail with this method depends on how well you follow the directions in this chapter. There are a lot of steps in learning the ready position. Do each of the steps each time you assume the ready position. As we used to say in the military, "Do it by the numbers"— every time out.

Resist saying to yourself, "God, I can't do that every time. For instance, what will happen in hunting?" You are in training.

Do each step in turn until there is no conscious thought. You are training your body to assume the same position in relation to the shotgun, the same angular relationship, every single time. So, when the time comes and you don't have time to do anything but react, your body will do what it has been trained to do, with unbelievable swiftness.

It's like a major league baseball pitcher. They go through the same windup every time—whether it is for a practice pitch or the World Series. It's the windup that creates the consistency in the pitch. In fact, if you asked them to throw a pitch without their patented windup, they probably couldn't do it—at least not very well. It's so ingrained in their subconscious, as they have done it so many times, that it cannot be separated from the act of pitching itself.

Similarly, our steps blend together into a lovely flowing single motion starting from the ready position, through the mount, the shot, and back to the ready position again. To us, the ready position and mount seem to be performed in a dreamlike state or something that happens fluidly underwater. To the uninitiated, the mount appears to be a movement almost too rapid to see, like those unfamiliar with baseball are awed by the speed of a World Series windup and delivery.

Remember: "We shoot like the rattlesnake strikes." And the rattlesnake always strikes from the coiled position.

When practicing the ready position without targets, we go to the goofy foot position. This is the position we used to fit the gun. And in practice, we are refitting the shotgun before every shot. With targets or while hunting, obviously, we do not always shoot from the goofy foot position. Actually, we have three versatile shooting positions. These depend on what the target is doing.

We are the only creatures in nature who have an odd number of legs. We have three—the gun leg and two bird legs. Bear with me for a moment, in case you think I am pulling your, er, leg. I have a serious point to make.

The Gun Leg

The gun leg, like the gun side, the gun arm, the gun shoulder, etc., represents the side on which you mount your shotgun. Your gun leg is always your right leg if you are right-handed, or the left leg if you are left-handed.

The Bird Legs

We have two bird legs, as the bird leg can be either the right or the left leg. They are simple to understand because they are hemispheric. If the bird/target is anywhere in the right hemisphere from straight ahead to straight behind, stand on the right leg. If the target/bird is anywhere in the left hemisphere, stand on the left leg.

The position is easy to assume since our shooting positions are simply half of walking steps.

For a right-handed person, to go goofy foot or to stand on the right bird leg (in this instance, they're the same), simply take half a step forward and come down on the right leg. Transfer all the weight to the right leg and lock the knee. We always shoot off a locked knee since we can rotate further off a locked joint than a bent one. Now simply raise the left heel. Keep the feet close together, about three or four inches apart, the same distance you would when walking in the field. The toes of the rear foot are about opposite the front heel.

Face the Dog

Remember, we are basically hunters who shoot clays, not vice versa. So in preparing for a shot, just think of facing the dog.

Modern clay techniques usually tell you to point your foot where you want to break the target and rotate back to the target thrower. Since many of these shooters are shooting in the rifleman's stance with the weight forward on a bent (read not rotatable) knee, they are limited to 45 degrees either side of straight ahead. For hunting, this is not practical or even smart.

So, why not face the dog, since it is the only one in your hunting party who seems to know where the bird is anyway? This way, you can adjust your stance depending on what the bird does. If you don't know which way the bird will go, you can rely on goofy foot. In other words, you're favoring the gun side. A bird or target flying into your gun-side hemisphere is the more difficult shot. A right hander has more difficulty with a left to right flying bird/target (right hemisphere), since he is winding up. A right to left flying target (left hemisphere) is easier for a right hander who is then unwinding.

The Test

(Trouble Shooting Test #1)

It is critical to perform The Test *BEFORE EVERY SHOT* when practicing instinctive shooting. (I call this The Test because it was the first of the trouble-shooting tests I came up with and didn't know there would be others.) Also, when practicing, even after you've learned to shoot instinctively, it's a good idea to go through the formality of The Test before each shot. You won't have the time to do it while hunting. That's why it's so important in practice. Hunting is usually bad practice for shooting. It sometimes forces us to be sloppy. We just go for the shot and hope our bodies have learned their lessons well. Therefore, it is critical during hunting season to intersperse trips afield with precise practice sessions. Remember— do The Test and do it by the numbers.

To be a good pianist, you play the scales. To be a great skier, you must practice to "make it look easy." To be a good instinctive shooter, you do The Test before every shot. In the field, the Predator takes over and you have no idea what you did. Luckily, enough of our conscious mind remains in control so as to keep things safe and even holler "hen" or "dog" or "person."

A. THE TEST FITS THE GUN TO YOU BEFORE EVERY SHOT.

B. THE TEST STRETCHES THE MUSCLES AND PREPARES FOR THE MOUNT.

Remember in the chapter on fitting, we agreed that the shotgun should, as nearly as possible, be fitted so it is 90 degrees to the shoulder both laterally and vertically. The Test sets this up.

1. FOCUS—First you've got to begin developing and protecting your focus. The target thrower (which represents the dog for us) is probably safely behind a barrier. Select a point on the barrier, a nail head, a knot, or even a dot from a felt-tipped marker, near where the target will appear. NEVER ATTEMPT TO LOOK AT AN IMAGINARY POINT WHERE THE TARGET WILL APPEAR. Your eyes will focus on infinity, since you can't look at nothing. When the target eventually does appear, it will be out of focus and you'll never be able to achieve critical focus as quickly. So, focus back on the dot where the target is originating. When you position the rear hand, it begins the pointing process. Continue to look at the dot and point your rear hand slightly under it. When the target does appear, the focused Predator will be instantly attracted by the movement and move to the focus instantly to the leading edge.

A focus point is a tiny (depending on range) dot, knot, bolt, or, in this case, a roofing nail and washer painted white. This dot is on the same plane as the target will be on when it appears.

2. POSITION THE REAR HAND—It all begins with the safety. The thumb behind the ball of the safety sets the entire fit of the shotgun. We use safeties with a half ball since it provides a solid surface to push against even with a glove on. It also represents a single point from which to fit the shotgun. You can use the rear corner of the safety, if yours doesn't have a ball, but make sure you always use the exact same corner. Let's say you have the ball safety that we prefer.

The thumb on the safety sets the entire fit of the shotgun. Dig the ball of the safety under the inner corner of the thumbnail until it is a bit uncomfortable.

Arch the thumb of the gun hand over the safety and dig the ball in under the thumbnail on the inside corner of the thumb. This is a mild irritant, which helps keep you from forgetting the safety. It also positions the gun hand properly on the wrist. Now, lower the gun elbow and rotate the hand slightly under the wrist or grip of the gun. The trigger finger is now supporting the firearm above the front trigger. The underside of the grip is resting on top of the outside heel of the hand. Keep your wrist straight and you've achieved good bone support. The middle finger should be from one-sixteenth to one-eighth inch behind the trigger guard.

3. PLACE THE HEEL—Place the heel of the stock in the center of your armpit. Let me emphasize that again. PLACE THE HEEL OF THE STOCK IN THE CENTER OF YOUR ARMPIT. This is all you have to remember. Everything that comes afterward is natural.

4. DROP AND ROTATE—Now drop the off-side arm to the seam of your pants. As you do, rotate the gun shoulder forward until the shotgun is sticking out from your armpit at 90 degrees, both vertically and horizontally. Be sure that the muzzles (and your eyes) do not leave the focus point.

With the gun hand firmly in place, drop the offside hand to the seam of the trousers and rotate the gun shoulder forward until it's at 90 degrees with the barrel. You have intense focus on the focus point. The trigger finger is pointing under the focus point. With the gun hand slightly under the gun, you can maintain this position for some time. This is a handy position to use while searching for birds.

Be sure you keep a normal, upright posture, head up, elbow down, shoulders straight across. If you're doing it correctly, you should be able to maintain this position for some time. This is the same position you'll use when kicking around for a pointed bird that's holding and won't fly. You're only a split second away from a shot, yet your off-side arm and the barrels aren't blocking your vision downward into the grass or brush. You can also maintain total muzzle control. If you're having trouble, it's probably because your gun hand is on the side of the stock and too high. You're holding the gun up with muscle support, and forcing a lot of weight to hang from the wrist. The shotgun remains at 90 degrees in relation to your body and gun shoulder.

Back to that ball under the nail—it still hurts a bit, right? Well, we want it to irritate you into remembering to turn off the safety during the mount. If you can't feel it, you'll forget the safety. The worst thing you can do with the thumb is to lay it on top of the safety. If you do forget the safety, and eventually you will, it will really get you ticked that you missed the shot. Worse, you may forget to move your thumb out of the way and off to the side. If you do, the top lever becomes a cleaver perfectly capable of inflicting great damage to your thumb on recoil.

The safety comes off at exactly the same time during the mount. It's automatic. NEVER DISCONNECT AN AUTOMATIC SAFETY. It's there for a reason and will become an automatic part of your gun mount. With our method, you'll never forget to turn the safety off again. No more missed shots because you forgot the safety.

5. POSITION THE LEAD HAND—The off-side hand controls the mount, so it must be positioned properly. You are already focused on the focus point and pointing under it with the forefinger of the rear hand.

Now, also point with your off-side arm—elbow locked, palm down, the hand in a gentle fist, pointing finger pointing, a couple inches to the side of the barrels. As you do this, be sure to keep

Now, point at the focus point with the offside hand, palm down, elbow locked. Be sure the hand is held along side of the barrels, not up in front of the face. Now in one slow, smooth motion, roll the hand and elbow under the barrels and grasp the barrels with the offside hand, so that the pointing finger is in the groove between the barrels.

your shoulders square. You must try to keep your 90-degree angles consistent. Do not reach forward with your off-side arm and drop your gun shoulder back at the same time—a common error.

Now, rotate the off-side hand and elbow under the barrels while keeping the elbow locked. No, you're not going to shoot with a locked elbow. But keep it locked at this point. Grasp the barrels with the thumb along the offside barrel; third, fourth, and fifth fingers grasp the gun-side barrel. Bring the elbow close to the firearm as well.

THE POINTING FINGER SHOULD LIE NATURALLY BETWEEN THE TWO BARRELS. If your pointing finger is pointing toward the gun side, your offside elbow is too high, creating a poor point and forcing muscle support. Rotate the elbow further under the firearm so the pointing finger points naturally up between the barrels. This also gives you some bone support. Keep your focus. The lead finger is now also pointing slightly under the focus point. THE LINE OF VISION AND THE PLANE OF THE BARRELS IS PARALLEL. If the focus point is high, do not raise the barrels to the focus point with your arms; the body must be rotated rearward at the hips to raise the barrels. You must keep those two 90-degree angles consistent: the vertical angle and the horizontal angle.

6. COIL—Okay, here we go. Here comes the rattlesnake, the lioness, or the Olympic sprinter. In this rather awkward position, unlock the offside elbow and coil the shotgun straight to the rear. Keep the 90-degree angles. Do this very smoothly and very slowly. This movement sets up the mount movement. Do it quickly with a jerk, and you'll have a quick and jerky mount.

Now, coil the firearm straight back. Maintain contact with your armpit. Do not raise or lower the barrels. They should remain parallel to the ground. Your barrels and vision line should be parallel. If the target appears at a high angle, you should shift your hips forward, your shoulders go back, all the while keeping the knee of your bird leg locked. Remember, to raise or lower the gun, you must do so with your body, not your arms. Do not bend backward at the small of your back. Keep your back straight. Raise and lower the shotgun by moving the body backward or forward.

COIL IN SLOW MOTION. DO NOT DROP THE BUTT. *KEEP THE COMB OF THE STOCK FIRMLY AGAINST THE ARMPIT.* Coil rearward until the fingers of the gun hand just touch the chest. Keep the barrels horizontal. When coiled, the line of vision and the plane of the barrel remain parallel. A common error is to drop the butt when coiling. The butt goes down, and the muzzles go up. When the shotgun is thrust forward in the mount, the barrels will slide forward at an angle and intersect the line of vision. You'll see the barrels and, as a result, shoot high. The barrels and vision must maintain this parallel relationship throughout the track and mount.

Chuck is now in the ready position and coiled. He will stay in this position during the track, which we'll discuss next. It only takes a second to perform The Test and Coil. It's a vital part of your practice sessions. Don't get sloppy. Do the entire Test and coil in slow motion. To be fast, you must learn to go slow. Remember the cowboy who tried to be a quick draw and ended up shooting himself in the foot. You'll never be aware of the speed, just smoothness.

7. ROTATE THE GUN SHOULDER FORWARD—This is one of the last things you'll learn how to do in perfecting your mount. But this is the part that self-compensates for additional clothing. Remember, we fitted your shotgun so it fit on a warm summer day. It's shorter than most. But since we shoot in a fully closed position, we can get away with this, whereas rifleman stance shooters can't. Rotate the gun shoulder forward. I think of it as pointing at the focus point with the tip of my gun shoulder. This helps to keep me square to the shotgun.

I know this feels like an awkward position, at least at first. I thought so too when I first tried it. But remember, the Predators have largely come up with this ready position. If they want it, it's okay by me. And, after a day of practice, you'll come to realize that *this,* not the rifleman's stance, is the natural position for shooting a shotgun.

This is where the ready position ends.

THE END OF THE READY POSITION IS NOT THE BEGIN-NING OF THE MOUNT.

While in the ready position, coiled, the shooter must also track the target or bird. We must maintain our critical focus.

FOCUS, FOCUS, FOCUS.

From time to time, I hear people talk about "the sweet spot." As I understand it, the sweet spot is that limited time in which the shooter can critically focus on the target. Supposedly, then, the shooter can only break the target at one point in the flight path. Frankly, in my opinion, that's not good enough. Certainly it's not good enough for an instinctive shooter. We can and should learn to focus on the leading edge or tip of the beak for the entire flight path of the target or bird. We should be able to break a target at any point in the target's flight path that we choose, or when the opportunity presents itself.

In addition, I hear a lot of talk about focus when many targets are in the air at the same time. Of course, for us this is simple—there are *never* a lot of targets in the air at one time. There is always only one target—the target is the one you're going to shoot. The others are just background noise, like clouds in the sky, until after the first kill when one of them might become the second target.

All of the above is simply a matter of training yourself to focus. And you needn't be shooting to learn it. Indeed, shooting while learning to focus only complicates an already difficult skill.

During a recent Workshop, Charlie D. turned around and said with amazement, "This is like mental weight lifting." And it is. But mental awareness and concentrated focus are skills you can learn.

In instinctive shooting, when I see the shot pass six inches behind the target, I know the student has lost focus. This missed shot won't pass seven inches behind, and not five, but exactly six inches. Misses in instinctive shooting are always very exact. And every miss should tell you exactly what went wrong on the shooter's end.

It's what we call "window watching." In other words, the student is looking at the window where the target is flying. A miss six inches behind is always because the student was not concentrating his focus on the leading edge. The student was window watching.

If I see the student continually hitting the back edge of the target, I know he was looking at the entire target, not focused on the leading edge. You see, a clay target is too big for our Predator to focus on. Instinctive shooters pick a tiny point and learn to intensely focus on it, from the instant the target appears until it breaks or disappears into the grass. That point must be the leading edge of a target, or the tip of the beak, if it's a bird. Every so often, especially before hunting season, graduates will arrive at the Workshop to tune up and practice clipping the leading edge off the target. Once the mount is perfected, it's usually just a matter of having them be able to redevelop that concentrated focus on the leading edge of the target. Sports psychologists talk now about batters looking to hit the laces off the ball. We saw the success in this type of concentration a long time before, with an intensive focus on the leading edge of the target.

Protect Your Focus

As an instructor, it's easy to know when a student is looking into space, at a point where the target will appear, instead of at a focus point on the barrier. When the target flies, the student's barrel gets left behind. Indeed the student remains behind until the eyes finally focus. And this may be long after the target has passed the shooter.

This could be why shooters have so much trouble hitting going-away targets. Because there is no single point on which to focus. In watching shooters trying to hit these targets, I notice a lot are hit on the left or right edge. The edges represent single spots, which good shooters look for when they point. Actually, a true going-away shot is relatively rare. Most shots will be slightly to one side or the other of the target's flight path.

There is a simple solution. If you find yourself slightly to the left side of the flight path, shoot the target's left edge. If to the right, shoot the right edge. True going-away shots for the instinctive shooter can be tough—apparent motion is at a minimum and there is no single spot on which to focus. For these true going-away shots, I usually focus on the left edge, drive the gun quickly but smoothly, and shoot under the target. Once you get the hang of it, going-away shots are easy for us.

The eye of the Predator is attracted by movement. When most of us hunt upland birds in the States, we are following a dog—let's say either a pointer or flusher. In most cases, we are looking at the dog while we are in the field. If a flusher, the dog is near the bird when the bird goes up, and focus is thus transferred from dog to bird. If the dog's a pointer, we transfer our focus from the dog to the cover toward which the dog is pointing. Again, focus is successfully transferred from dog, to cover, to bird. The problem occurs when the bird flushes. Our eyes are attracted by movement and, in the case of a game bird, this means the movement of the wings. Since instinctive shooters hit what they look at, and since the eyes are attracted by movement, a wing gets hit because it is moving faster than the head. So what does one do to avoid "winging birds"?

Simple: focus on the tip of the beak. Alright, I admit it's not simple. It's hard. It takes practice. You have to override the Predator's desire to focus on the movement of the wing and train the Predator to seek the movement of the tip of the beak. And again, like practicing focus on targets, practicing focus on bird beaks is best learned when you're not shooting. Get a birdfeeder and practice watching the bird's beaks that fly in and out of your feeder. You can train the Predator's ability to intensively focus while doing most anything.

The reason I mention this here is that focus is best established when setting up the ready position. To maintain that focus is a function of Tracking.

THE LITANY OF THE TEST

1. Correct foot position (when possible), focus on the focus-point.
2. Thumb on the safety sets the fit of the shotgun.
3. Heel of the stock in the center of the armpit (we call it a gunfighter stance).
4. Drop the offside hand away to the seam of the trousers.
5. Point the gun-shoulder at the focus-point.
6. Now, with the offside hand pointing alongside of the barrels, and with the elbow locked, roll the hand and arm under the barrels until the pointing finger is in the groove between the barrels.
7. Keeping the stock firmly against the armpit, coil the shotgun straight back until the gun-hand fingers are touching the chest.

8

TRACKING

Along with the Ready Position and the Test, Tracking is equally important.

Tracking is so important, in fact, that it has *two* tests to help find the problem if something goes wrong. And remember: "something's going wrong" is easily identified. If you miss two targets in a row and you don't know why, something has gone wrong.

When you execute your ready position correctly and follow it with a lovely and accurate track, mounting and shooting become pieces of cake. You will hit the target—every time.

The two tests for tracking are THE POINT and THE RELATION-SHIP. First, though, let's take a look specifically at tracking. Tracking takes you from the point where you establish the ready position to that point where you mount the shotgun. Throughout the track, your body remains in the ready position. It is during the process of tracking that the Predator receives target speed, range, angle, height, and size.

The instinctive shot begins when the master eye first perceives the target. Not, as some believe, when the gun is mounted. By then, the shot is almost over.

Tracking begins when the master eye perceives the target and the shooter has already achieved the coiled position, either by the numbers, as in practice, or with blinding speed, as in dense-cover hunting with the shotgun possibly broken open.

Imagine that flying targets and flying birds have an imaginary line hanging under the leading edge or the tip of the beak. The line extends all the way to the ground. The barrels of your shotgun ALWAYS STAY ON THAT LINE IN A RELATIONSHIP WITH THE TARGET. Now what does that mean?

The Four Lines of Concept

There are four (invisible) lines of which the instinctive shooter must always be aware. These lines are conceptual rather than actual, but they are as real as the shotgun and the target. Ignore any of the four and a miss is almost guaranteed. Slop through any of the four, and your technique will not be graceful and stylish.

1. **The line of relationship.** This invisible line hangs under the target's leading edge all the way to the ground. Your barrels must always be on this line, in a relationship with the target. When the target has been tracked into the kill zone, the shotgun may be slid straight forward to a point under the target where it may be fired. Remember, the shot string is 2/3rds to 3/4ths on top of the barrels, so that you can focus on and track the target until the instant of impact.

2. **The stasis line**. This line begins with the focus point on the barrier, behind which is the target thrower or the dog. As the shotgun is coiled in the ready position, the chin is thrust forward and pointed toward the focus point. This movement establishes the stasis line. As the target appears, the stasis line is transferred from the focus point to the leading edge of the target.

3. **The vision line or the line of focus**. This is the invisible line which extends from the eyes to the focus point before the target flies, then moves to the leading edge as the target appears. As you can see, the vision line and the stasis line converge and meet at the target. I believe this slight convergence may give the Predator range to the target and maintains balance for the shooter. Think of this as the Predator's optical range-finder and gyroscope. If at any time the vision line wavers from the leading edge, especially in a high-angle shot, depth perception and balance are lost and the shooter stumbles.

4. **The barrel line**. This line is the fourth line in the lines of concept. The barrel line extends from your leading finger to a point somewhere under the leading edge of the target. It is established during the ready position on the focus point. The eyes are focused on the focus point and the fingers (both your front one on the barrels and the rear index), are pointed slightly under the target. (Never point the barrels, always point your fingers.) The barrel line and the vision line remain parallel at all times. This is especially true during the mount. If you rotate the barrels upward or drop them downward, the parallel lines are lost and a miss is likely.

Our shotguns are fitted so most of the shot pattern stays above the barrel. Therefore, when we point at the target, we will always point slightly below the leading edge, so the target can be seen right up until the shot hits.

We do not want to lift the barrels during the mount or we will impart upward momentum to the firearm. Upward momentum, or inertia, can cause us to shoot high, especially in fast close-ups or extreme ranges.

Therefore the muzzles must move with the target and rise as it rises, maintaining the relationship. As the kill-zone is reached, the shotgun is thrust straight forward to arrive at the precise spot beneath the target to ensure centering the leading edge of the target *on* the pattern.

But in so doing, the line of vision and the plane of the barrels must remain parallel. And, the two 90-degree angles, both vertical and horizontal, must be maintained. How do you do that?

Simply move the shotgun with your body and not with your arms. Let's put that in caps.

MOVE THE SHOTGUN WITH YOUR BODY, NOT WITH YOUR ARMS.

Okay, now we're ready to look at a track.

You are a right-handed shooter. This target will move in the left hemisphere from the dog or target thrower to your left. Remember for all shots, you're going to set up for it like a hunter—face the dog. In this case, face the target thrower. It's behind a barrier, so focus your eyes on a preselected spot (focus point) on the barrier near where the target will appear.

You'll assume the ready position on the left leg (the target's going to fly into your left hemisphere). So do The Test and coil. (Say the Litany out loud or have someone read it to you so you don't skip any one of the steps. Memorize it. Yep. It's that important.)

THE LITANY OF THE TEST

1. **FOCUS** on the focus point.
2. **THUMB ON THE SAFETY** sets the fit of the gun.
3. **HEEL OF THE STOCK** in the center of the armpit.

4. DROP AND ROTATE the offside hand to the trousers and
    the gun shoulder forward.
5. POINT with the offside hand under the focus point.
6. COIL till the fingers touch your chest.
7. ROTATE AGAIN to keep the gun shoulder forward

Notice, this target is going to fly higher than your eye level. So kick your hips slightly forward. This raises the barrels a bit. All the weight is on the bird leg, knee locked. The heel of the right foot is raised. There is no weight on the right leg. To turn, you will not push with the right foot or you'll knock yourself over. Simply let the right knee sag against the left. This will turn your body, which moves the gun sideways. At the same time, raise your right heel and thrust your hips forward, tipping your upper body backward to raise the firearm. DO NOT bend backward at the waist. Keep your back straight and bend at the hips—this way you won't hurt your back.

The whole idea is to keep your two angles as near to 90 degrees as possible and maintain the parallel lines of vision and barrels. DO NOT, under any circumstances, look at the barrel or attempt to float the target on the muzzles. Simply think, "I'm pointing under the target," and your Predator will do the rest.

Your eyes are locked with laser intensity on the target's leading edge and your body moves in graceful symmetry with the target. "Dancing with the target," we call it. Indeed, later, as you begin to master the technique, it is this "dance" that motivates.

The "dance" is the moment of ultra-intensity for the Predator. It is time suspended before the lioness charges, before the fox leaps, before the rattlesnake strikes. It is that moment before the pistol sounds for the sprinter. It is the moment supreme; the moment of anticipation; the moment before the kill.

The shot is an anticlimax.

Every day, before you begin shooting, practice the test known as The Point. In fact, practice it as much as you can with songbirds in your backyard. You don't need a gun.

To do it, you need a good ready position, and good tracking. With targets available, set up as if you were going to shoot. But leave your shotgun over your gun arm and point with the lead (offside) hand, arm extended. Call for a bird. As the clay target flies, focus on the leading edge. Turn with it. Point slightly under it (think one or two inches), moving your body to keep the two angles of the pointing hand/arm 90 degrees. As you finish The Point, don't drop your arm. Stop a moment and check your position. Have you opened up the angle of your pointing arm and your body from 90 degrees to 130 or 140 degrees? It's a natural error in the beginning. Continue to point as the target passes you, but push the right (gun) shoulder around constantly trying to maintain the 90-degree arm-to-body angulation.

Do four or five, or as many as needed to obtain sharp focus on the leading edge of the clay. Think of it as the tip of the pigeon's beak. Follow the leading edge of the target until it disappears. A single pigeon flying in a large flock is especially good practice. Point at the tip of its beak wherever that pigeon flies. Do this downtown, or in the park (but leave your shotgun at home). People may think you're a little crazy as you continue pointing at birds for no apparent reason. Indeed, some may close in to see what's generated so much of your interest. Usually they will comment—I didn't know pigeons had spots on their backs—or some other input to the effect that they were really seeing something for the first time. Their Predators focused in too!

Learn to focus intensely and an amazing thing happens. You begin to control the speed of the target. You can slow it down in midair. Ted Williams could see the stitching on the ball. Tennis pros return impossible serves. And *you* will control any target's speed. What was once an impossible close-up becomes a floater. Now you've got all the time in the world. Your shooting becomes hypnotic. Suddenly it's tracking—it's the "the dance" which you crave. After all, you *know* you're going to break the target if you shoot. And shortly, you'll break them all. You shift your desire from the kill to the dance and you don't want "the dance" to end.

Helen and I were working below the tower. We call it "The Witch" at the Wingshooting Workshop. Three times I watched her gracefully slide through the ready position and coil. Like a dancer she thrust her hips slightly forward to raise her barrels. She was totally relaxed—and focused.

"Birrrrrd," I crooned softly, just audible to the trapper and not to stimulate sudden movements with the word "pull."

Three times the target arced lazily over us at about 40 yards. Three times Helen turned, seemingly in slow motion, with her targets. Gracefully, she leaned her slender body rearward as the target rose, then gently forward as the targets vanished into the grass. Three times.

Stepping back, I admired her performance. She had truly perfected the dance.

"Er, aren't we forgetting something?" I said, not wanting to break what was obviously a moment of total concentration.

"What's that?" Her voice, almost a whisper.

"Well . . . you're supposed to shoot at it," was my obvious comment.

"Oh no!" she said, "Not yet."

"How's that?" I was still baffled.

"I was flying," she said in a near whisper. And that pretty well sums it up.

What Helen was doing was the test called The Relationship. The Relationship is The Point, expanded to include your shotgun. In The Relationship, the shooter maintains the Ready Position throughout the entire flight of the target: focused on the leading edge; barrels on the imaginary line hanging under the leading edge; moving the barrels sideways with the legs, up and down with the hips; pointing at that point under the leading edge where the target will be centered up in the pattern. But the shooter does not mount. To the experienced instinctive shooter this is the most enjoyable part of the shot— savoring that magical moment of ultimate intensity before the kill.

But eventually the hypnotic moment of The Relationship must be broken. And it is broken by The Mount.

9

THE MOUNT

And so we have come to this, you and I—the moment of truth. But is it really? Isn't the mount simply the natural, smooth-flowing conclusion of what you began just moments ago?

Oh, sure, I know, it's taken a while to read the other chapters leading up to this. But in reality, in the real world, the execution of these chapters takes just seconds. It takes a hell of a lot longer to explain them than to do them. In the bird field, they may happen in fleeting moments that, to you, seem suspended in time. The bird slows to a near halt. The senses of touch, smell, taste, and hearing are put on hold. The Predator takes control through its eyes. There's only enough of you left to mentally scream, "Hen!"

That's the good news. There *is* enough of you left to hit the brakes. The shotgun is at your shoulder for less than an inch of travel sideways before the dismount begins. The vision beneath the shotgun and arm is blocked only briefly. This makes the technique very safe. This is especially true when measured against a shooter who swings the firearm's muzzle a foot or more. Measured at forty yards, a muzzle swing of twelve inches *mounted* translates into a muzzle sweep some thirteen yards down range. That's *thirteen yards* that the shooter's vision is blocked beneath the shotgun and arm.

Now, let's take a look at our instinctive mount and its test.

First it's important to realize the mount and shot is really divided into three parts: mount, point, and shoot. Sometimes, in places such as thick grouse or woodcock coverts, the parts of the mount, point, and shoot are nudged pretty close together. Often, you have less than a second so the litany becomes: mount-point-shoot. Nevertheless, the parts are still there and they are still done by the numbers. But because of a bit of rush in hunting, it can be definitively stated that hunting is bad for shooting. We tend to get sloppy. So during the hunting season, days afield must be interspersed with critical clay target practice. Not enough time, you say? Then be prepared to suffer the consequences. Where at the beginning of the hunting season you *Homo sapiens* could hardly miss, by the end you can hardly hit—without practice sessions.

Before spreading gloom and doom all over, let's get back to the mount and see how it looks.

We want to avoid building in upward inertia. Therefore, we use the shotgun as the Predator has used a food-gathering tool for eons. We use the shotgun as the Predator has always used the spear—we thrust it. It's a natural movement. For hundreds of thousands of years, thrusting a spear was as natural as taking a drink of water. It is a movement built into our genetic memory that's as natural as pointing or focusing. We have used it as recently as the bayonet thrust. Our own minds recognize the movement as soon as it is felt the first time. We like it.

The thrust carries many benefits. The greatest of these is that it eliminates muzzle movement. True, the muzzles are moving sideways, but only because your body is turning, keeping the muzzles on the line hanging under the leading edge of the target. The muzzles are also in a relationship with the target. So when the muzzles are thrust forward, they neither have to move up nor down, but simply straight forward, arriving at that point under the target where the firearm is discharged. The target is automatically centered up in the pattern. Is there a forward allowance? Probably. But we can't see it, nor do we allow for it. Luckily for us, we simply point at the target and pull the trigger. The Predator does the rest.

HOLD IT! WAIT A MINUTE! BACK UP THERE, BUB! THERE'S GOT TO BE MORE TO IT THAN THAT!

Oh, well, okay, if you hold my feet to the fire, I guess I'll have to admit there is more—a lot more. But to the casual observer, that's all there seems to be. After the shooter moves slowly with the target, seemingly almost asleep, the shotgun slides forward, goes off and is dismounted as the shotgun and gunner return to the point of origin—the trap or the dog.

How about this puzzlement? If the muzzles slide straight ahead and we maintain parallel lines of vision and barrel, how does the toe of the stock get all the way from under the armpit up and into the pocket inside the ball joint of the shoulder and under the master eye? All this with the comb firmly anchored against the lower jaw, which is thrust forward, pointing at the target's leading edge. How does all that happen?

It's all in the cam, man. It's all in the cam. It's automatic, because that's the way our bodies are built.

Other shooters are taught to shoot with the gun elbow elevated. That's wrong for instinctive shooters. As the mount begins, the shotgun is in its coiled position. As the thrust starts, the first thing that happens is the safety also moves forward—in the first inch of travel forward. As the butt clears the armpit, the gun elbow is lowered, which automatically cams the stock upward to the lower jaw. The muzzles move straight forward, the shotgun simply cams upward behind them, pivoting on the muzzles, but there is no upward movement of the muzzles. The rear hand stays in a slightly under position, trigger finger under the wood, also pointing out the target. As the comb hits the lower jaw, there is a slight hesitation, about a quarter of a heartbeat before the finger slaps down off the wood and into the trigger, either front or rear.

This is where the mount ends and the follow-through begins.

In the first half-inch of travel forward, both fingers pointing slightly under the leading edge of the target, the safety is moved forward. For those having trouble with an offside eye, the safety also controls the wink. If you're doing everything right, and you're still not hitting, chances are it's an eye dominance problem. You'll lose nothing by winking the offside eye.

As the stock clears the armpit, the gun elbow rotates downward. Be sure that both hands are working together. Move in slow motion. Keep pointing the target through the mount.

*The action of the elbow downward cams the rear of the shotgun upward
to the anchor point alongside the lower mandible (jaw). The cadence
is always, "Mount, Point, Shoot." Keep that cadence. Say it to yourself
right now, "Mount, Point, Shoot." Don't hurry it. Keep the same cadence
as you say it. The usual fault is to hurry the shot, especially in the
beginning. You've got lots of time. When you're learning, turn down
the target speed so you have time to learn and practice. Trust me—the
Predator loves fast targets—the faster, the better. We've thrown them so
fast that another quarter of a turn on the spring tension of the thrower
makes the targets break coming off the arm. It makes no difference
to the Predator. Whether the target flies in a straight line, or in a long
lazy loop like the Jefferson National Expansion Memorial in St. Louis,
the Predator will break the target when and where you decide ahead of
time. But always remember, SHOOT IN SLOW MOTION. Don't hurry. The
speed differential between you and the leading edge of the target is
always zero, goose egg, nada, nuttin'. Take your time.*

A lot of other things happen at the same time.

As the pitch of the stock begins to move the toe down its one half inch on recoil, the trigger finger leaves the trigger and returns to the wood.

As the stock slides down, DO NOT ALLOW THE SHOTGUN TO ROTATE. DO NOT ALLOW THE MUZZLES TO MOVE UPWARD. Both hands must work together to keep the vision line and barrel line feeling parallel.

The stock is returning to the armpit (we assume you hit the target; we always do), and the muzzles are returning to the dog or target thrower. Since we didn't swing in the beginning, there is absolutely no reason to begin swinging when the target breaks. That simply means the muzzles are getting farther away from the point of origin. After all, the dog may be holding another bird, or a flush may have happened on report. So our follow-through takes us back to where it all started. Makes sense doesn't it?

The dismount is also our follow through. It must be as smooth and graceful as the mount. It begins with the half-inch downkick created by the pitch of the stock. If it is a single target, the downkick or demi-dismount, begins the dismount. The elbow rises again, while the shotgun continues back along the same path as the mount to the focus point. The shotgun ends its journey back under the armpit (where it began) and returns a track back to the focus point (dog). This, after all, is what it's about: to begin and end where you started—in exactly the same position, focused on the same point. During it all, the vision line and barrel line have remained parallel.

"Ha-ha! Gotcha," calls the doubter. "Suppose there's another bird flying alongside or maybe a few feet behind. Your technique won't work."

Sorry, Bub. It won't wash. Remember that we actually have three dismounts based on our pitch: the full dismount, the demi-dismount, and the no-dismount dismount.

Each has its own use, depending on what the bird is doing or birds are doing. Remember, we pitch our shotguns so that the natural recoil causes them to recoil downward one-half inch at the shoulder.

In the case of a single bird or target, the firearm simply continues its return to the coiled position after the initial one-half inch down-kick on recoil.

If two targets are following, one behind the other, as in a following pair, we can do a very stylish dismount. I call it the demi-dismount and the lazy gun. The idea is to track the first target into the kill zone and kill it. Then, while the shotgun kicks down its half-inch, the gunner looks back with his head, while the shotgun remains motionless, waiting in ambush for the next shot. The eyes pick up the new leading edge and follow it into the kill zone, and he remounts the half-inch, kills that one, and then dismounts back to the focus point (dog). We use this dismount because we can—it's fluid and graceful.

If two targets or birds are flying one behind the other, we use the demi-dismount with the lazy gun to handle the situation. Rather than wait to come up behind the rear bird, which may be too far to the rear, we simply follow the first target and break it as usual. However, after the half-inch downkick, we simply look back with the head, leaving the shotgun where it is. We follow the second target into the shotgun with our head. The shotgun is remounted the one-half inch and the shot taken. The muzzles simply wait lazily in ambush. We already have target speed, and we eliminate that ugly waving back and forth of the barrels so typical of the swing-through shooter. The result is deadly and simply lovely to watch. Naturally, after the second shot, the follow through is normal. The muzzles return to the dog before the shotgun is broken open to reload.

When two targets are flying side by side, the shot is simplicity itself. The biggest problem with a true pair is really no problem at all, since a true pair really isn't a true pair. It is simply two singles that are conveniently flying at the same time, somewhere near each other. So, all you really have to do is decide which bird to shoot—A DECISION YOU CAN MAKE BEFORE THE BIRDS FLY.

True pairs are simple—we use the no-dismount dismount. Simply hang onto the gun and don't let it downkick or change your body position from 90 to 120 degrees from vertical. This creates slightly more downpitch (which equals less downkick), which makes the shotgun remain in place. This is an advanced method. Be careful with true pairs, however—as this photograph shows, there's an optical illusion involved here. As the pair approaches, the away bird appears to be in the lead.

As they pass you, it becomes obvious that they are really side by side.

But, wow, as they continue past you, the near target now appears to have passed the away target—this presents a problem for swing shooters, but not for us. Simply think of them as I've stated: the away target and the near target. Know ahead of time which target you are going to shoot first. I always shoot the away target first, since it's getting farther away all the time. Then, come back for the near one. Never think of them as the leading target and the trailing one. Just focus, focus—leading edge, leading edge, shoot, and dismount back to the focus point (dog).

You can do it any way you want. Personally I always shoot the farthest target first. Since the range is constantly increasing, I ignore anything else in the air and shoot the away bird first. And then, "Oh, hey look! There's another one!" So I simply point/point. Be rather swift about it. This is very unsophisticated. Just focus leading edge/leading edge. Bang/bang. In some cases, observers have actually seen our muzzles back up for the second target.

The exception to this is if one target is dropping more quickly than the other, as a bird sometimes does. It's trying to escape into the grass. Take the dropping target first, and then point the second.

Avoid the concept of taking the rearmost target first. It can get you into trouble. There's an optical illusion here. As two targets are approaching, the far one appears to be in front, the rear behind. As they pass they appear side by side. After they've passed the near bird appears to have pulled ahead of the away bird. Trying to swing through the behind bird to the lead bird can be confusing, since they appear to change position as they pass.

Also avoid flock shooting. Shoot one and then the other. Often you'll hit both, but don't count on it. I've seen two targets, just inches apart, taken with two shots, the second target never touched by the first shot.

Okay, so you've been hanging around waiting—what about that one-half inch kickdown? Well, for the true pair, we simply employ the no-dismount dismount. We just hang onto the thing and shoot again. Remember, the gun arm is lowered, near the ribs. You have bone support. Somehow, the Predator simply resists the slight down-kick. Some shooters, however, will let the downkick happen and remount the one-half inch, which only takes a fraction of a second. Some do a full dismount, even between shots on a true pair, using time compression to make up for the extra second it takes. If you like to do it, and you hit 'em, it's okay. But it simply isn't as pretty as the no-dismount dismount. (As you become accomplished you can simply lean away from the targets, removing the one-half inch downkick and the butt will simply stay stuck to your pocket).

Now, what about a test for the mount? We've got one—it's called The Fundamental.

As I said at the outset, the mount and shot is really divided into three parts: mount, point, and shoot.

Sometimes, when we've hunted overmuch and practiced not at all, things start to go wrong. What do I mean by that? Well if you miss two shots in a row, and don't know why, something has gone wrong. Don't continue to shoot.

Go directly to the Fundamental.

THE FUNDAMENTAL. This is your life preserver, and returning to this is what saves you when something goes wrong. What does that mean? We really don't miss very often. But, if you have missed two targets in a row and don't know why, something has gone wrong. To find out what, go directly to the fundamental.

The Fundamental is first introduced to students at the Wing-shooting Workshop during day one of the school. Because teaching a new technique like this is best done in tiny steps, the Fundamental is a logical step between mount practice with a dot on the wall, to mount practice with a target on a metal pipe or post, but still using snap caps. (For those of you unfamiliar with the term, a snap cap is a nonfunctioning shot shell with a spring-loaded primer.) Never dry fire your side-by-side without something to catch the firing pin, or a broken pin may result.

Once the instructor is certain the student is hitting the target with snap caps in the shotgun, it's time to replace the cap under the front trigger with a live shell. By the time the student is smoking the targets every time on the post, it's time to move the target, but always using the Fundamental. This allows the instructor (or you, if you're working alone) plenty of time to check the entire mounted position before a shot is taken.

Okay, here's how it works. The student performs the Test as always, fitting the shotgun. We do this before every shot in practice, constantly training the body to assume the same 90-degree angular relationship behind the shotgun for every shot.

Now the instructor directs, "Mount."

The student performs the mount, just as in mount practice on the post and with a live shell under the front trigger, pointing at a preselected spot on the trap barrier or house.

Now, the instructor has an opportunity to check the entire mounted position before calling for the bird. The most common fault at this point is lowering the chin. It's hard for people who haven't done it to believe that the target really can be hit without looking down the barrel. You also want to check that the gun shoulder hasn't slipped rearward. A sore shoulder on day one makes a three-day school difficult on everyone.

Now, the instructor calls for the bird using the call "Birrrrd" rather than "Pull." "Birrrrd" is a soft, smooth sound and will generate a similar response in the student. "Pull" is fast and jerky and produces a similar response in the students.

When shooting instinctively, always think, "Slow, Smooth, Take Your Time." Rushing will frustrate a good instinctive shooter. Remember the quick-draw artist who tried to be fast and shot himself in the foot instead.

As the target flies, the instructor directs, "Point."

The student follows the leading edge of the target with the eyes, and points with the leading finger under the leading edge of the target, the same place the student did in mount practice. Naturally, the entire body is moving the lead arm so the body stays in its proper 90-degree relationship to the shotgun.

When the instructor is certain everything is aligned and the shot will hit, he calls, "Shoot!" And the target breaks.

The student does not know when the instruction, "Shoot," will come. The student's only job is to look at the target's leading edge, turn with it, and point under it. The direction to shoot comes as a total surprise. The finger comes down off the wood and slaps the trigger. This proves that at any point the instructor calls for the shot, the target will be hit. In other words, an instinctive shooter can hit a target at any point in its flight path—from the moment it appears, to that instant before it drops into the grass.

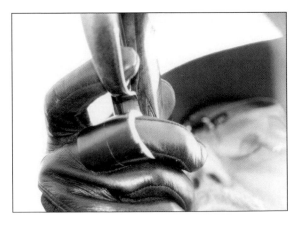

Trigger pulls are less important to an instinctive shooter than to a shooter who mounts with a finger already on the trigger (ugh). Notice also, only the pad of the finger touches the trigger. This way the finger is arched. The shooter is pulling trigger, not wood.

After a graduate leaves the school he can use the Fundamental by talking himself through it and having someone else, like a trapper, call "shoot."

Okay, but this is shooting with, in effect, a premounted shotgun. Doesn't this violate every rule of instinctive shooting?

Not really. Remember, the Fundamental is simply a training tool.

In use, the direction to mount and the call for the bird get closer together as the student hits the correct mounted position every time. Finally, they pass one another. Then the instructor is directing the more normal "Bird . . . Mount, Point, Shoot."

By skillfully altering the time between the call and the direction to mount, confidence builds up. But always keep in mind if two targets are missed in a row, and eventually they will be, return to the Fundamental. Something has gone wrong. Catch the problem now, and confidence continues to build as the student realizes this technique is completely self-repairing. At first, it's repaired by the instructor, and then by the graduate during practice.

Okay, so far so good. But the shot doesn't end with the recoil. Don't quit on the technique. Always follow through.

Summary

I don't want to keep harping on this, but I almost hated writing the last three chapters. Too often people will read something like this and then get all hung up on the individual parts of the technique.

Once I read a wonderful book titled *Quantum Golf.* Now I'm not a golfer, but golf and instinctive shooting when performed correctly, are very closely allied. The premise of this wonderful book is this: "I'm going to teach you all the parts of the golf swing. Now that you've learned how to do them, forget about the parts and just let it happen."

And the same is true for the technique we teach at the Wing-shooting Workshop. It is not the parts, but the whole, that interests us. In fact, once you're over the 95-percent bracket, hitting targets loses some of its appeal. You expect to hit the target. Okay, then what do you do? The answer to that is to work on your technique or, even better, develop STYLE. A concert pianist first learns how to play the piano. But lots of people do that. What earns a great pianist the right to play in a concert hall is style—a unique style that is that artist's signature on the work being played.

A great wingshot is the same way—our graduates, after their Year in the Wilderness, draw a crowd when they practice on the range.

HOLD UP THERE BUB! WHAT'S THIS YEAR IN THE WILDERNESS?

Well, I try to get each entering student to commit to what we call a "Year in the Wilderness." That is, a year in which they will go forth and practice the exercises and tests they have learned. They also promise, as near as possible, to eschew their peer group. Graduates practice alone or with another graduate for this year, so that they can concentrate on the technique without some "helpful" bystander calling out, "Say there fella, you gotta get y'r head down. Ya can't shoot with y'r head up that way."

Trust me—everybody wants to be a shooting instructor.

One evening John L. called. He was chuckling.

"Buz," he said, "were you ever right about staying away from other shooters when I practice."

"Okay," I responded, "tell me about it." I grabbed a pen hoping a good story was on its way, one that I could tell you.

"Well," John said, "I was waiting for a skeet field so I could shoot alone." (He'd made previous arrangements with the club owner to have a private field.)

"A couple of guys were just finishing up," John said, "and they were godawful."

John went on to explain that after they'd finished with scores in the low teens, they lingered to watch John practice. He'd almost finished his Year in the Wilderness and was shooting well, high in the 90 to 100 percent bracket.

"At any rate," he went on, "these two guys started giving me a hard time about the way I was shooting. Now mind you I wasn't missing any targets, but I was getting a lot of verbiage about what I was shooting (a side-by-side, naturally). Finally, I'd had it."

"Say," John seemed a bit chagrined about this since his anger had subsided, "I watched you two shoot, and I've gotta say you aren't that good. Why do you feel you can criticize me?"

The more outspoken of the two left John with his mouth hanging open. "Well," the loudmouth said, "our best friend is the club champion."

So here's my best advice. Keep to yourself while you're learning. When you have learned, be a gentleman or a lady. If you feel the need to prove you're the best to someone else, do it on the target range. Never take competition into the birdfield.

When you can shoot as well as this, you have nothing more to prove. You know it. That should be enough.

If you're running the hunt, make sure everyone has an equal chance to shoot.

I've heard of people who don't want hunting companions. They want observers—an audience—someone to admire how well they hit the birds. Well, here's the truth of it. I expect you to hit and kill every bird you shoot at. Very rarely does anyone totally miss a game bird. Oh, true, the bird may not come down, but it probably took a pellet or two, maybe more depending on the pattern.

The Audience Seekers are nothing but a game hogs. They care nothing about the birds, limits, or their hunting companions. They want to shoot everything that flies. And when they miss, they have a million excuses as to why. They blame the birds, gun, shells, companions, sun, rain, and dogs . . . on and on, ad nauseam.

You are not like that. I know, because I trained you.

10

YOUR YEAR IN THE WILDERNESS

Everyone has a shot that's traditionally difficult for them. For me it's the low, going-away shot. If I'm going to miss a target or bird, it'll be the simple low, going away, or slightly quartering away. A true going-away shot is quite rare.

The way to handle difficulty with a shot like that is to not handle it. At least, not try to handle it directly. The worst thing to do is to try to confront it head-on by setting up a difficult-for-you shot and then doggedly shooting at it, regardless of the results. You'll end up missing. And missing begets more missing.

Some time ago, I went out to do exactly that—work on those pesky low and away birds of mine, confronting my problem head-on. I set up the shot with an automatic, stand-alone thrower. I started shooting and, occasionally, missing. (Oh sure, it happens to all of us. The difference is knowing how to identify the problem and then fix it.) Going-away shots are particularly difficult for instinctive shooters because of the lack of *apparent* motion. Remember: the eyes of the Predator are excited by movement. In a going-away shot, the target is moving, alright, but because of the angle, there is little *apparent* motion. Therefore, it creates little excitement for the Predator.

I shot at a number or targets. The ones I missed were missed in exactly the same way.

"Why are you doing that?" Harry L. asked me. Harry and I were out to shoot a practice round of shots and angles that we'd found pesky in the hunting field.

"You always tell us to stop shooting if you miss more than two and, then, identify the problem."

"You're right." I said. "What am I doing wrong?"

"You're shooting behind it."

"How far?"

"About six inches?"

"About?"

Harry knew what I was getting at: "Okay, exactly six inches."

Trained and accomplished instinctive shooters very seldom have random misses. Their misses, when they do happen, are accurate and predictable. The few times that I've seen random misses in school were when the student was trying to miss or on drugs.

Now don't get all upset—drugs can mean something like anti-histamines. People who take them daily don't seem affected. But for most, taking an occasional cold and flu medication before shooting can ruin your whole day.

On even rarer occasions, when someone is trying to miss, it has been because the person in question is testing my ability or the guarantee. The result is always the same. If you're not shooting up to our minimum standards, you're out of the school. Luckily, we have only a 1.5 percent failure rate in the school, with people coming in under the guarantee.

"So what does shooting six inches behind the target mean," I asked Harry, who had graduated some five years before.

"You've lost focus," he said immediately.

"Okay, how do I fix it? Or, an even better question would be what's the problem? I'm a pretty good focuser, so what's going on?

The problem was more complex than you'd think.

To practice, you don't simply walk into a difficult shot and begin banging away. You sneak up on it.

The way you work into a difficult shot is by starting with an easy one and gradually, four steps and one shot at a time, walk into the more difficult one. Shoot, hit, move. Shoot, hit, and move again. Shoot and finally the miss—don't move. Shoot again. It's what we call "Tapping."

Chuck Gossett is demonstrating how we practice. It is a system called tapping. Here he sets up at about twenty yards from the line of flight, about thirty yards from the target thrower. He intends to practice the hard right to left, quartering away shots.

Push your Predator into a situation that's unfamiliar, or confusing, and it will shoot high. About a foot high—it varies slightly between Predators. If you continue to shoot and your Predator continues to go high, stop shooting. It's a standoff.

Immediately, go back to where you hit your last shot and start again. Work into the new shot, taking one step toward that shot at a time. Usually the Predator will accept the former miss and may even go a few steps beyond. But somewhere close by, you'll get another high miss. Again, go back. DON'T PUSH THE PREDATOR INTO A SHOT HE OR SHE REFUSES TO MAKE! It can continue to shoot high forever. Just tap on a new situation; if it doesn't work after a couple of tries, go on to something else. Sooner or later your Predator will accept the new situation. It's not unlike training a good dog. Be gentle. Push, but not too hard. Know when to back off and try another day. Above all, be patient—which is good advice whether you are dealing with a spouse, a dog, a gun, or with your Predator.

Here's how we solved the problem of my low and away misses and, in so doing, identified the problem. First, I went back to a fairly easy shot. I was facing the target thrower. Harry was pulling for me. I was standing about fifty yards from the portable trap house. The target was flying thirty yards away in my left hemisphere moving right to left—fast, but still an easy shot.

Okay. Next, each time I shot, I took three, four, or five steps toward the target thrower. Finally, I was six feet away, in about the same position I had been in when I was missing. But this time, I was hitting all the shots. Why the improvement?

In the first instance, I'd been facing toward the target thrower— that was correct. But, I'd been looking at where the target would first appear. But it's impossible to look at nothing. Instead, my eyes were focusing on the nearest thing to that spot. Since my eyes couldn't focus on nothing, they settled for a tree one hundred yards away—infinity, compared to where I should have been focused. When the target did appear, it was horribly out of focus to my Predator. At my age, with a target traveling at that speed, refocusing was impossible. And, so,

I made out-of-focus shot after shot, and all passed exactly six inches behind the target. The result was confusion. Had I continued to shoot, my Predator would have registered this confusion by shooting high. We would have lost the six-inch-behind indicator, which is so vital to solving the problem. Somewhere along the way, I remembered an instinctive shooting truth: on going-away shots, DON'T HESITATE. Drive the gun hard and shoot the back-edge of the target (it is an exception to the general rule of focusing on the leading-edge). AND, NEVER POINT THE BARRELS AT THE GOING-AWAY TARGET. Point your finger under the going-away target and fire.

Remember, we are hunters who shoot clays. We would never face away from our dog. This protects our focus in hunting. So in target shooting, always face the target thrower (the dog). However, you will be able to apply this method even if you can't face the thrower as you become more advanced—we are talking about practicing the method here. At this close-up distance, I had to turn with the target at near hyper-speed. Focus was protected and I picked up the leading edge immediately. The result? Back to 100 percent hits.

As he approaches the target thrower, Chuck still faces the dog (thrower). Gene, the trapper, is protected by a steel barrier attached to railroad ties. Chuck must face the dog, then pivot as the target flies. Target shooters will face in the direction the target will fly. But this is not realistic for hunters, nor is it necessary.

So how do *you* conduct *your* Year in the Wilderness?

The purpose of your year is to allow you time to practice all the shots and to practice them enough times so they no longer require conscious thought. This way, your Predator is rarely, if ever, confused no matter where you find that particular shot or combination of shots. This can be true, out to the maximum range of the firearm or as close as a few feet.

The graduates commit to one year of practice, one hundred rounds a week—this is the Year in the Wilderness.

Jon L. called me one winter's day from the Northeast. Jon used to call a lot. I was teaching in Mississippi and was in for the 3:00 p.m. lunch break. I have what some may consider a strange rule—never eat while you're shooting. It's a sure cause of hitting the wall. It dulls the Predator, as much as alcohol, and has the same effect.

"Buz," Jon was shouting! "Can you hear that?"

"Hear what?"

"THAT!" He blared, as he held the cell phone out at arm's length.

Over the receiver, I could hear the moan of the wind, as it sliced through some nearby barrier and whistled around buildings—or maybe it was trees.

"What *is* that?" I was almost shouting by now, too.

"THAT'S A BUTT-KICKIN' BLIZZARD. AND I'M UP TO MY ASS IN SNOW, SHOOTIN' MY ONE HUNDRED TARGETS. I JUST THOUGHT YOU'D LIKE TO KNOW!"

And so it goes. Jon has the fire in the belly to become a great shooter. He walks the walk. He talks the talk. He wears the look. And, he practices his one hundred targets a week.

"Buz," he asked two years after his graduation, "does the Year in the Wilderness ever end?"

"Not if you want to keep shooting like you are," I said.

Even for me, it's still true and I am sure professional athletes will readily give testament to this as well. If I lay off practice for two or three weeks, my focus and timing are affected. It takes a period of practice to get it back.

So what do you do?

The first thing is, shoot alone if you can. Modern traps with delayed release buttons are great for this, as there is no pressure while you practice. Well-meaning friends or bystanders can screw things up royally by offering advice while you're tapping. When you miss, and you will, they'll be on you like white on rice.

Remember, you're shooting ever more increasingly difficult targets looking for that point at which your Predator will miss. They see the miss as a failure on your part, not an information-gathering exercise. That miss gives them an excuse to offer "help."

Okay, so you arrive at the skeet or sporting clays range having prearranged to have a field to yourself. Pay extra, if you have to, for this courtesy. And let's say you've decided to work on left to right shots, medium-high.

Crank up the high house or pick the appropriate field to give you the shot you're looking to practice. Work on the shot, from all angles and all distances. Start in the middle of the field, for instance, but if you are using a skeet field, stay off the blocks or "stations." You want to shoot instinctively. For our practice, you will shoot moving gradually into more difficult angles or ranges. Keep going until you find yourself with a miss. If it's a high miss, go back to where you hit the last shot and start over. If it's a predictable miss, like six inches behind—focus, make the correction, and continue. If going back or making the correction doesn't work, apply the four Tests to test the technique.

DON'T PANIC! You haven't suddenly forgotten how to shoot. Panic has its own set of faults. You begin to lower your head to look down the barrels and thus shoot high. You drop the gun shoulder to the rear, the shotgun butt slips right, and the barrels move left. So, don't panic. Simply apply the tests and work yourself through the fault. The more often you work through the problems, the greater your confidence. Shooting well is simply the fundamentals applied over and over exactly the same way, while maintaining the confidence that you'll hit the target every time.

You'll hit every time, that is, until you hit The Wall.

Let me assure you, The Wall, sometimes referred to as **THE WALL**, is as real as your shotgun or boots. The problem with it is, you can't see it, you can't feel it, but when you hit it, the reaction is similar to hitting a concrete abutment with a race car at 120 miles per hour—everything stops. And it stops real fast.

We deal with The Wall in the Wingshooting Workshop all the time.

An instinctive shooter can shoot for an average of two and a half hours a day. That's actual focusing time. But, somewhere out there, when you focus on that first leading edge, whether you shoot or not, The Wall rises up, and with each subsequent shot (focus) gets nearer and nearer. Finally, you hit it.

To an experienced instinctive shooter, it's pretty easy to spot The Wall as it approaches.

One typical indicator is forgetting the safety. I mean, here's a shooter who hasn't forgotten the safety all day, suddenly he or she damn near straightens out the first trigger. Another good indicator is snapping the gun shut. Focus will begin to slip. I can hold a student off The Wall once it arrives for about ten shots, and then that's it.

"Leading edge," I say, as the target flies. Or a gentle coaching word to "kill it," instead of directly the student to "shoot." It's enough to sharpen focus for a bit. But finally, it's gone.

The first day of the Wingshooting Workshop, I try to keep a student away from The Wall. The trick is to balance what can be accomplished in trying to achieve one perfect shot, yet stop before hitting The Wall.

The big danger is the "just one more shot" syndrome.

By the end of day one, the student is usually hitting well over 95 percent—this for a shooter who had been lucky to card 50 percent on good days. Of course, the student doesn't want to stop shooting. He or she is afraid that this level of success may never happen again.

"I'll bet this is just a fluke," he thinks to himself. The level of self-doubt is huge. The shooter simply cannot believe that the ticket to good shooting was this easy to come by. And yet all of his life, he may have labored under unlovely, inaccurate, and often dangerous shooting. Naturally, human nature wants to keep shooting. But, eventually you must stop, and you want to stop before you hit The Wall. Because hitting The Wall is as devastating to you as hitting the wall is for a NASCAR driver. The natural reaction to hitting the wall for a shooter is, "Ohmygod, it's gone." It's not as deadly as NASCAR's wall—it will return—but the shooter has walled out for the day.

So, the first day, we stop before hitting The Wall. We want to stop on a perfect shot. That night, as the student is falling asleep, the student is instructed to make that shot, beginning with the feet and visualizing it, ten times. Again in the morning, when the student is first awake, we ask the student to visualize another ten shots. The results are dramatic—this is not just sports psychology, it is beyond that entirely; this is about building on the previous day. What yesterday was strange and awkward—today is about becoming graceful and smooth. Unless the student falls to the Second Day Syndrome (SDS).

SDS occurs when a student who has shot brilliantly on day one returns on day two and decides to "hit 'em even better today." Wow! This is a recipe for disaster. The student is tense, trying too hard, and quickly gets discouraged: "See, I told you it was a fluke." It can take thirty to sixty minutes just to get back to where we were on day one. On day one, the student had nothing to lose and relaxed. By day two, the student may feel like he has a reputation to uphold. You may have run into the same problem, even after the school, after a brilliant day in the field or with clays.

But by the end of day two, the student is already showing signs of the shooter he or she will become. Sure, they're all hitting all the targets, which is expected. What I'm looking for is the grace and style that has begun to form. Some people would swat a fly with a floor mat, while others can do it with a flick of the finger.

And, so I'm going to push them into The Wall, because at this point they need to know what it feels like. On the second day I want them to hit it with the force of a car crash, so they know what it feels like when they hit it.

Recently, I shot with a graduate who was scheduled. Later the same day, I shot with another who had just shown up. We were shooting some very low percentage shots—between the trees, dropping at range, and ultra-close-ups. Suddenly, I missed a floater—a target that sat suspended in the air, totally out of steam. And, I proceed to miss two and I quit.

"I'm Walled out," I announced. Later when I counted up my shooting time, it stood right at two and a half hours. I'd hit the wall so hard they probably heard it in a nearby town.

It's important for a second day student to hit The Wall. They have to know what it feels like.

Some take more doing than others. Barbara A. never hit the wall during her first time in school. I pushed until I was exhausted—nothing. She just kept right on smacking targets. Ward S., on the other hand, hit The Wall at forty-seven minutes, and he did it consistently, give or take a couple of minutes. I have one student who can hit ten targets in a row and, then that quick, it's over. Luckily, she is a hunter and ten hits are fine. Her practice sessions are short.

Barbara A. called one day, devastated.

"I've forgotten how to shoot," she moaned.

"Nonsense," I said, "you probably just hit The Wall the first time."

I convinced her not to do anything self-destructive and try it again the next day. I also cautioned her to keep her head up when she started.

"Boy, that Wall is awful," she admitted the following afternoon when she called.

Beware of The Wall. If you decide to become an instinctive shooter, become as familiar with The Wall as you are with the fundamentals. The Wall can be devastating. And avoid the "just one more shot" syndrome. That exacerbates the problem of The Wall.

Ronda R. and her husband Frank arrived in one of the few couples' classes that I hold. To be honest, I don't like them and try to avoid them by encouraging individual lessons. It's hard on me to teach what always results in two completely different classes at the same time. Frank is a surgeon and Ronda a race car driver. To say they both have a degree of forcefulness is a mild understatement. Ronda hit The Wall hard, on the second day. "Just one more shot," she said after a good day in which she missed rarely. She enthused, "I know I can hit it."

Foolishly, I let her shoot again. Miss!

"I *know* I can hit it," she promised.

"You've Walled out Ronda," I said, hoping against hope that she'd listen.

"I *can* hit that bird!" See, in the world of race car drivers, you win by driving yourself harder, working harder, forcing the focus. This rarely works in instinctive shooting.

She was hard to convince, but Frank finally got her into the car after we'd cleaned the shotguns. She was visibly upset. She saw The Wall as some kind of failure on her part. It isn't. It's normal. Instinctive shooters learn to accept it. We're brilliant until we hit The Wall—then we're slobbering troglodytes.

The next morning they arrived in better humor.

Frank said, "I'm going to tell you something," while Ronda punched him in the arm. "Ronda doesn't want me to say it, but I'm gonna say it anyway. She was asleep yesterday before we hit the first turn on the driveway out of the school."

And so it goes. Instinctive shooting is different than "normal" shooting. We're lucky to have it. We're lucky to know as much as we do. Is there more? Probably. But look on the positive side. You are

one of the privileged few who have walked into the almost unbelievable world of the Predator. You have flown backward thousands
of years and met the same *you*, only from a different time. It was a
time when the world was simpler, more easily understood. It was
a world in which your skills, your Predator, determined if you and
your family, or your tribe, would live or die by your skills. It was a
primitive world. Perhaps, in reality, things haven't changed so much
after all.

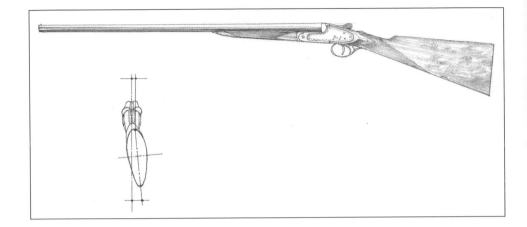

11

SELECTING A SHOTGUN

In this chapter, I'm not going to tell you which shotgun to buy. You may have already decided which shotgun to use. You might even have decided to try to get by with your old vertical format shotgun. So be it. Some people just won't be helped.

Let me tell you up front that I don't pretend to be an expert on the mechanics of shotguns. I have the knowledge to shoot them well and do routine maintenance. Beyond that, I let the real experts take over. We're talking gun selection here, which requires a rudimentary discussion of some of the mechanics. In gun selection I have some experience, which I would like to share with you.

So, in this chapter, I'll tell you what *I* do and what most of my graduates do, based upon experience. The graduates, after all, have had the benefit of the Wingshooting Workshop. They know the technique works.

Often, I run into people who proudly announce they own this or that side-by-side. When I see them shoot I'm usually shocked by their truly atrocious fundamentals. Then, I'll hear something like, "Well, you know the side-by-side is the most difficult firearm to master," or "The wide sighting plane takes a while to get used to."

They're using the side-by-side as an excuse for poor shooting technique. The reality is that was among the original and most traditional of upland guns.

Let me say it one more time: THE SIDE-BY-SIDE SHOTGUN, IN THE HANDS OF A SHOOTER WHO UNDERSTANDS IT, CAN AND WILL PERFORM AS WELL OR BETTER THAN ANY OTHER ACTION TYPE OF SHOTGUN.

Our technique has been designed around the properties of a side-by-side shotgun. Other firearms can be used as well for this method, but you will not want to use them other than possibly for a brief demonstration. Side-by-sides simply work best and are the easiest to fit and use in your quest to become a master gunner. There, now I have some enemies with this line in the sand. However, it is said that "you can measure your power by the strength of your enemies."

For your Year in the Wilderness, pick one gun, make sure it is fitted to you, and then shoot it to the exclusion of all others. It should be a shotgun which fits our preferred profile. It should be appropriate for your body size. It should be new enough so that parts are readily available. Plus, you should already have located a side-by-side gunsmith to take care of it for you. If I thought there was better a firearm for the upland gunner, I would be the first convert.

Maybe I'll make a few more enemies, but I'll also state that most gunsmiths are not qualified to work on side-by-sides, nor do they have the requisite experience to offer you much helpful advice if they lack the experience. When you go looking for a gunsmith, ask specifically for his side-by-side references. Not just *shotgun* references, but *side-by-side* references. There's a vast difference. Just because a gunsmith does a lot of work on semiautomatics or over-and-unders on a daily basis doesn't qualify him as a side-by-side gunsmith. A suitable gunsmith is rare for side-by-sides on this side of the pond. Some good smiths are arrogant and obnoxious, as I will concede, as are some instructors. You don't want either. One smith may be able to do the job, but at what price to your self-confidence? Still others have ability, yet an inflated view of their own importance (read: high price). They quite often take advantage of a new shooter because they sense inexperience. As you can tell, I'm not wild about most gunsmiths. But, there *are* good ones out there. I don't profess to be a gunsmith, but I hope you will find one that helps you and doesn't try to change you.

What you are looking for is a good smith, qualified to work on side-by-sides, who will do so at a reasonable price and who will do the work in a reasonable length of time—weeks, not months or years. As I said, a good side-by-side gunsmith is a very rare breed indeed, especially this side of the Atlantic, and let's face it: we side-by-side shooters are in the minority on any continent these days.

Rarer still, is a good gun dealer for side-by-sides. There are a few reputable ones left in this world. If you know a gun dealer who will always give you an honest deal while making a reasonable and fair profit, while standing firmly behind his firearms and transactions, welcome him into your family. Beware of the dealer who is less interested in what you want than in what he has in stock. Beware of the dealer who belittles your firearm of choice, running it down, only to build up his own brands. Beware of the dealer who demeans the lower-priced, entry-level firearm you are looking for, and tries to convince you that only by purchasing an expensive shotgun will you become a better shot. Beware of the dealer who lies when the truth will do.

The Wingshooting Workshop is a clearing house for stories about dealers.

A graduate called one day to say he'd found a particular type of side-lock, side-by-side at a dealer located near the graduate's home state. "But, that dealer doesn't have any of those guns," I said. "He's been calling all over the country trying to buy them."

"Well, this guy said he had the gun I'm looking for in stock."

"Tell you what. Call this dealer back, and tell him you're overnight mailing him a certified check for the full price, plus an FFL from a dealer in your town. Tell him to send the firearm UPS, next day air. Let's see what happens."

My graduate called me back to say the dealer had finally admitted it would actually take nine months after the check cleared to get the gun. It wasn't in his stock. By the way, the price of the gun was exactly double the price most side-by-side dealers were asking for the very same model.

My graduate finally bought the gun from another dealer all the way across the United States, at a price just half of what the first dealer had quoted. It still took nine months to order and receive it from overseas, but at least he knew what he was dealing with, as the dealer told him this up front.

The Utah Side-By-Side Association and the Order of Edwardian Gunners keep track of dealers who play fast and loose. It doesn't mean that an argument is always customer-weighted. What some buyers see as a bad deal may simply be a misunderstanding—often the result of bad communications on the part of the dealer, the buyer, or both. But if a particular dealer accumulates a list of incidents, it certainly indicates when there's smoke, and possibly fire.

In every case, when you're looking for a supplier of goods or services, ask for references, and check those references out. When asked for references at the Wingshooting Workshop, I usually give the name of the student who is in the school at the moment, or at least a very recent graduate. That way, no one graduate takes calls for references for too long. And, callers know there are many recent successes, not a handful of friends from decades past. A dealer or a gunsmith should operate the same way, as should anyone looking for business these days. Friends are willing to help friends out, but if your last friend was ten years ago, what does that say about you?

Okay, what kind of shotguns do we use in the school?

For years we have used a very simple, but high-quality boxlock shotgun by Ugartechea—a Basque gunmaker from the northern part of Spain. By the way, call them Basques. They don't like to be called Spanish, or French, for that matter.

The men in our school typically use 12-gauge shotguns; the women typically use 20-gauge. This is not to intimate that some women shouldn't consider a 12-gauge. We're talking upper body strength here. The 12-gauges weigh in at around six and a half pounds. The 20-gauges weigh five pounds, four ounces. Put another way, during the three-day school, men lift some 1,625 pounds, women, up to 1,350. This usually fits their physique, but there are exceptions.

Here are the specs on the school shotguns:

Men: 12-gauge; 28-inch barrel length, no ejectors, straight stock, splinter fore-end, wooden butt, choked .004" right, .008" left, forcing cones lengthened to two and a half inches, chokes and forcing cones polished to same quality as barrel, and no tooling marks (polished to final dimensions). Stock lengths are adjustable in quarter-inch increments. School guns have varying amounts of cast-off for right-handers (or cast-on for lefties). Today, most of our men are using casts of around one-half inch, and drop varies from two inches to two and a half inches, depending on the shooter. Pitch on the men's guns is typically one and a half inches at twenty-six inches. Left-handed guns have the triggers reversed, naturally, and the barrels are choked the same with the more open barrel on the left. There's one 12-gauge shotgun with 25-inch barrels, which we reserve for men typically of small stature. This gun's stock goes down to twelve inches and had to be weighted in the butt in order to achieve my preferred balance of one-half inch ahead of the hinge pin.

No, we're not saying all men should shoot with 28-inch barrels. Indeed we select barrel length based on the body proportions, not the final use to which the firearm will be put—that's silly. That's like saying if you had a shotgun for use in heavy woodcock cover, it would have to have short barrels, so that you won't hit brush and so that you can swing fast. That's rubbish. At least it is for us. If *that* were so, you couldn't use the same gun on open flats when hunting sage hens. And of course *that* gun could never be used in the goose blind. I don't know about you, but once I've gone to the expense of buying a fine shotgun and fitting it to me, I want to have it work in all my shooting.

Oh, sure, I'm only going to put the equivalent of a 28- or 20-gauge load in my 12-gauge gun. That's three-quarters ounce or seven-eighths ounce for woodcock, quail, doves, or pigeons. We use a full ounce of steel for geese. On occasion, I'll go up to a high-base shell with one and a quarter ounces of 6s, 5s, or even 4s on occasion for my second barrel. The point is I want to use my shotgun for whatever comes along, adjusting the shot, not having to have six different guns for all my shotgunning (and never really mastering any one of them because of their varying differences). Further, there is no need for such variety.

Philip B. bought a fine side-lock from Armas Garbi, after the school. He was a hell of a shot upon graduation. Not long after, he was invited on a dove hunt. Since he'd reputedly been to a "fancy shooting school," the hunt leader put him on a stand, which was under a large tree (the hunt leader was a rat fink), so Phil couldn't even see the sky. Out of necessity, Phil sat flat on the ground, legs at 45 degrees, supported by the shotgun in the ready position. He shot the first ten birds one-for-one. Then five birds passed his tree before he filled out his limit with two more shots. All head shots.

A properly fitted shotgun for our method fits in any shooting position—standing, sitting, kneeling, or even lying flat on your back. You shouldn't need to shoot lying on your back very often, but my point is that it is not dependant on your foot position. This is a fascinating photograph. I had Chuck shoot these photos of me. There was a strong wind blowing out of the east. The object was to smoke the target between the two poles. We took several photographs and they all looked fine to us. When photos were developed, we discovered that every one of the targets was hit directly above the eastern pole. The conscious mind perceived the puff between the poles. But, because of wind drift, the Predator had to break the target over the windward pole and let the slow-thinking conscious mind perceive the hit as centered. The Predator is very perceptive, more so than us.

The hunt leader—already furious because Phil refused to wear camouflage clothing, preferring khaki clothing and remaining perfectly still as our way of fooling birds—demanded to know why Phil had let five birds pass without a shot.

"Because I felt like it," Philip responded. "I didn't want the hunt to end too soon."

Meanwhile, the hunt leader took two boxes of shells, more or less, to fill out his twelve-bird limit. I could go on and on with these stories from doves to geese and woodcock coverts to sage grouse flats. In our method, the same gun works in all of these places, with just varying the shot.

We chose barrel length depending on our body size. We choose the barrel length that looks right for our proportions. For instance, a six-foot-four guy with a 25-inch barrel looks a little strange. If the firearm is a small gauge, the portrait gets even weirder. A five-foot-two guy with 30-inch barrels looks strange in the other direction. The barrels should be proportionally correct for our body size and arm length.

Take that five-foot guy with 30-inch barrels. Remember also that we shoot with shorter stocks than most people do. Now you've created a shotgun with 30-inch barrels and a truncated 12- or 13-inch stock. Not only does the shooter look strange, but the shotgun looks deformed and is very difficult to balance with those long barrels and short stock.

The choice of shotgun should complement the shooter, and should be proportionally correct with his or her body size and type. Since we don't swing the gun, per se, we can pay more attention to our overall appearance.

The five-foot guy should be looking at 25-inch barrels, maybe twenty-six inches at the most. After that, the barrels begin to draw attention to the shooter's smaller stature. The reverse is true with a tall shooter. The shotgun should complement the shooter. The length-of-pull lengthens or shortens depending on arm length and depth of chest: deep chest = shorter stock; slender chest = longer stock.

For us, the two fingers distance from nose to knuckle is a good rule of thumb when squared away to the shotgun.

The women's firearms follow similar proportional suggestions. Our school guns for women are 20-gauge. The 20-gauge barrels fit most women's hands more proportionally than do a 12-gauge. Again proportions should be your guide. Large hands hold the larger barrels more securely than do smaller hands. The 20-gauge guns have the same general features as the 12s, but are choked .003" and .007".

Also, the women get a half-inch recoil pad. It's possible to change pitch by changing the angular relationship of body to gun. If on a high shot the shooter simply stood up straight and didn't keep the angular relationship 90 degrees, a great deal of up-pitch would have been built into the stance. Remember, up-pitch makes the butt kick down. In the case of a woman, the kick down is right into her breast. After the school, do these women shoot without recoil pads? Of course, but in the beginning, it's best to have a little padding to guard against an occasional bad mount. See, one bad mount can ruin women from shotgunning forever. Ask most daughters of the serious shotgunners you know and you'll usually hear a story about "the time when dad took me out and I shot his shotgun three times, before. . ." This is what we are trying to avoid at all costs, as women's physiques are, obviously, different.

The best thing about all of this is to use common sense. A woman who just went through the school a few months ago, decided that she wanted to go directly into a 12-gauge after school. She is five foot nine and has excellent upper-body strength, and she found a really dynamite deal in a 12-gauge. Her name was Sarah L., and she modeled the gun with 28-inch barrels in front of a mirror. I agreed with her self-diagnosis, "It looked great."

And that's the reaction you want. Get sideways in front of a mirror. Go through The Test into the ready position and the coil. Now check out the mirror again. How does the gun look? If you like what you see, you're a step closer to owning a gun. But there are a few other things you want to check first.

Should you have a sidelock or a boxlock? What's the difference?

You can recognize the difference by the construction of the action body. The boxlock, as name implies, has a boxy look to the rear of the action body. Boxy, that is, unless the manufacturer has covered the straight up and down line with a side plate. Some argue this gives a nice canvas for engraving. I feel it's a little dishonest (like a wolf in sheep's clothing—and, in this case, there's nothing wrong with being a wolf). There's nothing aesthetically wrong with the look of an honest boxlock. They also tend to be from a few hundred to many thousands of dollars less than their counterparts—the sidelocks. Sidelocks are more expensive to make, and most have extra parts. The locks themselves must be fitted into both the action body as well as the stock. Sidelocks usually have a second sear, a safety sear, to

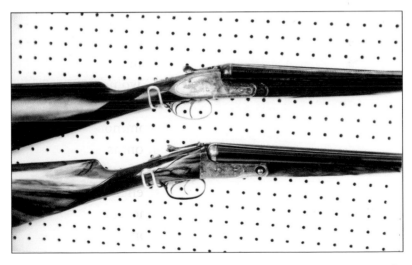

The boxy look at the junction of stock and action body is a dead giveaway for the box lock. If you can't see pins upon which the hammer and sears rotate, it could a side-plated boxlock. Sometimes the only way you can tell is to take the side-plate off.

catch the tumbler should the main sear slip. You can run into such exotic features as self openers, side openers, removable triggers, and . . . well, you get the idea.

Sidelocks are readily identified by the side plate on the right and left sides of the action body. The locking mechanisms are attached to the inside of the lockplate. Some experts go on and on about front-action locks and back-action locks. Some will also try to tell you the sidelock has a faster lock time (elapsed time from trigger pull to "bang"). Any human being that can actually feel a difference, if indeed there is one, certainly has my respect. I've always felt it's something of a "Princess and the Pea" syndrome.

There are a couple of advantages, aside from price, to the sidelock.

They're pretty, that's true, but they're readily removable. Some are even hand-detachable. There's a lever on the left side that allows you to rotate the lever partway and push out the right-hand lock. Then reverse the lever-screw and push out the left. Some sidelocks aren't hand-detachable. Big deal, they have three screws that have

Most side-by-sides have very thin slots in the screw heads. Special screwdriver blades are needed to turn them. About the only mechanical work I do on these firearms is to align screw slots. On most guns, these are set vertically. A good set of thin bit screwdriver blades can be had from Brownell's. A quick glance at the shotgun will tell you immediately if a screw slot is out of adjustment. I check this before and after each day's shooting and if they have come loose, I give them a quick turn.

to be removed to get the locks off. It's easy enough to do since the screws aren't torqued down, but it does take a special thin-bit, firearms-specific, screw driver.

So why do you want to remove them anyway? The big reason is rain. My rain-gun is an Ugartechea sidelock, named Raymond. (Oh, yeah, the school guns all have names. It's a lot easier to remember Lord Ripon or Hopalong or Far Killer or whomever, than a serial number. This also comes in handy if a graduate has forgotten or lost his/her dimensions, but a particular school gun had fit him or her perfectly.)

So what happens if Raymond takes a bath? Nothing much—off come his sidelocks. I dump them in a small bucket of mineral spirits to drive out the water while I blow out the rest of the gun with my air

When a sidelock gun gets wet or needs servicing, it's a simple matter to remove the three screws that hold the locks in place. A hand-detachable sidelock has only one screw with a lever to turn it. Back the screw off about half the threads (look on the other side), then push the screw to unseat the right hand lock. Take the screw on out, then drop the lock onto a piece of anti-screw-and-small-part-rolling-carpet. Mineral spirits (upper left, clockwise), drive water out of the locks and do not leave residue behind like some other solvents. A hairdryer is handy to dry out the interior of the gun after your air hose has blown all of the remaining moisture. Be sure to blow the moisture up and out of the trigger area. Finally, a quick coat of new fluoropolymer grease that stays put and doesn't migrate into the wood when the gun is stored.

hose. A hairdryer finishes the job. I take the sidelocks out of the bath, then blow off the mineral spirits, which leaves no residue behind. Finally, I grease them with good, high-tech grease.

Be sure you cock the shotgun before you remove the sidelocks. If you don't, the firing pins will be in the way of the tumblers (hammers) and you'll have trouble installing the locks again.

Boxlocks are another matter. When a boxlock gets a good dousing, it goes into the gunsmith for a tear-down and cleaning. As you've already suspected, I don't pretend to be a shotgun expert, let alone a gunsmith; I rely on the expertise of my gunsmith to do his job well and I'll stick to doing mine well.

The locking mechanism of a boxlock is contained entirely within the action body, where there are lots of little nooks and crannies for water to hide. To get stuff out of boxlocks, you have to remove the stock. Since I'm no 'smith, normal cleaning and keeping screw slots north/south and firing-pins in shape, is about as far as I like to go with it.

What do I mean by keeping the firing pins in shape?

Firing pins in most side-by-sides are dead soft. That's probably to protect the firearm if a firing pin is stuck in the fired position (out) and the gun gets slammed shut. In this scenario, the ejector or extractor in the extended position comes down hard on a firing pin(s) that's protruding from the face of the standing breech. Most ejector/extractors are chamfered (rounded) so they will ride over an extended pin. It's possible, however, for an extractor to be stuck out. Maybe it's dirty—whatever. I think, but I can't prove it, that manufacturers have decided to sacrifice the firing pin in such a case rather than bend the ejector or extractor rod.

Knowing this, it's in your best interest to carry a couple of extra firing pins and springs in your field vest. Most of the shotguns we use have firing pin housings that are removable in the field.

Look at the face of the standing breech. If there are circles surrounding the firing pin openings with two or three wrench holes in them, the firing pins should be removable in the field. Removable, that is, if you have a firing-pin housing wrench and extra pins to replace the broken number.

Firing pins on the school guns are replaceable in the field. When cocked, the disks are easily removed either with a factory wrench (upper) or a homemade device fabricated out of a steel-bladed (not chrome) screwdriver. Remove the temper by heating the blade cherry red and allow it to air cool. Grind and file the blade into a couple of points which will fit two (some shotguns only have two disk holes), of the disk's holes. If you haven't torqued them into place, they should come right out. Kneel down on the grass, and allow the disk, firing pin, and spring to fall into your coat. If the pin won't come out, it's because the rear end of the pin has mushroomed out like a rivet. I remove my firing pins about every five thousand rounds and turn them up in a drill press. While spinning, it's an easy matter to lay a file against the bulged-out portion of the pin's rear end. You can do this several times before the pin has to be discarded. Never let a well-meaning but ill-informed gunsmith talk you into a set of hardened pins. Instead of the pin bulging, the hammer that works on it will be damaged. Besides, if you close a side-by-side briskly on a stuck-out pin and the extractor doesn't ride up and over, the pin is supposed to shear off. A hardened pin will dig a divot onto your disk's firing pin hole and it'll look like a football. Not cool. And you could bend the extractor shaft.

Be sure *before* you go afield that the housings haven't been torqued into place. Finger tight is good enough. We show students how to make a proper wrench, which can easily be made from a vest-pocket screwdriver.

As you zero in on a shotgun purchase, you'll be exposed to an intense amount of merchandising. The advertising world calls it "features and benefits." They've been dousing us with "features" ever since they found they could put hammers on the inside and sell them as hammerless shotguns. To be absolutely truthful, they changed the hammer's name to "tumbler." Nobody ever claimed they were tumblerless shotguns. It's just good business—right?

It's not unlike the pharmaceutical companies discovering a cure before they've discovered the symptoms. Remember "simple nervous tension"? If you don't have simple nervous tension, you're dead.

Nevertheless, firearms manufacturers have to point out the features and benefits so you'll select their merchandise over that of others.

Remember, what you are looking for is a good, well-designed, and simple entry-level shotgun.

But in studying the merchandising claims, you'll run into a lot of terms. Most of these "features" will be used to sell you or raise the final cost of the firearm.

You're going to see features like:

1. Articulated front triggers
2. Side clips
3. Leather-covered recoil pads
4. Screw-in chokes
5. Narrow-sighting plains
6. Lumps
7. Crossbolts, third fasteners, and doll's heads
8. Ejectors

Let's take a look at these features one at a time. I'll be treading on some pretty sacred cows here, so remember these are strictly my own feelings and what I've found useful in my shooting.

1. Articulated front triggers

The front triggers on these firearms are hinged. This is to keep the front trigger from hitting your trigger finger when you pull the back trigger.

In all my years of shooting, I have never been hit by the front trigger. The trigger guard would have to break off the middle finger for the firearm to recoil backward far enough for the trigger finger to be hit by the front trigger. This is a complicated way of saying "forget it."

In my book, double triggers are an absolute necessity, but an articulated front trigger is not.

I've never really understood articulated front triggers. Yet, most expensive shotguns have them. I find them unnecessary and, possibly, one more thing that can break.

2. Side clips

These are wing-like projections that extend forward from the fences and are fitted tightly to the very rear of the barrels. Their purpose is to keep the barrels from moving laterally at the receiver. Sounds like a good idea until you remember that the lumps are fitted tightly into a recess in the bottom of the receiver. Both lumps would have to be ripped off the barrels for any lateral movement to develop. We have an awful lot of firearms with no clips and many hundreds of thousands of rounds through them that show no signs of lateral movement. Granted, we treat the shotguns gently, keep them clean and well greased, and shoot loads only strong enough to do the job. On the other hand, I did manage to cut my hand once, on an over-sharp clip. Personally, I'll pass on side clips.

3. Leather-covered recoil pads

You already know that I don't like recoil pads. They're usually a sign of poor technique. But if you expect to bounce the butt of your shotgun off a rock (splitsville), then a recoil pad (read "rubber bumper") is a must. Problem is, recoil pads stick to your clothing and preclude a really beautiful mount, which is exactly why they're covered with leather and then lacquered—to make them slip-pery. Now, you may have a perfectly legit reason for installing a pad. Maybe you need to lengthen a too-short stock. Perhaps you have two or three pads to accommodate different members of your family or a growing member. Okay. But I've seen too many pads, installed by so-called firearms restorers, which were

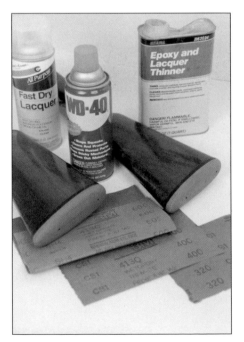

I've never cared much for leather-covered recoil pads. When done correctly, they're pretty expensive, and they don't slip very well, which is necessary for a proper mount. I much prefer to lacquer my recoil pads, if a pad is necessary. Mask off the front of the pad with masking tape and newspaper to protect the stock. Then, after contouring all the straight lines off the pad with medium sandpaper, proceed to polish the pad with wet-and-dry sandpaper.

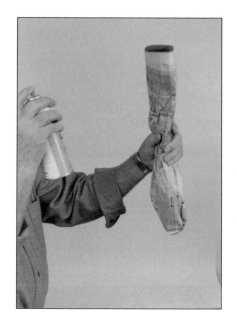

Keep the pad moist with WD-40 and polish away with 240-grit (for about an hour) until it's as smooth as it'll get, then switch to 360-grit. Keep smoothing. If you want a fine finish, you can go on to 400-grit. Just keep polishing and keep it wet with the WD-40. When it's as smooth as you can get it, take off the WD-40 with lacquer thinner.

Then, using clear lacquer from a spray can, fog on ten coats about ten minutes apart. Many light coats are much better than a few thick ones. Oh, sure, I know the pad will bend and the lacquer will craze a bit over time. Just sand it off, re-mask, and re-spray. After a while, the pad will harden up and stop crazing.

simply recoil pads with leather stretched over them and slapped back on the firearm.

When installed correctly, the pad is ground down the exact thickness of the leather all the way around. When the leather is installed, the final pad and stock have the exact same dimensions. There is no bump, or rise, where the stock meets the pad. In most cases, this is a time consuming, and therefore expensive, job. Sometimes this can be used as a sleight of hand.

One very well known purveyor of outdoor gear sold one of my students a "custom-fitted" shotgun. The salesman had gone on at great lengths about the leather-covered pad. As the student was handing the shotgun across the table I said, "They ripped you off."

This was perfectly obvious while the gun was still being handed to me. It was in no way a custom anything. It was a standard off-the-rack shotgun, the stock of which had been bent from cast off to cast on. That is an acceptable fix, except in this case, the triggers had not been reversed. The front trigger fired the right barrel. The triggers should have been reversed and the choking changed so the more open barrel was on the left and the front trigger fired it.

Later, when we tried to fire the gun, we discovered the "carpenter" who installed the pad simply cut the stock off at 90 degrees to the new length (which was also wrong). This gave the stock some five inches of downpitch. Remember, downpitch makes the gun kick up the way we use it. Even a swing shooter who mounts the stock on the shoulder would receive a vicious upper cut each time the firearm is shot. We sent the gun to my 'smith, reversed the triggers, changed the choking, cut the shotgun to the new length-of-pull (luckily the shotgun was still way too long for our graduate the way it had come, even though it was supposedly custom) and corrected the pitch at the same time. We were also able to bend in the correct amount of cast on.

Since the student, now a graduate, wanted to use the shotgun in the high country where there are lots of rocks, we reinstalled a

I always recommend the same pad, a Pachmayr Old English half-inch recoil pad. Recently, they discontinued the traditional red ones and went to something of an unattractive brown color. By the way, the pad isn't there to protect you; it's protection for the stock. A sharp blow (think falling down on a rock) will split the stock. A pad helps prevent that. The finished pads have the same look as the stock, and they slide beautifully from the armpit to the anchor point and back.

half-inch Pachmayr Old English pad. This was rounded properly and then polished, using WD-40 and wet-and-dry sandpaper, available at your hardware store.

I guess you can tell, but I'm not wild about leather-covered pads either. I wouldn't pay extra for one, especially on an entry-level shotgun.

4. Screw in chokes

Boy, I'm not going to make many friends here. Personally, I would rather see you invest the money in shooting lessons and practice sessions than in screw-in chokes. Remember, our whole thing is to take a little bit of shot and put it through as big of a hole as possible so it enters the air round. That way the shot stays with its fellows and makes a uniform pattern. I should say small shot. I really haven't experimented with shot larger than #4, as I can see no use for it. Small shot flows through a barrel better than large, so I'm not going to make any statements about large shot because I don't use it. Some of my students have used #2 shot on geese and report excellent results. Remember, we're going to shoot birds at ranges not greater than forty yards. Do you know what an ounce of steel shot (or Bismuth for that matter) in the brain of a goose will do to that goose?

Right.

We regularly break targets at seventy yards. Well, okay not regularly, but often. But we do break them regularly at fifty and sixty yards with #8 shot which is the only shot we use in the school.

I have shotguns with screw-in chokes—two of them; that's how I

I'm not crazy about choke tubes. So when I came up with my formula of .004 and .008, I gave up on choke tubes and spent my time learning to shoot with those two chokes, which are ideal for nearly all types of shooting.

came up with the .004 and .008 configurations. When I was doing my original testing, I kept ending up with those chokes. I finally left them in the guns, as they are really ideal for 95 percent of all of my shooting.

When our shooting grounds were open to the public, I saw guys screwing in chokes between each sporting clay station—constantly changing tubes. And most of these shooters were constantly asking the better shots, "Which chokes should I use?" These are the same guys who over and over again ask what the range is and "How much do you lead it?" Even with that information, they still shoot less than 50 percent. I consider it an increasing preoccupation with gadgets and the result of a certain level of a succumbing to marketing scams to sell you gadgets.

So, for myself and my graduates, I'll stick to my .004 and .008 and spend my time practicing, not screwing.

5. Sighting planes

Many years ago, when shooters were deserting side-by-sides for the vertical-format shotguns, side-by-sides were roundly criticized for having too broad a sighting plane. You've already learned we shoot with our heads up and make every effort to ignore the barrel (if you see it or are even aware of it, you'll miss). So side-by-sides obviously *have* no sighting plane.

A humorous aside here always makes me chuckle. The pumps, semiautos, and especially over-and-unders were adored and received lavish praise for their "narrow sighting planes." By that, I assume you peer down the rib, align the beads, and achieve a perceived relationship between barrel and target. In my book that's aiming, but practitioners proclaim loudly that they're pointing, not aiming. To me the term "sighting plane" means just that, sighting (aiming).

At any rate, a few years ago, several over-under manufacturers made a discovery and came out with the wide rib. And guess what their reason for this was? So the shooter would have a broad sighting plane. (Can you hear me chuckling?)

6. Lumps

All the shotguns I own have lumps. I think most modern side-by-sides do as well. The "lumps," as you already know, are those chunks of metal that hang down under the breech end of the barrels. The little cutouts at the rear of the lumps are the bites. Actually, the rear one is tapered downward on the lowest side. This is to accommodate the cross bolts or under lugs, the rear one of which is also tapered, like a wedge. They both slide forward into the bites. The rear one cams the breech end of the barrels downward, locking the gun shut. The reason "lumps" are in this section is that there are several different kinds—chopper, dovetail, through, shoe, and monoblock—all of which are really a choice in the method of construction.

Dovetailed chopper lumps are easy to spot, but not so easy to photograph. There a lots of kinds of lumps on side-by-sides, but only one true chopper lump. Look very carefully at the lumps on the Garbi (right). Notice a faint line down the center of both lumps. Those are chopper lumps. No line, no choppers. It's that simple.

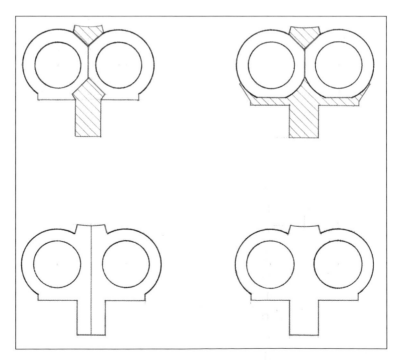

Here's another look at chopper lumps. Dovetailed chopper lumps are on the lower left.

The chopper lumps are often used on the more expensive side-by-sides, although chopper lumps sometimes turn up on our entry-level Ugartecheas as well.

Chopper lumps are easily identified by the line that runs north and south down the middle of them. When the original billet of steel which will become a barrel is cast, the chunk, which will become half of the lumps, is already there. As the barrel is machined, the half-lumps are as well. When two barrels are joined, each barrel contributes its half to form the whole, which is then silver soldered or brazed into place. They're called "chopper" because a barrel with its attached lump reminded someone once of a hatchet or axe.

At any rate, I see the term bandied about by salespeople who wouldn't know a chopper lump from a dovetailed one. I object to using the term to up the price. The other kinds of lumps aren't necessarily better or worse, but they might make the breech ends of the barrels heavier and broader. So you should know the difference. You should know what you're buying.

For instance, the dovetailed lump was used on the famous Winchester 21. The strength of the dovetailed lump can be seen, since the dovetail as well as the brazing takes the strain of locking the firearm shut and the resulting recoil.

The shoe lump is simply brazed to the underside of the barrels. It's a large surface, therefore safe, but it can create a heavier, poorly balanced firearm.

The through-lump wraps around the barrels not unlike a figure eight with the outer sides cut off. It's strong enough and safe as long as some mechanic hasn't compromised the thickness of the firearm's chamber walls in fitting the lump to the barrels. But, again, it can make the breech end broad.

The monoblock is a method of construction in which the entire rear section of the barrels is machined as one piece. The tubes are then slipped through the holes and sweated or brazed into place. When done correctly, this can result in an invisible joint and a well balanced firearm.

7. Crossbolts, third fasteners, and doll's heads

Frankly, I wouldn't pay extra for any of these terms. And, in the minds of most people who know more than I do, they're unnecessary. Let me explain why.

Back in the days of the newly invented breechloader, cracks (read, "Oops, it broke") often appeared at the corner where the face of the standing breech and the water tables meet. The effort of barrels against the action body is fierce. As the ejecta (shot and wad) speed down the barrel, friction causes the barrels to be forced forward. Since the barrels are attached at the hinge pin, they press to swing down as well. This creates a near hammer blow on the forward edge of the action body. Result? Splitsville.

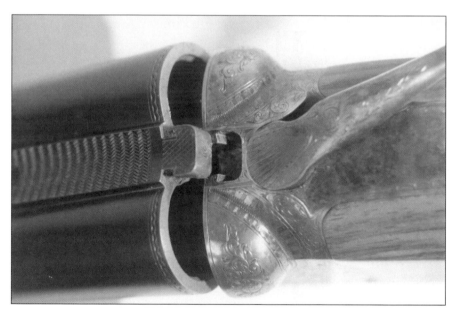

This doll's head on a Parker reproduction is more like a T-head, but nonetheless functions in the same manner.

So the manufacturers of the time set about trying to pin the top of the barrels to the top of the action body. Nineteenth-century gunmaker William W. Greener came up with the crossbolt. This is a round bolt, a round steel rod that passes through the upper part of the action body and an extension which fits behind the face of the standing breech.

Other manufacturers resorted to the doll's head, a round and tapered extension at the top of the barrels that fits into a corresponding recess in the top of the receiver.

Still others rely on the third fastener. This is a square projection which extends through the extractors and fits into a recess in the face of the standing breech. A bolt in the top part of the recess of the breech moves forward and back, fitting over the top of the projection, and locks the barrels into place.

Now that's the most technical I'm going to get. If you'd like to examine the engineering of the thing, forces and counter forces, I suggest you obtain a set of three books entitled *The Modern Shotgun*

The third fastener was Purdy's answer to the same problem. Notice the recessed notch in the upper part of the standing breech. In the top of this hollowed-out notch is a projection which slides forward and back and is controlled by the top lever. When the shotgun is opened, the projection is withdrawn enough so that the block, which sticks out through the extractors, can fit smoothly into the recess in the standing breech. When the gun is closed, the projection moves forward and successfully locks the upper part of the barrels to the standing breech.

by Major Sir Gerald Burrard. The set was first published in 1931 and has been reprinted several times. Unfortunately, at this writing, the company that published them has gone out of business. If you can scrounge up a used set, you'll be lucky indeed.

The bottom line is this: With our modern, more elastic steels, radiusing the angle between the breech face and the water tables, and a well-fitting pair of lumps and under lug, you should get all the bolting you need. Maybe the top extensions have some merit in guns intended for truly massive loads, but you've already learned they're unnecessary if your shooting compensates with accuracy. Shoot low-pressure, high-velocity loads, and shoot for the head. Limit your bird hunting to forty yards and there should be no need for tooth-cracking recoil.

In side-by-side shotguns, as with most things, you get what you pay for. Usually, what you pay has a direct relationship to what you get. It's not always true, of course, but it's a good rule of thumb. Occasionally, bargains do come along. But you really have to know what you're doing to identify the difference between bargain price and cheap quality, or worse yet, something dangerous.

A cheap-quality side-by-side is no bargain. It may not point very well. Its balance may be all screwed up and, sometimes, it may be a danger to you and those about you. A good-or fine-quality side-by-side is a joy forever.

8. Ejectors

For 99 percent of my shooting, I'd just as soon not have ejectors. Extractors are fine.

In a side-by-side, the ejector hammers, sears, and springs are all contained within the forend. When you open your shotgun, you cock the tumblers (hammers) in the action body. As you close the action, you cock the ejector hammers. This puts quite a bit of strain in a fairly small area—the forend. Most of us do not let the empty shells fly when the shotgun is reopened. We prefer to save the empties for reloading or disposal, not only at the range but to avoid littering while hunting. So we put our hands over the breech end of the barrels and let the empties pop into our hands. Well, logic tells you this: cocking the ejectors speeds their wear. Why not either remove the ejectors until needed or simply use an extractor gun for all shooting where ejectors are unnecessary. If you head for the British Isles, on a driven shoot, or to South America for a dove fandango, pop your ejectors back in, or have your gunsmith do it. Ejectors can be a real plus when many shots are taken in a short time. Ejectors, a loader, and self openers all came into being because of volume shooting. But the shells all land in a relatively small area at the peg of a driven shoot or in a dove blind. When the shooting's over, it is an easy task to pick up the empties and take them out of the field with you. Not typical shooting for most of us in the States, where extractors will suit the vast majority of us much better.

When selecting a side-by-side, remember this—the side-by-side is simplicity itself. When taken care of, it is not normally subject to breakage. Fewer parts equal fewer things to go wrong in the field,

I'm not wild about ejectors. The Parker reproduction forend still has them in place. The Garbi forend on the upper right has the ejectors removed. They are placed in a little plastic bag with some oil, in case they are needed for a day of driven shooting.

where a broken part can ruin your whole trip. Take along spares of those parts you feel comfortable replacing after a tutorial by your 'smith. The best insurance against a disastrous trip spoiled by a firearm that goes down is to carry a second identical gun on all trips. It's good insurance. And, if you have the opportunity to shoot with a loader (a person who loads for you), you're never really out of ammunition if you have a pair of guns at the ready.

With your Predator safely tucked away in your mind and a pair of well-fitted shotguns, you're ready for fine shotgunning, anywhere in the world. Now it's time to work on becoming a Master Gunner.

12

MAKING OF THE MASTER GUNNER

Many years ago, I wrote an article called "Instinctive Shooting—Making of the Master Gunner." The more we discover about instinctive shooting, the more appealing the concept of the Master Gunner. But what *is* a Master Gunner? Is it an advertising ploy to get students into a shooting school? Or is it a quasi-Zen concept designed to make the technique seem mysterious, magical?

This is a shot of my brother, Mike, just before his passing. Mike personified my concept of a gentleman and a master gunner.

The truth lies somewhere between the two. What I discovered about the technique was a concept which had to be incorporated into the teaching curriculum. The concept was truth and logic.

The truth would out even though it conflicted with time-honored concepts.

Everything in the technique would first have to pass the test of logic. Is it logical? If not, toss it out.

So what's the rest of the Master Gunner concept? The answer to that, I believe, is a little different for each person. To explain, I can only tell you what the Master Gunner means to me and to those graduates who have shared the power of the thing (Predator) with me.

Originally, the concept was to create gunners who were the consummate source of knowledge about shotguns, in general, and side-by-side shotguns, in particular. That is because I, like so many of the shooters I have met, had been misled by gun dealers and gunsmiths. I figured that if I garnered as much knowledge about firearms as possible, I could protect myself against any misleading information. In that, I've become successful, but as you can tell by the previous chapter, I make no claims of being an expert in the mechanics of side-by-sides. Where I take my claim is that I have become expert in how to shoot side-by-sides and to successfully teach that method to others in a way which is replicable. But I have learned to rely on a competent and trusted gunsmith to care for my guns.

I mentioned truth and logic—those became the cornerstone of the Wingshooting Workshop. With them came their natural tagalongs—honesty, generosity, courtesy, and honor. These, then, became the traditions of the Wingshooting Workshop.

The traditions are evident in the way we shoot, the way we conduct ourselves, the way we handle our firearms, treat our companions, love and train our dogs, and respect the people who allow us to utilize their property. We also dress the part of respectable sportsmen and women.

Recently, I attended a graduate hunt at a hunting preserve in Oregon. There were six graduates from our Wingshooting Workshop. Some knew each other, some didn't. But the four days made me as proud as any father could have been with successful progeny.

What do I mean by that?

Well, let's take gun handling. Total muzzle control is a way of shotgunning-life for them. Not once did I ever feel uncomfortable—not while handling guns, not in the field, not in the lodge. Not once did a pair of muzzles cross my body, not even in cleaning—never even close. I wish I could say that on all sporting trips.

Dog handling was as fine as I've ever seen. Not a harsh word was uttered. The dogs behaved as they do in magazines. This was amazing among six people who didn't train together and, since I don't teach dog handling, it was interesting that they had all developed such exemplary dogs.

Gunning was impeccable. The "other guy" was always given the first shot. Partners took turns flushing and never shot the other's bird.

This was at a hunting preserve—Great Expectations near John Day, Oregon—about which I had decided to pen an article for *The Double Gun Journal*. As a preserve, the regular season limits on game are not imposed. But hens were passed, at the request of the manager. Great Expectations is an unusual hunting facility. At the time, only roosters were released, but plenty of hens have been reared as well. Each spring, numerous clutches of chicks are hatched in a special preserve area where birds of either sex are safe once within its boundaries. Remember, these graduates, if they so choose, can hit anything that flies. They have nothing to prove nor any reason to show off. So killing another bird is not vital or an issue. Ensuring their hunting partners get a quality hunt was what was important to them. I was proud.

This was also an article circulating on the then newly formed Order of Edwardian Gunners, nicknamed "the Vintagers." The dress code was turn-of-the-century English shooting party, as practiced by royalty of the United Kingdom and their peerage. The dress, therefore, was formal—tweed coats, knickers (or breeks, as they're called in the UK), neckties, and, of course, side-by-side guns. Many of the new members were quite astonished to find, by the end of the four days, that the clothing was entirely practical and extremely comfortable.

I have a degree of arthritis which affects my knees. I learned long ago that when I wear either shorts or breeks, I get an extra three hours in the field and a full day in school without pain. I adopted them out of practicality, not snobbishness, before they were popular on this side of the pond. Many of the new Vintagers also discovered their practical application.

But there's more to my reasoning here than just style. Remember, logic is always our guide. While teaching, it's vital for students to see my knees, as the legs lock and unlock, shifting weight, depending on what the target is doing. In a pair of long pants, the students can't see those movements. In shorts or breeks, they can.

And think about this: in professional sports, when players are either practicing or playing their game, they are always wearing shorts or knickers. Even some professional golfers are returning to knickers to get the freedom of motion afforded their knees.

Let me explain about the word "knickers." When I was a kid, the truncated trousers were called "knickerbockers." The pants were roundly hated by children my age, because they were required wearing by most Depression-era mothers, since they could be bought long or blousy, and then as the kid grew, the pants kind of grew with them, at least more so than trousers.

The knickers we wore as kids were kind of a puke-colored tweed with knitted cuffs, which fit into the tops of our long stockings. Or if you had an "okay" set of parents, you might have had the privilege of a pair of high-top lace-up boots with a knife pocket on the right hand side. But boots or not, we hated them. I vowed never to be caught dead in knickers, no matter what they were called. But, vows are made to be broken.

When I moved to Idaho, I was able to do a lot of whitewater rafting. In Minnesota, I learned to love whitewater canoeing. My wife and I were on the rivers every chance we had. On my first Idaho whitewater trip, I was doing an article on whitewater rafting, steelhead fishing, and chukar hunting—a combination cast-blast-and-raft trip. I rowed my own raft, so I could film the other rafts, which consisted of guests of a professional rafting company. I had my beloved English setter, Fizz, aboard. It was fall and the weather was cool. The water was cold. I noticed immediately most of the professional guides were wearing breeks—actually West German military surplus, wool (loden) breeks. I was wearing the obligatory Levi's blue jeans. By noon the first day, I was wet to the crotch. They wore sandals, no socks, and these military breeks. They stayed dry.

I stayed wet. I bought my first pair when I got home. They were German surplus, boiled wool, and cost a whopping $14.95.

When chukar hunting in long pants, I could manage two, maybe three hours before my knees felt like marathon prayer celebrant's on a rocky beach. Long pants pulled the patella down with every step. My kneecaps felt lubricated with sand. Steep hills made the chukar hunting almost impossible for me. Finally, I got smart. I decided to wear the wool breeks and the results were dramatic. I was able to hunt five, sometimes six hours before my knees began sending signals.

Old photographs of my father and grandfather always showed them in fedora hats, vests, and neckties. It looked quaint, and old-fashioned. Little did I know that I would also return to these roots.

On a golden, fall day, while sage grouse hunting Idaho's Pahsimeroi valley, a friend's large German shorthaired pointer got slapped by a porcupine. What a quill pig was doing so many miles from the safety of the trees is beyond me. But there he was, out in the middle of the sage brush, and slap the dog, he did.

Tom, the owner, panicked in an effort to help his dog. He grabbed a handful of quills and pulled. He was rewarded with a bite from his faithful dog. Luckily, I had a spare shoestring in my pocket and I wasn't prone to panic. I came up with a bright idea. We were able to pass the string over the dog's muzzle, cross it under his chin and tie it up behind his neck. We pulled the quills, one at a time, with my hemostat, something I found useful to my hunting kit. The dog attempted to bite us with every quill, and the shoestring didn't do a good job, as it dug into the dog's muzzle. Finally, those neckties my dad wore made sense and, perhaps, had more practical application than I had thought.

After that, I began to wear one in the school, out of respect for my students. Later, I discovered more practicality in that the necktie is actually like a scarf (and this is why the fashion developed, after all). It is snug on a cool morning. It holds in heat. As the morning warms, it can be loosened or removed. If needed, it can be retied as the sun begins to set.

In season, I almost always wear a necktie out of respect for my students and the sport which we're a part of.

The necktie, particularly a silk one, can also double as a sling. Here in the West, it's sometimes necessary to sling a shotgun while both hands are used to climb. Often, while photographing a story, my tie becomes a sling to get the shotgun out of the way to take a few photos. We've also used neckties, twice in fact, to splint up legs of dogs that had been torn by barbed wire. Once I used it to repair a shoulder strap on a friend's game bag that had broken. The necktie is a handy piece of emergency rope.

A shotgun with a permanent sling is worse than useless, in my opinion. It ruins the balance of the shotgun. Plus, the forward swivel is right where I want my offside finger to be. The necktie is a great sling, if you find yourself needing one. It's light, strong, and, in my case, always there. But it's not there when you don't need it.

But the most obvious use of the necktie is this: The upland hunter has a very high profile these days. Many Americans still fish, but we are now in the minority as hunters. And, few of us own the land where we hunt. We are seen along roadsides in rural areas. We must ask farm families for permission to hunt. We travel to hunt. We frequent local businesses, restaurants, and motels while we are there to shoot their game. Is Rambo the image we want to convey?

On one memorable occasion, my hunting partner, Russ, and I approached a farmyard to request permission to hunt a birdie-looking creek bottom. A dirty pickup was just leaving, spinning its tires in aggravation. Three unshaven types with blaze orange vests were in the cab; a Labrador retriever hung precariously over the side of the pickup's bed. As they passed, the passenger tossed an empty beer bottle past the front of our car and yelled, "Don't bother, that bitch won't letcha hunt."

We ignored their advice and proceeded to the farmhouse where we were greeted by a lovely lady who explained the three coarse-looking men had frightened her.

"They were rough-talking and smelled like beer," she explained, though an explanation certainly wasn't necessary.

Both Russ and I had on tweed shooting jackets, breeks, shirts, ties, and rubber knee boots. No matter what clothes I'm going to hunt in, I always ask permission in the coat and tie, and it comes in handy later at the restaurant for lunch or dinner, as well. In between, I may pull on chaps and a canvas coat if there are briars.

"But you boys look real nice," she said smiling, "so I'm going to tell Carl that I said it was all right for you to hunt. You know, we really don't let people hunt here very often. It makes Carl nervous, what with the cows 'n' all. . . ." her voice trailed off hoping that we'd understand.

We got three nice roosters out of the creek bottom. We stopped in the farmhouse and offered them to the lady, who appreciated having two of them for her family dinner. I'll bet you if we go back, even ten years from now, we'll still be welcomed to hunt and, probably, well remembered.

Another time, a necktie saved my life. It was my last chukar hunt.

We'd climbed above Idaho's Salmon River in a precipitous section of the canyon. Fizz was with me, as always; although she hated white-water, she loved to hunt chukars, so she tolerated the raft. She'd hide behind me in her little yellow life jacket, gripping the cargo net, her eyes tight closed.

Back in those days, we were still taking a step toward the weak side, as is taught in some schools. Well, anyway, I took the step and connected with the first bird. When my foot came back down, there wasn't anything under it.

Greedily, I was trying for a double and took the second shot even as my body was beginning to fall—backward.

My shoulders hit the talus slope and immediately the slippery shale began to toboggan me down. I managed to roll over. I was still sliding. I could see the drop-off, fifty feet ahead. I was desperate. I reluctantly let go of my shotgun; this one was named First Son.

Toes digging, knees digging, hands digging, chin digging, gradually, I began to slow down. I stopped. My head and shoulders were over the cliff face. I watched First Son fall one hundred feet to the Salmon River's rocky beach.

All I could think was, "Boy, I hope First Son's got a good safety," as his barrels were pointed up toward my face as he was falling to the beach below.

He did. But I was still in deep trouble. My feet were above my head. Every time I tried to push back, I slipped forward. My hunting companion came to my aid but was afraid to get too close for fear I'd go and pull him over as well, as the footing was very insecure and the slope was severe. I hung there in the balance for quite a long time. He looked for help.

Finally, a professional rafting guide named Mike eased his way to me. He slipped his belt through mine. One of my hunting companions arrived and tossed his belt, along with a fine, silk necktie from one of London's best shotgun makers, which was then tied to the guide's belt. The belts were looped, buckled, and tied to the tie.

Now, both guys were able to daisy chain to a stout bush. By pulling on the makeshift rope, they eased me away from the cliff face to the safety of the shrubbery.

Moral of the story? Never move your feet while tracking. Always wear a stout, quality belt with a good, solid buckle. AND, always wear the best-quality silk necktie you can afford while hunting with me.

And, while we are talking about style, don't litter! Every time I talk with farmers or ranchers about litter, they say the same thing about their land as you'd say about your front yard. You don't appreciate other people's trash in it.

What leads their list of litter? Empty shotgun shells. Imagine. You allow someone to hunt on your land and they return the favor by leaving their empty shotgun shells all over the place. They're brightly colored, the brass reflects the light, and they don't belong in someone's field. How would you feel if, the following weekend, the same farmer turned up on your front lawn with a picnic lunch and he tossed the empty sandwich bags, napkins, bottle caps, and cans into your flower beds? You wouldn't like it. Trust me, neither do farmers. Several I've talked with have closed their land to hunting simply because of hunters' slovenly ways.

Gates are right up there too.

The best policy is to leave gates as you find them, unless you are told otherwise. Nothing makes a farmer or rancher more upset than to arrive at a pasture with half his herd to discover some hunter has "thoughtfully" closed the gate. It's nearly as bad as leaving a gate open and letting them all out.

I suppose if there's a bottom line to becoming a Master Gunner, it's following the golden rule.

The original instruction handed down to us was "lead by example."

"Do unto others . . ." springs to mind as well."

Both are still good advice.

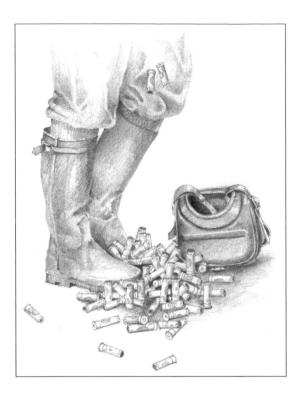

13

PRACTICE, PRACTICE, AND WALKABOUT

Each shooter who graduates from the Wingshooting Workshop commits to what we call "A Year in the Wilderness." By that, we mean each student will go forth and practice what has been learned, on a weekly basis for a minimum of a year. Not as others would practice by shooting trap, skeet, or sporting clays, and not even by hunting. No, they commit to practicing the exercises learned in class. Then, if the practice sessions go well, they may shoot a walkabout or go hunting, sort of as a treat rather than as the form of their practice.

I know it seems like I'm beating this business of practice to death, but the more I teach the school, the more I realize how important practice is and how to make practice sessions really worthwhile.

Failure to follow this method of practicing will result in backsliding and loss of technique.

There's nothing wrong with trap, skeet, or sporting clays. But they aren't practice venues. These are games operated by ranges, the busiest of which make more money by pushing people through as quickly as possible. Not that this is their goal; but to make money, this is something they generally have to do. I operated a sporting clays range for a while, and I'll tell you it's not a big money-making venture. We lost money if we didn't move squads as fast as possible. There are various ways to do it, from throwing true pairs, pushing our widely separated fields as close together as possible, and promoting such games as flurries or Annie Oakley competitions with three to five shooters and just one clay.

I love to shoot leisurely. I love the time to chat, stop, and admire guns or tell tales.

"That's what a clubhouse is for," one operator told me, "where they can buy food and visit the pro shop. We don't discourage talking on the field, but we don't encourage it either. Keep 'em moving." Now not all ranges are that way, but many have been forced to think along these lines. And sporting clays to Annie Oakley are all fun games, but like hunting too, they are not good for practicing shooting.

Practice is different than that; practice is what the name implies— practice. Very few shooters actually practice.

Set up each practice session ahead of time. The Year in the Wilderness is comprised of one hundred targets a week for a year. That's not much, is it? You can shoot more. But, shoot less and your skill slips. If you want to become a Master Gunner this is what is required. Do you think a college (or even high school) ball player shoots at least one hundred hoops a week?

Try to find a range where you can shoot alone. People mean well, but trust me, everybody wants to be a shooting instructor. "You're shooting behind," they'll tell you, in the sure and certain knowledge that *you* don't know *where* you're shooting. So "shooting behind" is a safe suggestion. And, it puts *them* in a position of power.

I visited a skeet field on a rare trip away from my home range, and saw one poor fellow was having an awful time. His buddies were doing their best to "help" him. But it took only a casual glance to realize they had him shooting at least four feet in front of the target because of their constant "you're shooting behind" barrage. They had no more idea where he was shooting than he did. Without the focus learned by instinctive shooters, seeing the shot pattern is quite difficult. Instinctive shooters have no problem seeing the shot of other shooters; many instructors do, too. But your average shooter cannot see the pattern.

On another occasion, I visited a graduate, Rob E., on his home range in the East. He, by necessity, shot on a skeet range. The resulting damage was apparent on his first shot.

He felt it necessary to "hurry up" so he wouldn't hold up other shooters. As a result, he'd discarded The Test, which we perform before each shot in practice sessions. His shots were rushed, and the beautiful thrust was gone, replaced by the "lift," which is so common with aiming shooters. The beautiful mount was gone.

That's the bad news. The following spring, he returned to the Wingshooting Workshop. The good news is it took a mere twenty minutes to wipe out the damage caused by the skeet shooting.

So I'll say it again: if you can, shoot alone. Find a range and time when there's no one else around. Or, set up a stand-alone trap, battery operated and remotely controlled, that you can move from location to location.

Decide ahead of time what you're going to practice that day. Write it down if necessary, so that you stick to the plan. There are always some shots you prefer over others. But the unpleasant shots must receive as much attention as the favorite ones.

For instance, I hate low, quartering-away shots. I find myself avoiding them. But I force myself to practice the shot. I may never get miraculous on low quartering shots, but I practice them, as they are my nemesis. In practice, I hit all of them. I just don't love them. In the field, I may not drive the gun hard enough when this shot appears, or worse yet, I start to think about it with the conscious mind. One thought and you lose focus. You miss. Hesitate the merest moment, even a nanosecond, and you'll miss.

Okay, let's take a typical practice day. Let's make it easy. Chuck is our shooter. He's decided right-to-lefts are the order of the day (and he's right-handed).

He's using a standalone trap that's mounted in a small trailer. Lots of graduates buy their own (often, following my model) and set them up on land that they own (or they arrange a little lease from a farmer or rancher). You don't need good land; offer to lease some of their worst ground. The owners are only too happy to have a little income from it. If you can find a place with a cliff, so much the better. Retired gravel pits are a good choice. Best of all, you can promise the owner that there will never be more than two shooters at a time and you'll pick up your shells.

Chuck starts by doing a few simple but vital stretching exercises. This is a good idea anytime you shoot—practice, competition, or hunting. Stretch out the muscles that you'll use in the activity. Go goofy foot, then turn your leg, waist, back, shoulders, and head as far as possible, standing on the gun leg to your weak side. Push gently against any locked-up muscles and tendons. Eight or ten gentle stretches against the locked-up joints and tendons are good. Then, rotate to the strong-side leg and again push against the locked-up muscles, joints, and tendons. Be gentle. You're trying to stretch, not dislocate. Do this as many times as necessary to feel loose. If you have your own stretching exercises, by all means use them. This is a true sport. To perform instinctive shooting well, you should be loose, supple, and relaxed.

Today, Chuck sets the trap up for right to left shots, shooting in his left hemisphere. He's also using my trapper, Gene, to trap for him, although, he could use a remote control trap machine.

Chuck starts by facing the trap. It represents the dog in a hunting situation.

He begins with the test called The Point. It's the quickest way to sharpen your focus. He sets up on the left bird leg. His shotgun is hanging over his right arm and he is pointing with his left index finger. He focuses on a spot, the focus spot, on the trailer, and calls for a series of targets. He practices keeping the angular relationship between his pointing left (offside) arm and his body constant,

Always begin a practice session at twenty to thirty yards from the flight path and about the same distance from the point of difficulty which you intend to practice. Begin each session with the Test called "pointing." Chuck is doing the practicing, here, while Gene is "pulling" for him.

A common error in pointing and, therefore, in shooting, is pointing with the arm and not keeping the body at 90 degrees to the arm, both vertically and horizontally. Chuck has opened his stance to almost 180 degrees.

90 degrees up and down, 90 degrees side to side. He locks on to the leading edge and focus throughout the flight path of the target.

It's sometimes helpful if you have another person who is familiar with our method to know what to look for while you're doing these various exercises, perhaps your trapper. At one point, for instance, the trapper might say, "Excuse me, but your left arm is getting past 90 degrees." Another time it could be the hips are staying still. Chuck then starts raising his left arm by lifting his hips rather than by raising his arm.

He does the Test called The Relationship, two or three times. It's the same as The Point, but now with the shotgun in the ready position and coiled. He practices keeping the shotgun at 90 degrees to his body throughout the track. Finished with the Tests, he's ready to begin shooting.

The relationship is the same as the point, except now the shotgun is in the ready position and coiled. The shooter's barrels stay on the line hanging under the target's leading edge. The stasis line and the vision line converge at the leading edge. The barrel line and the vision line are parallel. The barrels are on the line pointing slightly under the target, depending on fit. All of these lines are conceptual. The shooter cannot see the barrels, nor is he aware of them.

Chuck starts with his easiest shots. Everyone's different, but I always begin at about twenty yards in the center of the field, halfway from launch to landing.

Chuck goes through The Test and coil before he calls for each target. He's careful to point with his chin before he calls for the target. This refits the shotgun before each shot and sets the head and vision in the proper relationship to the shotgun and barrels (parallel). He is careful that the head is raised and the chin pointed during the coil.

The trap I use for these practice sessions is really a good one for these types of practice sessions. It allows for a built-in delay, after the remote button is pushed. It has an adjustable cam, which turns off the power to the arm during each rotation. By adjusting the cam, a shooter can shut off the power immediately after the target

The trap Chuck is using here is a Quickfire II, by Hunter's Point. The release, simply overrides a micro-switch which, starts and stops the motor. A cam, seen here, stops the motor by depressing the switch. A shooter can build in a delay by setting the cam so it will turn off the motor sooner. When the release switch is pushed, the motor turns, the arm moves to the magazine, picks up a target and throws it. A delay, of a second or so, is built in. This is plenty of time to push the release if it's attached to the shooter's belt, do the Test, and be ready for the target.

A WORD OF WARNING HERE. TRAPS ARE DANGEROUS! Become a professional before handling any trap. You must know a trap better than you know your own body before you attempt to adjust one. Traps are *not* forgiving. If you have a remote, put it in a safe place before reloading the trap from behind. Disconnect it from the power source and uncock it before retiring a trap for the day. Never leave an unattended trap cocked. Never leave a trap running. Keep trap enclosures locked. TRAPS ARE AS DANGEROUS AS FIREARMS. TREAT THEM WITH RESPECT. Follow the manufacturer's directions exactly and by the book. Do not take short cuts. Ever!

is dropped, but before the target is released. A one-or two-second delay can also be programmed in. By building in a delay, the shooter allows time for The Test when shooting alone.

Chuck takes his first shots. He's got a good ready position. His body tips back gracefully as his left hand rises with the target. The left forefinger points at the line hanging under the target's leading edge, *in a relationship* under the target. This is so that when the shotgun is thrust forward in the mount, it will arrive in the exact right spot to center the target up in the pattern. His focus is hard on the leading edge. Chuck is working on style here, so he's careful to control the speed of the target with focus and to shoot in slow motion. He concentrates on the leading edge, but keeps the mount smooth and graceful.

This time, Chuck has decided to work on quartering-away birds. Last fall, he missed a couple of quartering birds and knows the work must be done to improve his performance with this shot. But, take notice, Chuck starts with the easy 20-yard crosser at a medium speed. The Predator likes the 90-degree angle and will usually shoot well at one, whenever the Predator is left to its own devices. At 90 degrees, the speed, angle, and height are easiest for the Predator to determine. As the angles decrease, the target information is more difficult for the Predator to estimate. Once the target angle is under 10 degrees, things get tough quickly. Finally, on the going-away target, target speed and the like are almost not apparent. The Predator sees the target rise, but that's about all, it is not excited by this small amount of movement. And remember, the eyes and brain of the Predator are excited by movement. The greater the *apparent* movement of the target, the easier it is for a Predator and an instinctive shooter to hit it.

With each practice shot, Chuck completes The Test—being careful to keep his shoulders at 90 degrees to the shotgun. He even occasionally thinks, "Point the gun-shoulder at the focus point when the offside hand drops to the trouser seam." Pointing the gun shoulder is one more way to keep the body at 90-degrees. As the gun-shoulder points at the focus point, it's actually ahead of the 90-degree angle. But each of the steps in The Test and Coil move the shoulder back slightly, so that by the time the mount happens, the shoulder is in exactly the correct position.

With each practice shot, Chuck gradually works himself toward the trap house, three or four steps at a time.

With each shot, Chuck takes three or four steps forward toward the target thrower and sets up for yet another practice shot. It's a lot like the game of HORSE, in shooting hoops. You work around the circle until you miss.

Chuck is gradually working into the more difficult shots as he nears the target thrower. Notice that Chuck always faces the target thrower. In skeet, shooters face away from the target thrower on the number one and seven stations. This is an unrealistic shooting position for hunters. Never once can I remember standing and gazing into the sky when one of my dogs was on point. The Predator looks where the birds are likely to arise.

There is a difficulty for hunters when practicing with clay targets. Targets are going as fast as they will ever go (wind excepted) when they come off the throwing arm. They decelerate throughout their entire flight. Real game birds are just the opposite—they take off and accelerate to maximum velocity, then slow to a glide. But there's nothing to do about this paradox. It is neither fair nor good sportsmanship to practice on game birds. Opening day hunters who touch their shotguns little, or not at all, before the season opener are to be decried. With the hunting license fee should go the promise to treat the birds with respect and to never shoot unless a quick, clean kill is guaranteed.

Chuck has worked himself into that angle which caused those two misses the previous season. Sure enough—about ten yards from the trap house, his Predator shoots high—twice in a row.

Chuck has worked himself into that position where he missed last season. A quartering-away shot like this easily fools a gunner into believing he's shooting a going-away shot. True to our technique, Chuck is still facing the trap house (dog), and must turn with the target as it flies. The left-hand edge of the target has become the leading edge. Chuck will watch to be sure that the target pieces bounce to the right.

"They're going high," Chuck announces and questions himself at the same time.

"Yeah, I think so. Shoot again," Gene replies.

Again, the shot passes about twelve inches over the target.

"Time for tapping," Chuck mumbles under his breath and walks back to the spot where he hit his last target. "Tapping" is the word we use to acknowledge that Predators will, for the most part, shoot high when confused or unsure of a shot. This might be a new shot, which the Predator has never seen, or even a familiar shot that has been missed twice. Why?

"Easy shot!" Chuck calls out in a loud voice so his Predator is sure to hear. Chuck has already hit this shot, so he's sure he'll hit it again. In reality, his Predator clipped the front edge off the target—a head shot.

"Right in the lips," he murmurs and takes a *single* step toward the trap house. He shoots again. Again, resulting in a hit. And, again straight in the head. He continues, one step at a time for several steps, past the point where his Predator refused the first time. He continues until another pair of shots miss high. Again he "taps" back to where he hit the last shot, and he begins again.

If your Predator goes through this process, and twice refuses to progress, go on to something else—such as increasing the range, just a few steps at a time. Eventually, your Predator will hit the target it refused on the previous attempt. They always do. But not always when you want them to.

Gradually throughout this practice session, Chuck trains his Predator that this quartering-away shot is really not as hard as first perceived. Finally, the shots are breaking 100 percent of the time. Even when Chuck is nearly behind the trap house, at severe angles where the leading edge of the target has rotated to the left-hand edge, the targets break handily or better on the left hand edge.

The problem with most quartering-shots is that as they approach zero degrees, shooters tend to handle them as true going-away shots. They aren't the same. A true straight-away shot is rare. For us, it's difficult in that we tend to point *at* a straight-away target and, thus, miss it. Remember, our shot pattern is at least two-thirds on top of the barrels. If you point right at a target, most of the shot will go high. If you point *at* a quartering target, your shot will end up going off to the opposite side. That's why you must focus and point at the edge of the target which is on your side. If it's a game bird, try to see the tip of the beak. Ignore the wings and focus on the tip of the beak. In my opinion, that's why so many going-away game birds are missed. There's really nothing to focus on except the rear line of the target's lower edge, which is not where you want to be—you want to be on the near side of the beak (which you often may struggle to see).

We have now had some five hundred students through the Wingshooting Workshop. That's quite a few, but probably less than a lot of shooting schools. At our school, they go through one at a

For students in the Wingshooting Workshop, this is how I rate the shots, from the easiest to the most difficult. The number one easiest shot is the crosser at 90 degrees.

The incoming shot at 45 degrees is the next most difficult.

Low and high incoming shots are fairly easy and quite rare. If this high shot is even a few feet to one side or the other, it becomes a high crosser.

time—which probably sets us apart in numbers. Individual lessons help individual Predators, as each Predator seems to have difficulty with different targets—and each Predator has its nemesis.

In a very general way, this seems to be the way most instinctive shooters rate the difficulty of shots, ranging from easiest to the most difficult:

1. Crossing shots at 90 degrees.

2. Incoming shots at 45 degrees.

3. Low and high overheads. These are relatively rare shots. Even a foot or so to one side or the other makes the shot a crossing target again. This is the reason for most shooters missing this "easy money shot." Two shooters can be hitting all the overheads. One moves four or five feet, usually to the weak side, and then someone promises, "Bet you a buck can't hit this one." The second shooter treats the shot as an overhead, drops the inside shoulder, cants the barrels,

The "money shot" or overheard shot on the weak side can be quite difficult, especially if the shooter tries to take it as an overhead. To take a crosser as an overhead shot forces the shooter to drop the inside or weak shoulder. The shotgun may cant, and the shot, which is all on top of the barrel, flashes by ahead of the target. It's an easy shot, if you treat it as a crosser—turn with the target and keep your shoulders level.

The high, quartering incomers are relatively easy as well. Just keep the angular relationship at 90 degrees. Think of it as if you are pointing your belly button at the target while it flies.

High, quartering away targets are not too difficult, if you remember the near edge has become the leading edge. Keep the cadence, "mount, point, shoot." Drive the shotgun forward. But be smooth. If you hesitate, you're lost.

and misses. Seventy-five percent of his shot is on top of the barrels causing a miss ahead of the target.

4. Quartering incomers. Easy shots, if you handle them as in #3.

5. Quartering-away targets. Again, easy targets, if you focus on the near edge and drive the shotgun toward them. By that, I mean don't hesitate on this shot. Make it easy, by shooting quickly, but smoothly.

Probably the most consistently missed shot is the going away. Even Chuck missed this high shot several times, until I reminded him to focus on the focus point below the lip of the tower.

The low, going-away shot can be dangerous in the hunting field.

All manner of creatures can be in the line of fire for low shots in the hunting field. Low, crossing, or going-away shots should probably be restricted to the clay-target field, where they're fun.

The target thrower is placed in a block house made of railroad ties. From this thrower, the targets fly fast and low.

6. Going-away targets. Probably the most missed target. As I said, appearance of speed is diminished. The target looks like a floater and the shooter relaxes. "Oh boy, the big apple," he thinks and therefore misses—over the top.

Here's the most important thing to remember about shooting at moving objects in the air: THERE IS NO SUCH THING AS A DIFFICULT SHOT. THERE IS ONLY YOUR PERCEPTION OF DIFFICULTY. In other words, if you think a shot is difficult, your Predator seems to pick up the doubt and a miss is all but guaranteed.

You notice in this list I haven't mentioned presentations—rabbit targets, jumping teal, battue, or the like. The presentations are simply variations of the six shots described above. By changing targets, presentations, and speeds, the operators force shooters to think too much and, therefore, miss. Practice the fundamentals, learn how to shoot, and handle all the variations in the same manners. "Just shoot the sucker."

There are some targets that are just downright unfair. Be your own judge. If you run into a target that's unrealistic, simply pass on the shot if you don't want to shoot at it.

I went to a skeet field one day to be with some friends. I don't shoot skeet anymore, so I had the trapper throw following pairs, report pairs, and "take you by surprise" crossing pairs. This was a lot more interesting and forced us to use our hearing, as well as focus, so as to know which thrower had thrown and where to look. The targets had to be tracked mentally, as well as visually. The trapper said he had more fun than he ever had, since he could toss in delays or whatever he wanted—which was as often as he wanted to change things up. We call this unpredictability the "you against me" method of testing our wits.

Once you have your fundamentals down well and once you can hit any target from any angle (high, low, or in between), you are ready for a walkabout.

The Walkabout

The Walkabout is, for an instinctive shooter, like dessert after fine dining. You get a Walkabout only after you've done a good job at the practice. Remember, a Walkabout isn't practice. It's designed to make you do a lot of things—some that you don't necessarily want to do—such as hurry, lose focus, hesitate, miss the mount, shoot in uncomfortable positions, and shoot into the sun.

A Walkabout goes like this: All that's needed is a single target thrower. You can spice up the mix by having two, but they're not necessary. The target thrower should be able to throw eighty to ninety yards, since this lengthens the Walkabout. A remotely-controlled thrower is very convenient. If you use a trapper, be sure to position the trap where the operator is behind a protective barrier (at all times). This protective barrier should be able to stop

A walkabout can be set up using the same remotely-controlled trap used in more formal practice, or it can use a trapper on a hand-operated trap. The remote trap is really best, since there is no trapper to worry about. It can be moved and set up easily. An ATV stand can even be pressed into service. In a recent school that I did out of state, I took this very same trap with me and used it for three weeks. Even though I had two deep-cycle batteries with me, I never had to even recharge the first one. Both are fitted with battery boxes with dials indicating the condition of the battery's remaining charge. The first battery was never pulled below half charge. Targets can be thrown through the small door seen here or the large door can be left open so that the shooters can see how many targets are left in the magazine.

When using a trapper in a walkabout, great care should be taken to keep the trapper behind a protective barrier at all times. At the school, our barriers are all made of steel. Naturally, these are impossible to move. Portable barriers can be moved, but they must be able to withstand a shot from the closest ranges in the walkabout. It's best to position the trapper and trap behind natural barriers found in the area to be used. Cliffs are handy. A target can easily be thrown and the trapper is all but invisible. Huge piles of logs, old buildings, hills, rocks, and the like can all be used. But never shoot when the trapper is visible. And NEVER SHOOT AT A TARGET IF IT FALLS BETWEEN THE SHOOTER AND THE TRAPPER. This is very dangerous, since it puts the trapper in a direct line of fire with the shooter. Use common sense. A trapper's safety is your responsibility. It's best to use a stand-alone, remotely-operated trap.

a shot pattern at point blank ranges and protect the operator from all angles in the walkabout. There are no exceptions to this caution. Never allow the target to fall between the shooter and the trapper. This is why a stand-alone trap is so sensible for this exercise.

In its simplest form, the trap is set up in an empty field. The shooter begins somewhere near the target thrower. He shoots one or two targets, whatever the game is, then moves along a teardrop-shaped path that will take the shooter out into the field, gradually away from the trap, gradually increasing the yardage away from the flight path.

If you're up to it, the range can increase up to fifty, sixty, or seventy yards, as the target reaches its zenith. Now the end of the teardrop nears and the shooter or shooters work their way toward the midpoint of the teardrop. These are now straight incomers. Be sure the trapper, if there is one, is not in view or in the fallout. A target that drops between the shooter and an in-view trapper is extremely dangerous. Always shoot the incomers at the peak of their flight path, if possible, to avoid accidents. If at all in doubt, don't shoot incomers.

For low overheads, simply cut across the teardrop anywhere along the midpoint.

Once past the midpoint, the shots reverse. Let's say on the way out, as you face the target thrower, the shots were all in the left hemisphere, right to left flying targets. Now they're in the right hemisphere and become left to right flying targets, and the range gradually decreases as you approach the trap. Finally, you're back to the trap, but now you're shooting quartering away birds left to right.

Right now, a word of warning: never shoot a Walkabout, until you have learned everything in our school or in this book—The Test, track, and mount with your finger off the trigger. Anyone who keeps their finger in the trigger guard during any part of this process is a danger to everyone. This is especially true in the hunting field. A hunter who puts his finger in the trigger guard before the shot is asking for trouble.

Walkabouts are so versatile; simply turning the trap slightly gives the shooter a whole new series of target presentations. This is where a mobile, self-contained trap is invaluable. I installed mine in a small, over-the-road trailer that's light enough to move by hand but sturdy enough be towed behind a vehicle to any location. The trap is battery operated, which can be recharged by a solar cell. I installed a Stanley gate opener, which has an 18-volt power source, so you have to have someone add a nine-volt battery into the mix to make it operate. It is relatively inexpensive and has a very long range. I've tested it to 250 yards. Why so long? Figure that if the trap can throw ninety yards and you can shoot seventy yards (sometimes), the time may come when you'll need to operate the trap at least 160 yards away—on the flat!

Now, let's talk about different, interesting terrains.

Once in Mississippi while teaching during the winter, my host took a small, 400-target trap, trailer-mounted and pulled by a four-wheeler, to a new area about to be opened for selective logging.

A logging road had been punched through the heavy forest of pines at first, then gum trees festooned with lianas. The road ended in a bottom. As we arrived, woodcock fluttered through the open spaces and they continued to fly throughout the time we were there. We had to take care not to endanger them.

We set the trailer on the road at the top of a small, fifty-foot rise. The targets had a clear path down the road into a low, boggy place. Beginning near the trailer on its left-hand side, we gradually worked our way through the trees. We shot every five or six steps. The game is this—you may shoot the targets, but you may not touch the trees or the vines, or anything else visible to your fellow shooters. The rough teardrop-like path was the same as with other Walkabouts. This provided shots from close zingers hauling at full bore to long-floaters dropping softly through the trees. The presentations were not unlike the flights of woodcock which were all around us, but not in season.

Naturally the visibility was poor. Our longest shots were no more than forty yards. But believe me, in that mess, forty yards was as challenging as anything I'd want to handle.

Later we took the same trap to an area so typical of the South, an open pine forest. The area was groomed. The forest had been logged, selectively. Trees stood well apart. Annually, the forest floor was selectively burned of noxious plants. Forest edges were planted with crops and plants attractive to game birds, mainly doves and quail, both of which abounded.

We placed the trap in a location where it could throw unimpeded ninety yards. It was a beautiful walkabout. It was early spring and crisp. The targets we used were all black, which made seeing the leading edge challenging.

"Don't shoot my trees," was all that my host said. We shot the morning away at a leisurely pace. Hardly anything was said. First one shooter led, then the next, till all had completed the course.

Then, we changed the angle. It was a whole new Walkabout. This time a cliff was about halfway down the flight path. Keeping a watchful eye out for the possible sunning snake, we worked our way around the most beautiful and challenging Walkabout that I've ever been on.

I have reports of Walkabouts from graduates off the tops of high mountains, across sloughs, and with the targets shot with nontoxic shot in preparation for the waterfowl season. Indeed the value of the Walkabout is limited only by available terrain and your imagination. Remember, you only have to move a trap slightly to have an entirely new Walkabout.

How about the other shooting ranges or fields?

Trap fields are of little use to us, since the angles are limited. However, one could be used if the course was deserted and there was at least three hundred yards of safe area down range. But trap fields, in general, aren't designed for some of the hard right, left, and incoming shots.

Skeet fields are very usable, for practice, if you just don't shoot skeet. Skeet isn't a practice venue for tapping—which is what we use to practice instinctive shooting. In skeet, the gunners shoot a prescribed number of shots, then move on. The ranges are also limited by the blocks on which the gunners stand. When tapping for practice, you want to be able to move around, always varying the angles and ranges with each shot. Skeet fields are a good place to practice. But just use the target throwers for that—throwing targets. Be sure to explain to the manager what you are about to practice, so he won't be alarmed. Use the range when there are no others there, in order to limit the amount of unwanted assistance from well-meaning, but confidence-damaging bystanders.

Safety is always first and foremost. Know where your shot is going and know what's there to receive it. Instinctive shooters are so accurate, they can hit a target at any point in its flight path without touching anything near the target. But you must learn everything in this book, before you try the more difficult shots and venues.

Vary your practice, from close-ups at the eighth station, to working your way toward the houses, to the longest ranges your field safely allows. That's an important point. BE SAFE! Never *just shoot* when practicing. Every shot has a purpose in practice. Analyze what you're doing before, and how you did after the shot was performed.

The same is true if you're shooting on a sporting clays range. Work alone. Be there when no one else is around. Let the operator know what you're doing. Practice on one station at a time only. You're not there to shoot sporting clays. You're there to practice—one hundred targets minimum, but not a round of sporting clay. You may shoot all one hundred at a single station or two, depending on your need and ability to move about.

That's how it goes, week after week, and one hundred targets minimum. If you hit The Wall, call it quits. Never proceed beyond where you begin to encounter unexplained misses. You're through for the day. Be gracious. But get off the field. Misses ruin you self-confidence. You need to *know* you're going to hit *before* you pull the trigger.

Practice the rules of safety even though you're alone. This is also true of ethics. I once heard ethics explained as doing the right thing when you're alone. There is no room for poor gun handling or bad ethics. This goes for others, as well.

If you see someone operating or handling a firearm in an unsafe manner, it's up to you to let them know about it. Don't be shy. You needn't be abusive; simply tell them what they are doing and suggest how to fix it. You need do this only once. If they ignore you and continue the unsafe practice, GET OFF THE FIELD! Remember, a firearms accident very seldom happens to the guy behind the gun. You're the one out front. So is your dog.

Oh, sure, they'd be very sorry if they shot you. Big deal.

You are attempting to become a Master Gunner. There are no halfway measures, not in safety, not in ethics, not in skill, not in behavior, and not in dress. You will lead by example. Set a good example and you will be a role model for young gunners on the way up. Be the best that you can be. Be proud of what you've accomplished, but be generous with your time and knowledge. Never use it to embarrass, always to enlighten. And never offer until asked unless safety is at stake.

Remember, practice doesn't mean just shooting. Practice means striving to attain the goal of Master Gunner.

14

SELECTING EQUIPMENT

Selecting Firearms

If you have been reading this book chapter by chapter, I have to apologize. Some of what you're going to read here was also previously mentioned. But there are some who will turn to the equipment section first, so I am trying to also entice those readers who want to cut to a particular chase. But let me warn them of the old adage, "It's not the arrow, it's the Indian." Some people think that there's something magical in buying a new shotgun. But that simply isn't true.

Perhaps the shotguns we use in the school seem magical, but that's because we have shaped and sculpted them, in what we call "parameters." For an instinctive shooter to be consistent, the firearm must be within the limits of fit. By knowing a person's height and dress shirt size, I can select a shotgun that for that person is "within parameters." Having said that, let me tell you how I arrived at the shotguns we use in the school, which we have discussed in previous chapters—but don't worry we'll also quickly move on to other equipment.

When I started out to become an instinctive shooter, I did the obvious. I used the firearm my mentor had used. Herb Parsons was in the film I'd purchased called *Showman Shooter*. It was produced by Winchester, I remember, and showed Herb doing his stuff along with his son Fred who, at the time, was twelve. But even at twelve, Fred could shoot better than I could. Both Parsons used

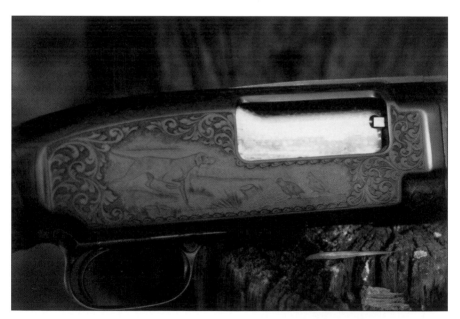

My grandfather's Model 1912 Winchester was, and still is, a beautiful shotgun. But, back in the years when I was starting my shotgun career, it took me to top-gun at several clubs on the Eastern Seaboard, and it kicked the livin' snot out of me. I shot it because Fred Parsons, the Showman Shooter for Winchester, shot a Model 12, as well. It wasn't until years later, that I discovered it had short, 2-9/16-inch chambers. When I had the problem resolved by a gunsmith, I was delighted to find the shotgun pointed like a side-by-side.

Winchester Model 12s. So I used my grandfather's Model 12—that's right, Captain Billy's. But the gun kicked so hard (it had 2-5/8-inch chambers, I found out many years later) that I soon opted for an over-and-under.

Luckily or unluckily I, like so many others, chose a Browning Citori. The problem was that the firearm was heavy, the top cartridge kept falling out in the field, and the safety wasn't automatic. I'd either forget to put the safety on or forget to take the safety off. Furthermore, the safety seemed to be on the wrong side. When a right-handed shooter pushes forward on the safety, he also pushes slightly to the left. Unfortunately the safety would occasionally slip into the crossbar position of the safety/selector pattern—under barrel on the right, over barrel on the left, with a cross/over slot to go from under to over. In my mind it looks something like a capital "H." In the crossbar position, nothing happens. The gun won't go off. I nearly straightened that trigger out on several occasions when a world's record rooster climbed skyward.

Besides, the selector moves from left to right. Why not use a gun that does the same thing? Better yet, why not use a firearm with one trigger for each barrel. That way, you can have instantaneous selection of choke and shot shell. I have never had anyone claim they change barrels with a selector when a bird is in the air. But we change barrels with double trigger guns while the birds are in the air all the time.

In the long run, the choice turned out to be a wise one.

My gauge of choice was 12. In a side-by-side the 12-gauge barrels fit my hands and a 28-inch set of barrels look about right with my six-foot height and arm length of thirty-four and a half inches. Twelve-gauge is a good choice for someone my size. It only weighs six and a half pounds and can fire loads suitable for all gauges. In other words, I can fire all the heavy loads for hunting plus I can also fire 1-ounce, 7/8-ounce, and 3/4-ounce shot charges. Those are loadings typical for the 16-, 20-, and 28-gauge firearms.

Remember, a shotgun is basically nothing but a piece of tubing with a wooden handle on it. The tubes are configured differently depending on the technique you use. Vertical format for gun aimers, horizontal for gun pointers. It's as simple as that.

When I got into the game the first two Ugartecheas I bought were $250 and $187 respectively. I found them in, of all places, the Target store in Marshalltown, Iowa.

The Ugartechea is a Basque-made shotgun from the northern part of Spain. At the time of this writing, the entry level model is up over $1,300 retail. It is still one hell of a bargain. The way the guns are choked at the factory is tight and tighter. But that's okay since I don't trust factory chokes very much anyway. I'd rather have my own smith adjust the barrels for the 12-gauge, .003 inch in the first barrel, and .007 inch in the second. Remember, the best shots the world has ever known didn't have the choice of choke tubes. They shot at all ranges with just two chokes.

My gauge of choice is 12. In a side-by-side, the 12-gauge barrels fit my hands and a 28-inch set of barrels look about right with my height, six feet, and arm length, thirty-four and a half inches. Twelve-gauge is a good choice for someone my size. It only weighs six and a half pounds and can fire loads suitable for all gauges under it. In other words, I can fire hunting loads if I need them, plus I can also fire one ounce, seven-eighths ounce, and three-quarters ounce shot charges (which are more typically, 16-gauge, 20-gauge and 28-gauge loads) and they work great in a 12-gauge.

Now before you go off about the micro gauges, listen on.

It takes a while to get a gun totally tuned and fitted. And, it's not cheap. Now let's say that's the gun you're going to do all your practicing with from here on out. Then, along comes hunting season and you dig out your 28-gauge chukar gun and you wonder why you can't hit a thing.

If you want to use a 28-gauge, fine. But like David Marsh, a graduate from 1992, you should shoot the 28 all the time—for everything.

Admittedly shells for the 28 are limited, so you'll probably have to hand load to accommodate the range of loads you will need to shoot everything you want to hunt from a 28. And, have you ever loaded a 28? It isn't easy. Some reloaders never really get the hang of it, crushing more shells than they load.

Personally, I'd rather use one gun for everything from waterfowl and geese to dove and quail (and just vary the loads, rather than varying the guns) and I would like to have a reasonable range of loads readily available, so 12-gauge readily comes to mind for men and 20-gauge for the build of most women.

Once, while I was in Mississippi teaching, I took a free day to hunt some quail on the plantation where I was running the school. An older gentleman sauntered over to me.

"Whatchashootin?" he asked looking at my side-by-side.

"A Garbi," I responded.

"No, I mean whatsa gauge?"

"I shoot a 12," I said holding the shotgun out for his approval. He jerked his hands away in horror.

"A twelve'll tear up them little birds," he nodded vehemently turning to his fellows for affirmation, "You gotta use a 20 on quail."

"Is that so?" I said, "Interesting? What shells are *you* using?"

He handed me a box of Winchester game loads, one ounce of 7 1/2s.

I said, "I shoot seven-eighths ounce of number eight shot, which I am sure I do not have tell you, is an eighth of an ounce less than you and smaller pellets, as well."

He looked at me, confusion spreading across his face. His friends, realizing he had blundered into deep dark water, turned away, as if the conversation no longer interested them.

Finally, firm resolve spread across his face, confusion giving way to faith.

"Yeah, maybe so, but those twelves'll tear up them little birds."

I shook my head and walked off realizing that for some, logic has no place in either selection of firearms or shells.

We are choosing a firearm for instinctive shooting. We are pure instinctive shooters and we shoot in an upright walking stance. We don't look down the barrel and shoot—our heads are up and forward, chin pointed at the target, stock next to our neck, and comb along the lower jaw. If we see the barrels, chances are we'll miss.

Because of the stock bolts in the vertically formatted firearms (pumps, semiautos, and over-and-unders), it's difficult to bend in enough cast for our technique into most guns. With such guns, you usually have to have one custom made—an expensive solution. With our side-by-sides, you just have a good 'smith bend the stock. In my case, we need half-inch bend, and in some cases more and a few cases less.

In the gun world, there seems to be an acknowledgment that while side-by-sides are fine, light, and quick little guns to carry in upland hunting, they have no place on the target range.

A couple of older shooters had followed my brother, Mike, and me around a sporting clays course near Phoenix. We'd shot about half the course when the bolder of the two older shooters approached us.

"You shoot pretty good," he said looking at my Ugartechea, "but you'd shoot a lot better with an over-and-under." Just about then, the trapper walked up with the score sheet.

"He hasn't missed any targets yet, Mr. Scott," the trapper said.

"Yeah," he went on undaunted, "but he'd shoot a whole lot better with an over-and-under."

Again, what can you do with logic like that? In the hands of a shooter who understands it, the side-by-side can shoot as well as, if not better, than vertical formatted shotguns, regardless of the target.

Okay, since this is my book, let's say you agree with me on the point that side-by-sides shoot at least as well as a vertical format gun. How do you pick a side-by side?

What I suggest to newcomers is you shouldn't throw a lot of money at the subject until you know if you like it. So begin with a good entry-level shotgun. I may be dating myself but when I got into the game, the first two Ugartecheas that I bought were $250 and $187, respectively, and I got very good deals on them.

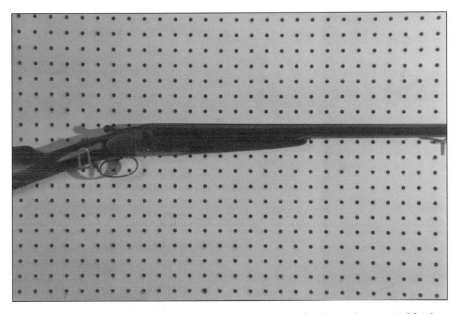

The Ugartechea is a Basque-made shotgun, manufactured in the northern part of Spain. Eibar is a small town which is renowned for its manufacture of firearms, in general, and shotguns, in particular.

At the time of this writing, the entry level model is up to $1,100 retail and beyond. It is still one hell of a bargain, even at that price, given what else is out there. Unfortunately, the gun is choked at the factory tight and tighter. But that's okay, since I don't trust factory chokes very much anyway. I'd rather have my own 'smith adjust the barrels to an open .004 inch in the first barrel, .008 inch in the second. I say first and second because they're different for left-and right-handed shooters. The guns are set up for right handed shooters. The front trigger fires the right barrel, the rear the left. A left-handed shooter will want to have those reversed, as well as the chokes. The front trigger for a lefty fires the left barrel and the rear fires the right. A 'smith can also switch the triggers for you, if you are left-handed. With really tight chokes, there's plenty of metal left so that the barrels can be reconfigured with the left barrel opened up to .004 inch and the right to .008 inch. With small charges of shot, the pellets tend to stay together giving the patterns uniformity to extended ranges, without using choke tubes. The best shots the world has ever known didn't have the option of choke tubes. The best shots in the world, from Annie Oakley to Lord Ripon, shot at all ranges within just two chokes. And, they shot ammunition that couldn't hold a candle to our modern loads, with paper wads and non-plated BBs.

The 'smith may have to bend the stock for you, from cast-off to cast-on. Certain 'smiths specialize in stock bending, which is important to know before you send your gun off, as this is about as important as someone who can bend a bow—though any person can understand the concept, few can do it with precision. The same is true with adjusting chokes—use a 'smith who specializes in chokes. You need exacting measurements and no tooling marks—none.

And the shotgun that you'll chose will have a straight stock, not a pistol grip. Try this exercise:

Select a distant focus point, at least across the room.

Stand square to the focus point and point at it with your offside hand, keep your focus on the point. Your hand should be about at the height of your chin.

1. Now, point at the spot with your gun hand, keeping it behind the lead hand. Don't let them touch each other.
2. Keeping one hand behind the other not touching, draw them slowly and smoothly back to your chin and then slowly extend them.
3. Keep this slow sawing motion going. Feels comfortable, right? Back and forth—back and forth.
4. Now slowly lower the rear hand slightly below the front one—not far, just two or three inches.

5. Whoops! The slow smoothness goes away. Awkwardness replaces it.
6. Okay, bring the rear hand back up in line with the front one. Smoothness again reappears.

There went your pistol grip. To be able to mount the firearm smoothly and swiftly, the hands must align with each other. When trap and skeet shooters discovered they could hit a higher percentage of the targets by premounting, they did away with the low-gun-and-mount and went to a gun-at-the shoulder before calling for the bird. At that point, the pistol grip became an advantage. Now the gun could be aimed at a spot on the trap house and controlled with the rear gun hand. The lead hand fully up the barrels became a disadvantage, as did the side-by-side. On going-away targets, the barrels of the side-by-side tend to hide the targets when covered—so the single barrel, autos, pumps, and over-and-unders became the darlings of the ranges. The lead hand could be brought back, since the rear hand was controlling. But another problem appeared—single barrel guns tend to be barrel light. Add this to the tenancy of some gun aimers to stop the gun and pull the trigger, and now you have many shooters who, in trying to solve what they perceive to be a problem, create another problem. To counter this problem, the manufacturers created heavier shotguns. It's harder to stop a heavy barreled gun than a light one. In other words, let technology solve what should be solved by technique.

So here is the entry level side-by-side you will buy:

1. Straight stocked
2. Splinter (small) forend (you want to hold the barrels, not the wood)
3. Double triggers
4. Barrels compatible with your build
5. The balance point, one-half inch ahead of the hinge pin (that's where I like mine)

6. Smooth, straight wooden butt (no curve in the butt)
7. Automatic safety
8. No stock bolt
9. Smooth or concave rib
10. Boxlock construction
11. Extractors only

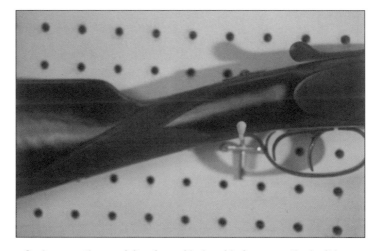

So, here are the requisites for a side-by-side for our method—it has a straight stock.

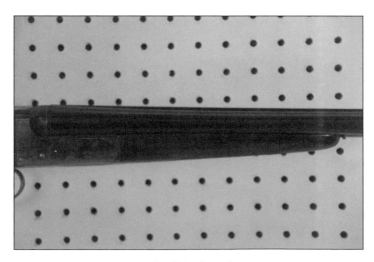

A splinter forend

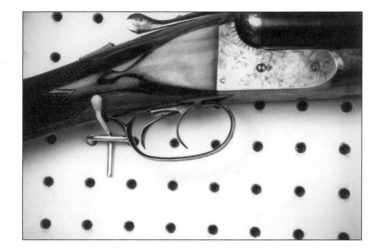

Double triggers

The balance point of my firearms rests half an inch ahead of the forearm, for my walk-up guns. For a driven shooting gun, I would elect to balance it one-half inch behind the hinge pin.

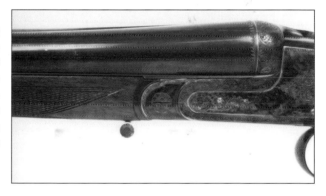

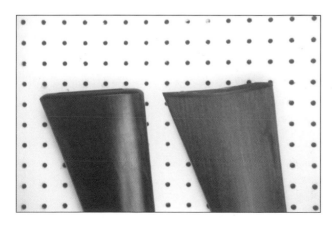

Because we mount the guns high on our shoulder, we prefer a straight, smooth butt, rather than one with a sharp point on the toe.

All of my firearms and all of the school guns have automatic safeties. The true safety of a firearm lies in the head of the shooter. But automatic safeties help insure that for those brief moments when the gun is closed, a random twig or a fall won't cause the firearm to discharge. Always remember, these safeties are only trigger blockers, not true safeties, on side-by-sides. These don't prevent the fall of the tumblers or firing pins, if the sear slips off the bent. Remember too, the safety also controls the wink of the offside eye in the case of a shooter with an eye dominance problem.

There is no stock bolt from which to attach the stock to the action body. Graduates use a lot of cast (one-half inch is not unusual). It's very difficult to get that much cast into a shotgun with a stock bolt, no matter what the gun's configuration, vertical or horizontal. This is why I prefer some of the guns that I do.

I prefer a shotgun with as little of a rib as possible, since I don't use the rib as a sighting plane— it serves little purpose except to add weight. If you've got a good 'smith, I suppose it would be possible to adjust a firearm's balance with the rib, if you wanted to use it for such, but no one does.

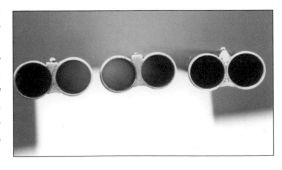

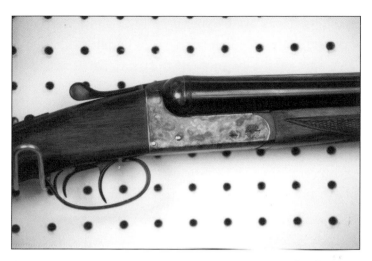

My entry-level school shotguns are of a boxlock construction. Boxlocks always cost less to manufacture than sidelocks. I advise my graduates to start with a good entry-level shotgun and find out if they really love side-by-side shooting. If they do, it's easy to add a second gun, a sidelock, which won't shoot any better, but will be prettier.

I prefer extractors only. Ejectors require cocking hammers, which put an awful lot of strain on the forend iron. Plus, most people I know put their hand over the breech end, in order to catch the empty shells. So, common sense dictates that if your gun has something that causes it to wear out faster and which you defeat every time it works anyway, why not remove that feature until needed. Remember, if you have an ejector gun, you also have an extractor gun. Simply have a 'smith remove the hammers and springs until needed, for those special days of driven shooting.

These suggestions are for an entry-level shotgun. At this time, the boxlocks are going for less than the sidelocks. If you live in a very wet part of the country and can afford it, a sidelock has distinct advantages (especially when it comes to drying them out). Also try to stick to entry-level guns for which parts are readily available. When a part breaks, and it will, you need a replacement right now. You should have extra firing pins and springs, at least two each. Keep them soft. You want pins that'll shear off, if stuck in the face of the standing breech and the gun gets shut firmly with the ejectors out.

The exception to the general selection of boxlock would be for a graduate living in an area of high humidity or frequent rainfalls. The sidelock guns are easier to take apart for cleaning and drying out.

Hammers break, especially right-hand hammers—so do main springs. There should be a ready replacement parts available. After one hundred thousand shots or so (even if you close your shotgun carefully), you'll need to replace the cross-bolts.

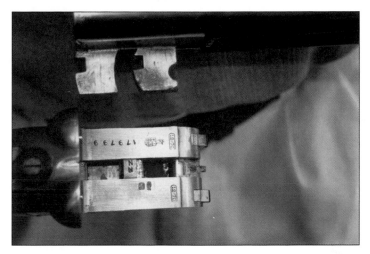

We protect the cross bolts by easing them into the bites of the lumps, and keeping bites and cross bolts well lubricated with grease. Some of the school guns have over 250,000 rounds through them. That's more wear than most guns get in a lifetime of regular use. But parts wear out. Once, when parts for Ugartecheas were hard to get, a tool and die maker made a cross bolt for me. Had he not been a friend, the cost would have been prohibitive.

Side-by-sides, like any machine, can experience failures from time to time. Parts break or wear out. Springs break and firing pins need to be replaced. Probably, with moderate use, you may get lucky and avoid this in your lifetime. But, even if nothing breaks or wears out, school guns go to the 'smith every six months for inspection and cleaning. My own guns go in yearly. The point is that we want to have parts that are readily available and a smith who can install them.

Once a cross-bolt wore out on a school gun and a replacement was not available. A friend of mine (an old tool and die maker) made a replacement. It took him seven hours. Had he not been a friend, the price would have been prohibitive, so readily available replacement parts are a real plus.

Selecting Accessories

Instinctive shooters are (or can be) the most under-accessorized shooters in the sport of shooting. All we really need is a shotgun and four boxes of shells, if we're practicing. Hunting's even easier. If a limit of chukar is eight, you should carry at least ten shells, so that it won't look like you're trying to show off.

But, and that's a big "but," just how will you go about carrying those shells? Long ago, I realized the shooting vest is no good for

Instinctive shooters can be very under-accessorized. Somehow, we seem to have filled the void with a few very necessary (to us) accessories. The speed bag is a capacity bag, sewn-front made of bison on pigskin. It is reinforced with solid brass, so it will hold its shape and has a solid brass hinge. The Spanish bags (our name for them) came from a design similar to those used in Seville, Spain, hence the name. The hat is a Buz Fawcett Special, by Priest Hat Co.

instinctive shooters. The large arm hole of the vest can catch the firearm's butt, as it slides along the body from the armpit to the pocket. Also, most of us put a box of shells in the gun-side-pocket which, of course, tightens up the fabric on that side. As you shoot, the tension on the fabric gradually changes. Changes, gradual or not, are the dedicated enemy of all instinctive shooters. So the shooting vest went a long time ago, as did the hunting vest. Besides, if we wore vests, we'd look like everybody else, and since the way we shoot precludes looking like everyone else to begin with—who cares?

In the field, most hunting vests have a large game pouch in the rear. Some extend this pouch, so it reaches around the shooter's body to the front. As you fill this pocket, you begin to feel like you're inside a bag full of birds. In the rear-only pouch, the weight of the birds pulls on your lower back. If you are hunting out here in the West, you may leave your car in the morning, not to see it again until dusk. You'll need some way of carrying, not only up to a limit of birds, but water enough for your dog at least and perhaps a bit more for you. And you may want a sandwich along about mid-day. I've found the carrier manufactured by Buck's Bags here in Boise to be excellent for this day-long hunt and some of my students report that the Quilomene San Carlos belt is also very suitable. Cabela's has a new waist belt as well, and I am sure, there are many more to follow. The Buck's Bags carrier is built along the lines of the float-tube cover, which originated here in Idaho for fly fishing lakes. As you fill the carrier, it gradually expands, but *away* from your body. It is kept from swinging by an inner belt, but it is held just far enough away from your body so air can circulate between you and the load. This helps cool the game to keep it from getting sour. With very little effort the birds can be distributed around the body so the weight is carried by the shoulders, evenly. The body of this carrier is usually made of heavy nylon mesh. This also aids cooling. There's plenty of room on the outside for pockets and a large one which will carry one large, or several small, water bottles. Yes the water tends to pull you backward in the beginning, but as you add game, the carrier can be loaded to the front to help balance the load.

If I'm hunting far from the car, I like to use this carrier by Buck's Bags here in Boise. It's kinda hard to see in black and white, but it is built like a float tube. As you fill it with game, it grows away from you so you don't feel like you're inside a bag full of birds. There's plenty of room for water also. Some of my students also like the San Carlos Bag from Quilomene.

I have very little use for the European bird carrier straps for our upland hunters in the States. Birds suspended by cords or leather straps tend to swing and throw me off balance. Having said this, the game-carrier is excellent for keeping birds together and cool, as long as there arc no flies about and as long as you don't have to do much walking with birds in them. Waterfowl hunters will find them handy for hanging birds inside the blind, as may dove hunters who wish to hang some birds along a fence, to be picked upon the return trip or just have a convenient way to carry them back to the vehicle. Horse hunters have long used game carriers to suspend their birds from a saddle, as long as the horse is cooperative and the birds stay in place.

The game bag is an excellent alternative for the hunter who is returning to the car often. A good game bag is leak-proof, washable on the inside, and will carry about a maximum of three pheasants. The game bag which I use also wards off insects.

This reminds me of a story some years ago when opening day of duck season was unusually warm, back in Minnesota. I returned to our camp to find one of my hunting companions had been suddenly called back to the Twin Cities. My hunting vest was hung on a nail outside while I hurriedly packed to accompany my friend back home. Now I'm not very proud of this, but on returning home, late, I opted to put my vest in the basement refrigerator, meaning to clean the birds the following morning. But fate meant to deliver a powerful lesson. Early the next morning I was called away on a motion picture shoot and ended up being gone a couple of weeks.

Yep. You guessed it. In that brief period outside, a bluebottle fly had found my birds. The game pouch was literally filled with maggots. Some had even slid between the grate of the refrigerator shelf, making the whole mess impossible to remove, except by removing the entire shelf itself. My wife was not pleased. Nor was she happy when I carried the shelf outside and dripped the occasional maggot on the carpet leading to the garage.

I tell this disgusting tale only so you never forget the cardinal rule—clean all game as soon as possible after it is harvested. Until it is cleaned, keep it away from flies. If it must be transported before it is cleaned, keep the birds in a clean, insect-proof bag—like a breathable feed sack. Now you folks in the East may not have access to feed sacks like we do out here in the West. So keep harvested game in a cooler and in large freezer Ziploc baggies until it can be cleaned. Some fish and game departments don't want you to completely clean game (i.e., they may require a head, leg, and/or wing to still be attached for identification) until it is back home, but be careful to preserve and protect your harvest.

On another occasion, I was shooting in a shoot-to-retrieve contest, in which I had half an hour to kill my released birds, while a judge followed and scored my dog's performance. Somehow in the hustle-n-bustle at the end, I missed a quail in the game pouch of my Barbour jacket, which went unscored. I always keep that thirty-year-old Barbour Beaufort in the back of my SUV for emergencies. About ten days later, even my "terribly operable"? nose knew there was something amiss in that truck. The resulting mess of a jacket was hosed out about a hundred times and hung in the backyard for the remainder of the season. In fact, I bought another Barbour coat, rather than being forced to use that Beaufort. I even bought another model, the Gamefair, as the memory of the Beafort was so noisome.

Trust me, I never put game in my clothing any more.

Game bags are nice, especially if you return to the car often. Since I forgot a quail in my Barbour's game pocket, I haven't been all that wild about putting birds in my clothing. Some hunters prefer a game carrier. This one is really nice, but in warm weather there is no protection from flies. They also seem to swing when I carry one. They're fine on horseback, in cool weather or for carrying waterfowl from boat to car.

My shell belt is always worn under my coat. In fall or winter, this keeps the shells warm. If you don't think it matters, put a box of target shells in the freezer overnight and try to shoot a decent score with them.

As I've said previously, I never dump a box of shells in a pocket when in the field. Instead, I use a shell belt. I had an old shell belt and it was this abused piece of equipment that led me to saddle maker.

Shells dumped in a pocket are subjected to the ambient temperatures. In the fall and winter temperatures fall way below forty degrees. This means as pocket-carried shells fall below forty, as well. And, their velocities drop. Shells in the field should be carried in a shell belt which is worn *under* the hunting coat. Body temperature keeps them warm. The cold ones, in your side-by-side, can be replaced with warm ones every fifteen minutes or so.

In winter, a belt with full shell pockets help in this effort. Shells are a little more difficult to remove, so the belt with half pockets is more convenient, in warm weather.

I had bought a full-pocket belt from a well-known purveyor of hunter's leather goods. Gradually, I became more and more dissatisfied with their products. They looked good, but fell apart in day-to-day use and in schooling and hunting.

For instance, the shell belt was a full pocket, single-thickness belt with tag ends sewn on to accommodate different waist sizes.

The first time I used it, I put shells in the pockets. But when I put it around my waist, the thin belt part bent up into the pocket, forming a friction brake. I couldn't get the shells out of the pockets.

When I wet the belt and reformed the pockets over shells slightly enlarged with clear, two-inch wrapping tape, the cartridges went in and out alright, but when the belt was tossed into the truck and turned upside down, the shells all fell out on the floor.

Let me explain how I use my shell belt. As I said, it goes under the hunting coat, with the buckle in the back. What is more, the belt always has an odd number of pockets. In the beginning, I put in different colored shell in the middle pocket—hole number thirteen in a twenty-five cartridge belt. Since 20-gauge shells are all yellow, I had 20-gauge shooters and put a snap cap or a wooden plug in the center pocket. This way, for a right-handed shooter, the shells to the right of pocket thirteen were for the right barrel, to the left for the other one.

These shell belts are made for warm and cool weather. Actually, if you keep 'em under your coat, it probably doesn't matter. Notice the middle slot, number thirteen. It's got a slot in it, so you can tell where shells for the right barrel change to shells for the left barrel. Notice how these shells are low base. The shells on my belt's left side are high base. These represent the second shot from the left barrel, the follow-up left barrel. As head shooters, the low base shells usually don't need the second (high based) shot, unless there are two birds.

On an early-season dove hunt, I would put #8s on the right hand side, and possibly 7½s on the left, for follow-up shots. For pheasants, it might be 7½s on the right, 6s on the left. Later in the season, it could be 6s and 5s, or even 4s, depending on how and where the birds are flushing. I've never known anyone who could hit a selector button and change barrels with a single triggered gun when a bird is in the air. But our side-by-sides have two triggers. So it's easy to change barrels instantly, without thought, reserving the heavier shot for longer ranges and lighter shot for modest ranges.

There is another feature of the single thickness belt that personally ticks me off. The rough side is inside. I always put the belt on buckle forward then turn it so number thirteen is in the front. The rough-out finish of the belt turns my sweater with it, so I end up looking, and feeling, like a corkscrew.

Saddle scabbards have traditionally been made for rifles and single-barreled shotguns. Traditional scabbards, with their sewn-bottoms on the muzzle end, rapidly removed bluing from the shotgun's muzzles. This side-by-side scabbard was hand-built for graduate Barbara Allard Ward in California.

I had a saddle maker make a shell belt from a single piece of leather. That puts a smooth side on the inside as well. The second layer of leather will also protect the shell-pocket stitching. It'll keep the belt from binding shells *and* make it easy to turn without twisting your sweater.

I also had him put a slot in number thirteen or on the middle shell pocket.

I reasoned that while I'm not fat, my sweater often bulges over my belt and I can't actually *see* number thirteen. With a slot, I could *feel* the separation between right and left shells without taking my eyes off the sky or dog.

I dreamed up a special design of shell bags, also called speed bags. The leather bags currently available in the States are alright for infrequent use. But in daily use, under a hot desert sun, they dry out rapidly. In trying to keep a preservative on them, I found they rapidly softened, and as the shells dwindled, the openings collapsed—so you couldn't get your hand in without looking down and doing some serious fishing. I guessed this was why the English made so many of them out of canvas. In their climate, I guessed leather bags would soften up even more quickly and lose their shape, though they don't have the aridness that we do.

So, I designed a number of different bags, based on my experience with hunting and teaching. They're also called speed bags because when shaken, a certain number will turn shot-end down, so that your hand always picks them up by the brass end. That's why you'll see a loader shake his shell bag from time to time, as he knows this will speed up his task of picking shells and shoving them down the barrels. This is especially true if there are two or more boxes of shells in the bag, as they seem to right themselves better when in company than when alone.

I designed a leg-o-mutton case, which was made the right way, leather over leather, then lined with soft material. The case is molded over a wooden form shaped to the dimensions of the individual shotgun. I used the old idea of a two-piece cleaning rod to hold the action and stock upright. The result is a bomb-proof case, which is gentle on the shotgun. The case also allows easy withdrawal of the shotgun, once the top is open.

The other items I really like are the leather bags that I call Spanish bags, because the first pair I had were from Barcelona, Spain. It's a bit of a misnomer, as a Spaniard would have no idea to what I am referring with this term. My Spanish bags are a pair of slim bags (big leather pockets really) attached by a belt. The leather on the originals, I suspect, is a goat leather of some kind (and is very hard to replicate). Over the years, mine have taken on a patina of age which is absolutely beautiful. Everybody who sees them wants a pair, but they want them exactly like mine, with the same patina. We tried every kind of leather, calfskin, pigskin, and the like, but nothing was quite right. Some were too stiff, some was too supple, some were pretty good and others rejected because they clung to the back of the hand. Finally, we developed a replica. The bags are quite narrow at the mouth, but the bottoms hang below the hem of the coat. This

Spanish bags have an unusual shape. They're designed to hang under an outer garment. When filled, they bulge below the hem and don't disturb the hang of the coat. If you want to be really cool, when you open a box of shotgun shells, grasp the box by the lower right-hand edge, and open flap toward you. Now, rap the left rear corner against a firm object like a table top above the table's legs. The flap will pop open on the left-hand edge. Flip it open with your right thumb and rotate the box slightly to your right. The inner flaps will slide apart and can be flipped open with your right thumb. Now, pour the shells into the speed bag. Shake it up and down and the gravity of the lead pulls the front ends downward (i.e., the brass ends are mostly up, which is what you want for ease of loading). My trapper in Mississippi, Taice Clayborn, taught me that when I taught at Dunn's Shooting Grounds.

way, if you wear a fine, tweed shooting jacket, the empties will fill the bag beneath the lower hem, and not bulge, nor change the hang of the garment.

With a waxed-cotton coat, at least one of the shorter ones like a Barbour Bedale, the lower zipper is raised about to the breastbone, and the empties can be put away with a minimum of effort into the leather bags. Keeping the fabric of any garment the same tension across the chest and over the shoulder pocket is very important. If loaded shells are kept in the lower right pocket and empties in the lower left, fabric tension gradually changes over the shoulder pocket and the vital pathway from the armpit to the shoulder and its anchor point.

It's important to keep the tension of the fabric over the shoulder's pocket constant. This is why I never place shells in my pockets. They represent counterweights that gradually move the weight from one side to the other, as the lead in the shell is expended. Luckily most waxed-cotton coats like this Barbour, zip up twice. Zip it up, first to keep the fabric tension constant across the chest and shoulder pocket. Then, zip it up from the bottom to get access to the Spanish bags or shell belts beneath.

Spanish bags help remove yet one more variable: fabric tension in the coat over the gun shoulder. Some people have liked the bags so well that they've had a saddle maker make a third bag or pouch which hangs at the rear. This one is lined and can be used for carrying small birds like quail or dove, or a bottle of water.

We finally settled on kangaroo as the best leather for Spanish bags. It most closely resembles the original Spanish leather. At this writing, the originals are about thirty years old and are still in use daily, so one set should last you a lifetime and, probably, meet your grandchildren.

15 »

MORE ON CLOTHING

Here, again, I can't tell you what to wear. We're all so different, and live in different climates and shoot for different birds on different terrains, such that we could never agree. I can tell you what I do. As a primary consideration, I try to dress in a manner that casts a good light on the upland hunter. After all, we are the most visible of the hunting fraternity.

As I've said before, in cool weather I like a shooting coat, breeks, a coat, and tie. Footwear can be anything from ankle-fit rubber boots to low-cut brogues (kind of a heavy-duty wingtip). If these are worn into the brush, I'll pull on a pair of gaiters. Otherwise, your high

Take the necktie for instance. As a kid, I never understood why my dad always wore a tie when he hunted. It wasn't until I saw him tie a splint onto a dog's leg with a pair of neckties from his hunting party that I began to understand. Perhaps it was a part of his generation, but it also still serves a useful purpose.

socks and flashes will end up full of stick tights and beggar's lice weed seeds. I didn't know what "flashes" were when I started wearing breeks. I wore wader socks that were so tight and high that they stayed in place. But as I bought some of the nicer imported ones, I found they slipped down. I tried pulling the breek bottoms over the socks to hold them in place. It worked for a while, but then they'd give out and started slipping. I tried bulling the stockings over the bottoms of the breeks. That also worked, if only for a while. Finally, I tied a leather boot lace around the stockings just beneath my knee and folded the tops over. That worked.

I met a couple of Englishmen and they told me about "flashes." Flashes are kind of a knitted garter strap, which takes the place of my boot lace in holding the socks up. Folks from the British Isles really like them in some wild colors. (I suppose it's the one area where the British show much color in their shooting fashions.) They're wrapped around the leg over the stockings. The tops are folded down and most of the flash stuffed up under the stocking top. The tassels are left hanging out. I asked the same two Englishmen whether the stocking tops are worn under the breeks or over the cuffs. They immediately began to argue amongst themselves. After a bit, I quietly slipped away. I wear the stockings both ways, and apparently the Brits do as well. I wear them at the bottom of the breeks, in mild weather. I wear them under as it becomes brisk and over when it's cold. Yep, you can get long underwear under the stockings and breeks.

In the back of the Suburban, I have a box, actually a big Rubbermaid box with a sealable lid, in which I keep extra clothing—long johns, sweaters, socks, caps, and, yes, military berets for windy days. The chaps are in there too. I have a set of shelves I had made that are carpeted, and two large dog boxes fit neatly on top of them. During the school, I keep gloves, earplugs, shooting glasses, leather hand guards, tape, first aid, and you name it in there. They're all in smaller plastic boxes, labeled with their contents. The carpet is easy on shotguns. Cases of shells and empty containers are stowed, where they're readily available. Anyway, this was all very unique at the time and there are several models which are commercially available now and very similar to my design.

But, back to that clothing box—there's everything in there to accommodate sudden weather changes, unexpected rain, snow, sleet, or whatever. Most of the time, it's not me that's dipping into it. I've loaned everything from earplugs to gloves to sweaters and long johns to students, graduates, and friends.

The rear of my Suburban has a false floor with two drawers in it. Everything is in Rubbermaid boxes, labeled so the contents are easily found. Most of the year, the boxes contain items which I need to run the Wingshooting Workshop. But come hunting season, two dog crates fit on top and the school boxes are easily switched for hunting gear.

Just ahead of the false floor are two large Rubbermaid boxes. The one on the Suburban's own left contains truck's emergency necessities: extra oil, power steering fluid, flares, inflator/puncture seal canisters, a large knife, machete, tow-strap, jumper cables, and etc. The one on the right is my slide-off-sack. It contains what I need for a three-day stay if I'm caught in a storm or cannot otherwise proceed home. It also has chaps, extra sweaters, coats, gloves, padding, hats, and ties for students.

In the winter or fall, I prefer breeks—knickers. Think about it, in this country, every professional athlete, when they're performing their sport, are either wearing shorts or knickers. It's true—with an apology to the pro bowlers.

In my late forties, my knees began to give me trouble. Lift your leg in a pair of long pants, and you'll see the fabric pull down on the patella—the kneecap. After an hour and a half of walking, my knees felt like I had a hot wire inserted between the knee and cap. Quite aside from the point, I was doing a lot of whitewater rafting. When I got to Idaho, I noticed a lot of the whitewater guides were wearing surplus NATO knickers with sandals during the fall and early winter months. They explained they could jump in and out of the boats without wetting long pants each time, and the heavy wool, actually loden wool, so popular with Europeans, would keep them warm even when wet.

I teach the Wingshooting Workshop in either shorts or knickers. It's important that students see my knees, as they lock and unlock to move the gun sideways. There's more to it. In my fifties, my knees started to go. Hunting a full day in the field played hell with the patella. As you can see, with each step, the material of long pants pulls down on my kneecap. After an hour or so, depending on terrain, my knees are on fire. In shorts or knickers, I get three hours or more without pain. With them, my knee is free to operate unencumbered.

The first knickers that I bought were surplus West German issues to their mountain troop. The German loden wool is tough, water resistant, and warm. Sticktites, beggar's lice, and cockleburs stick to them momentarily and are easily removed. They are still my favorite hunting pant. I now have five pairs that are used all winter. They are also great for cross-country skiing, rock climbing, and snowshoeing.

I got three pairs at a local surplus store, and they're still my favorites, though I've since gotten many pairs of civilian knickers. Knickers or breeks got a stigma in this country way back when I was a kid, back in the 1930s. Kids wore knickers, especially to school. They were kind of a tweedy looking corduroy. We wore long socks and often high-topped shoes to keep junk out. Really cool kids got high-topped boots, which were the coldest footwear in winter, but preferable to galoshes. I suppose we had to wear them because our moms were looking over their shoulders to see if the Depression was catching up with them. She could buy knickers way too long and too big around the waist for us. Then as we grew like young colts, we gradually filled out the overhangs at the knees and floppies at the waist. Suspenders kept the too-big knickers up and a sweater (also too big) hid the sins underneath.

Then the day finally came. We were twelve years old. It was the big time. All kind of things happened to kids when they turned twelve. They got admitted into churches and synagogues and some were given their first shotgun. But even more importantly, we were given our first long pants and low-topped shoes. The hated knickers or knickerbockers, as they were called then, were left behind forever. Well not quite. Remember what Dad said: "You'll learn."

So there I was, in my late forties, back in knickers. But wearing knickers has lore of its own. As advertised, the pain in my knees all but disappeared.

I learned early on that by adding my wader socks to the knickers, I could wear a combination of footwear appropriate to the occasion. Low shoes, wingtips—actually an outdoor version of the wingtip called a brogue by the Scots—were perfect for shooting at a range on crisp autumn days. For boggy terrain, the shoes could be exchanged for a rubber boot. Here in this country, La Cross makes several models sixteen and seventeen inches high. They fit at the ankle, so mud won't suck them off. In Great Britain, they wear rubber boots that they call Wellingtons or Wellies. On the continent, the French, always ones for style and practicality, have laminated soft thick leather to the inside of their rubber boots. Amazingly comfortable and practical, the French brand Le Chameau are equipped with an outside zipper that's gusseted to stay waterproof. Best of all, the leather keeps you from the clammy feeling, which you otherwise get from a day in rubber boots.

Knickers let you tailor the footwear to meet the need. (Clockwise from upper left) Wingtips are really stylish copies of the Scottish brogues (they can be worn alone or with gaiters, as can the stylish high-topped shoes favored by the British). Russ Laws brought these back from a driven shoot in England. The high-topped Maine Guide Shoes from L.L. Bean are excellent. Keep the leather well greased with Sno-Seal, so they won't leak. Below them is a pair of La Crosse's famous ankle-fit boots that may be ordered in either the insulated or uninsulated versions. The high socks can be high fashion or lowly over-the-knee wader socks. They won't irritate your legs like pants stuffed into damp boots will. The last pair of boots, on the lower left, are the leather-lined, French boots by Le Chameau. They are spendy, but worth it. By the way, in those last two pairs are garters (or flashes) to hold your socks up. The socks can either go under the breeks or over the lower edge. A hell of a row will result. Boot jacks (center) make life easier.

Out here in Idaho, up in St. Maries, an outfit named Peet makes a set of boot dryers that are an absolute must. They're nothing but hollow tubes with footie things, like shoe shine supports, and a warm heater in the base. Put your boots on them before you go to bed and you'll have warm, dry boots in the morning. When I travel, I carry a pair of boot dryers like little shoes with holes in them. Plug 'em into the wall, put one in each boot and again, dry boots by morning.

For luxury beyond belief, and to extend the life of your boots, own at least one pair of boot driers. These are from Peet in St. Maries, Idaho. There are also little metal foot jobs, which travel well and can be slipped into damp boots to dry them overnight.

For upland hunting you have different considerations. You may have a bit of low water, but you certainly don't want the weight of a rubber boot pulling on your leg all day. We used to say in backpacking, "Each pound on your feet is like five pounds in your pack." For upland hunting, I generally prefer a good, lightweight hunting boot, green or brown (never camo), and waterproof, as in rubber-bottomed packs from L.L. Bean, or a good Gore-Tex boot with ankle support. Russell Moccasins are also worth looking into for durable and comfortable hunting boots right out of the box.

Here comes the next problem if you follow my advice on breeches. Every cocklebur, stick tight beggar's louse, and hooky-thing hears your knee-length socks are in the field. Suddenly you look like you have a pair of brown fur socks between your boots and breeks. Interestingly enough, that stuff doesn't stick to loden wool. The answer is gaiters.

Why do American gaiter manufacturers think the only people who wear gaiters are cross-country skiers or archers? I wore gaiters even back when I wore long pants. They keep the creepy crawly biting things from crawling up my pants and sucking blood or transmitting an ugly disease of some kind, which was a real issue in the thickets and swamp lands of Minnesota. But when you go to the stores or look through catalogs, all you will find are blue, awful pastels, or camouflage. They're either waterproof so you end up as wet on the inside as if you didn't have any on in the first place, or they're Polarfleece so you end up wet *and* covered with cockleburs. Whatever happened to nice olive drab or khaki in nylon? I finally ended up buying some water-*resistant* nylon and having several sets of gaiters made in the hues I want. I've used the hell out of them ever since. One of my students reports that Mike Keetch of Grand River Outfitters is making a nice set of gaiters from leather and brown canvas.

Remember, I said you'd end up looking a little bit weird, but since you're shooting a side-by-side and using my technique, you already look different. So a little more won't hurt and you'll be a lot more comfortable with the breeks, boots, and gaiters, than you ever were in pants. Try them before you knock them.

How about gloves? I think every shooter should learn to shoot with gloves on. It's like learning to shoot sitting down. Guys who jump up in a blind not only scare hell out of the ducks, but risk getting their heads blown off if their partner doesn't jump up too. It happened in Minnesota. And what if you're hunting out of a canoe? How do you feel about jumping up in a topsy-turvy canoe or pirogue?

The school gloves are really handball gloves, which hold up and offer better padding than most shooting gloves. They're pretty beat up, but they have been in constant use for many years. Notice the padding on the middle fingers. Most students haven't learned to keep the middle fingers away from the trigger guard.

Learn to shoot sitting down. Learn to shoot with gloves on.

Once I even learned to shoot with mittens on. It's true. We'd hunted all day. Pheasants were so skittish in the late season this particular year that they jumped up a mile away, or tipped over and ran like torpedoes. It was cold too. I had a pair of mittens on, ones that you could fold back so that your fingers were exposed. They are a good idea. But on that day my setter, Blue, missed the only rooster holding tight in the entire state of Iowa. The lone pheasant exploded out of the snow behind me, screaming curses and voiding yesterday's supper. Everything went into slow motion. I turned on the off-leg, and focused on the tip of the beak momentarily. I wasn't aware of it, but the shotgun slid forward, went off, and returned to the ready position. It wasn't until Blue returned the rooster to me that I realized the mittens were still on and unfolded. How did it happen? I haven't got the foggiest idea.

Gloves protect your hands from the cold, to be sure. But they also protect them from the sun. I'm starting to get brown spots on my hands with age, which is something you never consider as a younger man. Doctors now recommend broad-brimmed hats and gloves—perhaps you'll heed this advice, as we didn't have anyone recommending this when I came up.

There's another reason to wear gloves—when you begin shooting a double-triggered shotgun, you may occasionally get hit on your middle finger by the trigger guard. After a while, you'll learn to keep an eighth-inch gap between your finger and the back of the trigger guard. But in the beginning, it is painful enough to make you lose focus for the day if this occurs. So simply go to the drugstore and you'll find boot and shoe padding. It's an adhesive-backed foam meant for bunions and ill-fitted shoes. Craft stores have lots of foam paper as well. Cut a piece that fits around the middle finger from the knuckle to the first joint. Don't cover the joint. You won't hit the joint if you keep your elbow down and your gun hand slightly under the firearm, as described earlier. With the glove on your gun hand, wrap the foam around the finger and fix it in place with tape. Now, the broad part of the middle finger is across the guard and it's protected with foam padding. As long as you have your shooting gloves with you, you'll automatically have a padded middle finger. No need for an expensive trigger guard, and this works better anyway.

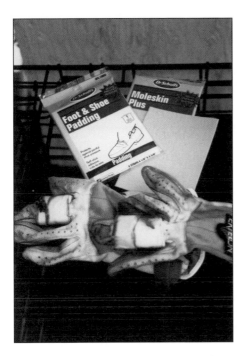

Foot padding helps protect the fingers from painful digs.

In addition, your barrels will get hot, so gloves will help with this issue as well. If your shotgun is getting too hot even for a glove, you might think about obtaining a leather hand guard. Not only does the steel-lined hand guard protect your hand from the blistering metal barrels, it also helps someone new to the technique to place his lead hand properly extended out, well on the barrels. With the hand guard in place—be sure the guard doesn't press against the forend release button—and the elbow under the shotgun, the forefinger should be just over the leading edge of the guard, pointing up between the barrels; the heel of the hand should now be against the nose of the forend.

To ensure the hand guard doesn't press against the forend release button (if there is one), the rear end of the guard should be reformed to slide over the release. My solution to this problem is to grip a 3/8-inch bolt firmly in a vice sticking out, and then, with a rubber hammer, I form the nose of the guard over the bolt to create a kind of tunnel. When the guard is slid back against the forend, there's no chance it will push the button. This can be disastrous with an ejector gun. With the firearm discharged, and the gun opened with the forend-release button depressed, the forend will be cammed down, off the gun, in an uncocked position (the ejector hammers cock on the closing stroke of the loading procedure). If you're in the field when this occurs, it can be especially embarrassing. The forend, with its ejector hammers uncocked, cannot be reinstalled on the firearm.

This is a situation with which I'm familiar, so trust me, it is something you wish to avoid.

It was a dandy, early-season dove hunt. I had a lovely one-for-one ratio going and, being a bit sure of myself, was certain every eye in the field was on me. (I was assured later that no one was aware of my plight.) Leather hand guards slide away from the forend slightly, with each shot, as the gun recoils under them. Reluctant to take my eyes off the sky, I put my trigger finger in the groove of the barrel ahead of the hand guard to pull it back. (If you grip the guard and try to pull it back, it forms a friction brake with the barrels and resists moving anywhere.) I pulled it back alright, but depressed the forend-release button. The next time I opened the shotgun, the forend fell off on the ground, which was slightly sandy. I tend to keep my shotguns well greased, especially around the knuckle. The forend hit the ground with its butt-end down, and the fine grit embedded into the grease. The ejector hammers were also uncocked. Remember the song, "Feeling Stupid"?

First things first, I took the empties out. The barrels were stuck in one side of my full-around game carrier, the stock and action body in the other. While I walked toward a fence line, one half mile away, I cleaned the forend.

From my tiny, roll-up cleaning kit, I retrieved a Kleenex and with as much care as possible, I removed all the gritty grease. I also cleaned the slot in which the extractor cam is located. With a Q-tip, I dug out as much grease as I could from the cocking-lever recesses. Then, I applied a slight film of grease from a sample foil packet supplied by a manufacturer. Small grease tubes are also available.

By the time I arrived at the fence, the forend was as clean as it could be, without full disassembly. Happily, the fence posts were relatively new cedar. I found one with a handy rock near its base. With a firm footing atop the rock, I pressed the ejector hammers against the top of the post, with the knuckle recess alongside. Gently at first, then with firmer pressure, I pushed on the faces of the hammers.

They cocked. This is a critical point. Be reckless, and the hammers in the near-cocked position can slip off the top of the post, causing your hands and the forend to shoot downward. At the very least, you might lose your balance. In the worst scenario, you fall and drop the forend into a little pile of grit at the base of the post.

Come to think of it, you might want to put the grease back on, *after* you recock the forend.

The downside of a hand guard is this: it can become a crutch. When I first started to use one, I put it on every time I shot. It was a very comfortable grip and positioned my lead hand in the exact right place. One day while hunting, I forgot the hand guard. Suddenly, a gun which I had shot daily, felt awkward and strange. I vowed I'd never use a guard again, unless for a logical purpose. There's another obvious negative. The guard slides into place. Over a period of time, it gradually removes the bluing from the barrel. Let a little dust or grit become embedded in the leather and you've formed a kind of leather sandpaper. Keep the guard dry and slide a piece of toweling through it before installing it on the barrels. Use the guard only when necessary.

The handguard, which slips forward as the shotgun recoils backward, can be pulled back into position with one finger on the forward end of the handguard, while keeping your eyes on the sky.

Now, I would like to have a word about shooting coats, sport coats, and, the more formal, shooting suit. As the name implies, our sport coat's ancestors were the shooting coat of the British Isles and the European continent. I tend to think of them as tweeds. Indeed, we've all probably used a tweed shooting coat to serve double duty to a dinner when the occasion requires a more formal attire and we have nothing else on hand. The sport coats for shooting are those with bi-swing backs. You'll see the deep gussets behind the arm and shoulder. These allow the arms to be thrust completely forward without the coat binding across the back.

Tweed sport coats and tweed shooting coats are somewhat interchangeable, as they are derived from the same idea. This one lent itself particularly well to the task. The coat has a bi-swing back, which keeps the garment from restricting the forward movement of the arms and shoulders, as long as . . .

. . . the liner of the coat is fitted with a large gusset down the center seam of the liner. The liner, like the coat, must not bind the arms and shoulders in the mount. The gusset opens up to allow this movement. And whatever you do, never use leather over the pocket of the shoulder. It may look sexy, but the firearm simply cannot slide from the armpit to the anchor point and back over a leather patch.

But check the lining. There should also be a gusset inside, in the lining. The most usual place is behind the main seam up the back. The seam is there, but when you pull on the fabric, the seam can open up to reveal the gusset behind. This double gusseted approach allows the shooter full freedom of motion, like shooting in a dress shirt. Years ago, my dad outgrew a corduroy shooting coat from Abercrombie & Fitch. It became mine. It was wonderful. The best feature was it had no lapels. When a side-by-side is slid into position against the lower jaw, it slides up the shoulder. If the lapel of your coat or shirt is too broad, the butt of the gun lifts the lapel up and slaps it against the shooter's face.

Accordingly, a dress shirt is always best for shooting our technique. The dress shirt is tailored more snugly in the armpit, so it can be worn beneath other garments such as coats and overcoats. When we coil the shotgun in practice, the fabric of a dress shirt does not interfere with the reward motion of the butt. Willis and Geiger used to make very fine heavy duty dress shirts in solids, stripes, and Tattersalls with bi-swing backs so the freedom of motion is carried from the coat to the lining to the shirt. They also had some great cotton poplins for safari. Anyway, you have to have them custom-made these days or search around, as a few merchants such as Orvis are trying to revive the style and functionality of these high-end garments, with some success at replicating the original quality.

If you are considering or have been invited to a driven shoot on the other side of the Atlantic, there are several pieces of information you may find helpful in advance. If you're on your own, be sure the times that you're to arrive to the shoot are spelled out, so you can be about fifteen minutes early. Your travel agent or host will hopefully help you to arrange for permits for your side-by-side and advise you as to the letter-of-the-law with ammunition and the like.

Find out also what the dress code is for the shoot you'll attend. Some hard-nosed Americans insist on wearing their hunting clothes from home, which most would now recognize as bad form, but you'd be surprised when I was coming up what some Americans would turn up in and think they were not out of place. When in Rome do as the Romans, and when in the U.K. be sure to dress in a manner appropriate for the shoot you're attending. You wouldn't wear blue jeans and a sweatshirt to a wedding, so be prepared to blend in with the other shooters and respect their traditions.

The dress code can run from informal to formal. Informal dress will still be breeks, but they could be your more comfortable pair and a waxed cotton coat that has been around for a while. It is in good repair, just experienced. You'll still wear a shirt and tie, perhaps with a Barbour coat or a sweater. But the degree of informality is mostly between a sweater and a shooting coat. If you're unsure, take both. You can always take off the tweed jacket, and a sweater can replace it. The Barbour comes in handy for rain over either.

But if the dress is formal, they mean a matching, three-piece-suit—breeks, vest and coat. Footwear can be stockings, complete with brogues or Wellies. Again, if you're unsure of the footing take both. If the weather turns, change. When you arrive, scope out the other guests and make any changes necessary.

The formal suit can be an expensive affair. A bespoke shooting suit can run thousands of dollars from a maker on Saville Row or Bond Street in London. There are now several dealers in the States as well, but the fit is generally more "off the peg" and not a custom look, which if you are easy to fit can save you some money.

In addition, there is the matter of style and cut. My breeks were more plus fours or fives than the plus twos which are stylish today. The "plus" refers to the overhang of the fabric at the knee. The golfers that you might recall from the photos and films of the '30s and '40s wore plus fours. So my plus fives hang well over my Wellies. My first sport coats also had leather patches. Whoa!

Now, the one thing you want to avoid like a plague is patches on the gun shoulder. I remember a sweater my wife gave me for Christmas one year. It was gorgeous, knitted in Scotland with very natty leather patches on the elbows and shoulder (just the right). Now why they'd want to put patches on the elbows is beyond me. The sweater was brand new. At any rate, I took it out to see how it shot. That's another point: Before you take any new piece of clothing, accessory, or what-have-you out on a trip, take it to the range to see how it shoots. Is it shooter friendly? Does it help your shooting, or hinder it?

The very first time I shot that sweater, it delivered me quite a surprise. As the gun slid across the sweater to the anchor point, it picked up the different surface of the patch, which slid along ahead of the butt. I ended up with most of the sweater up around my right ear.

Patches are out. Having said that, I'm reminded of a wonderful green corduroy shooting vest from France that my brother Mike gave to me. It has patches. But they're largely decorative and have the same "tooth" as the rest of the garment. A shotgun slides just fine from the armpit to the anchor point. So maybe patches will be back in again by the time this goes to press; just make sure they don't interfere with your mount.

If you are in the more formal side of shooting, you have already made the acquaintance of a tailor—hopefully a good one. Sheri is my tailor and she's a perfectionist. If she can't find a piece of thread to match the garment perfectly, she will take out a lining and unravel a piece of the fabric to get an exact match. And if the fabric has a pattern, it will match when she's through with it, even it didn't before.

So I took my new suit, as I had the sweater before it, and had it tailored. Sheri literally took the suit apart. The patches were inserted into the fabric, seams on top of the shoulders, then fitted into the seams where the sleeves meet the body. Only the lower edges, which can also catch a butt, are visible, and the inner edge is hidden by the lapels. If you look at catalogs from such makers as Holland & Holland or Purdy of London, you'll see they never have lowly patches on any new garments.

When I bought the suit, I bought trousers to match. My reasoning was that I might be able to wear it at functions fully apart from shooting experiences. Fat chance. Let me tell you, those suits are heavy and made for outdoors, not indoor events. Apparently they're constructed to deal with the worst weather the British Isles can concoct. Throw a waxed-cotton jacket over that suit and about all that will penetrate is a .45-caliber bullet.

Because a waxed-cotton coat is so waterproof, it can also become slightly damp from perspiration in a walk-up hunt where you're following a dog—what the Brits call "rough shooting." So the Brits, and the Scots as well, have come up with a new number called a "waterproof tweed." I bought mine with matching breeks.

"How about a vest or jacket to go with this?" I asked Hani Hafez of Euro Chasse in Greenwich, Connecticut.

"You won't need one," he replied, and wandered off. That's the first time in living memory that Hani, when asked about a particular garment or other, didn't have at least ten on the table in a heartbeat. But he was right. With the exception of a sweater, the waterproof tweed is all but bomb proof as well.

Now let me switch garments and tell you, if you've never owned moleskins, you've missed a great garment. Moleskin in the British Isles is about as common as denim is in this country. It's cotton, but brushed with a nap to make it feel like, well . . . moleskin—soft, fluffy, and suede-like. But, it wears like Wang leather. It is the fabric of choice for farm workers, estate and game managers, fishermen, and royalty. It is simply wonderful. I have many pairs of long trousers, in sages and dark greens, as well as one of each in breeks—all in moleskin. They aren't waterproof or anything, but like blue jeans, they fit wonderfully and feel, well…wonderful!

This chapter mustn't end without my opinion about hats. I love hats. They're vital to your technique and make a statement about who and what you are. In the eastern parts of the country, the driving cap holds sway. They're made in many designs and all kinds of fabric with the tweed definitely holding a predominant lead. There are several, well maybe six or seven, in my closet. One, of course, is of waxed cotton for those occasional unexpected rains. That number lives eternally in the poacher's pocket of my Barbour Border coat. Caps are ideal in brisk winds. If caps are being blown off, about all that's left is the military beret. But don't be out there without head cover. When a target breaks, its pieces fly quite some distance. And they're sharp. When I ran a range, everyone had to have eye, ear, and head protection. We even had loaner caps for bareheaded shooters. One fellow took the loaner and immediately removed it outside proclaiming, "I can't shoot with a hat on." He was, of course, a gun aimer. Fifteen minutes later he returned with a gash on his forehead. Wear your hat.

Hats are half the fun of upland bird hunting. The hats in the top row are Buz Fawcett Specials, made by the Priest Hat Company of New Plymouth, Idaho. Brett and Linda Brotkey make numerous versions of this hat for graduates. The hatband is the "Stutter Step" by Bud Shaul Elegant Leathers. There are three generations on the table (left to right) from the oldest, much loved and very stained, to the center hat, which is adjustable and the one you see on many of the shooters in this book, to the right, which is the latest version, a full beaver Buz Fawcett Special. It's kind of like a power hat.

My favorite hat is what has come to be called the "Buz Fawcett Special," made by the Priest Hat Company up in Eagle, Idaho. The style is as old as felt. In its broad-brimmed configuration, it's the Australian slouch or "Digger" hat often worn with the right brim snapped up so soldiers can march with their rifles at shoulder arms without hitting the brims of these hats. Of course, Australian cowboys use the same style as American cowboys. In its narrow-brimmed configuration it's sometimes called the field-trail hat. This same style was used in the 1930s, '40s, and '50s. It was, and still is, called the snapped-brim fedora. I remember in days of black and white movies, you could always tell the bad guy because he wore his hat with the brim down in back. Well, that's all changed. The only way to wear the shooting/hunting fedora is with the brim down in back so rain can run off fore and aft. In a driving rain you may want to bash the crown up so the rain won't fill the depressed crown and spill into your chipped beef-on-toast back at the chuck wagon.

There is more to the "Buz Fawcett Special Hats" than just good looks. The broad, snap-brim is pulled low over the eyes, shading the glasses and protecting the face from brush. It also keeps the chin up, for a good mount. Remember, we shoot with a high chin, so the brim must be lifted in order to see the target. The brim also shades the back of the glasses, so sun can't cause a sudden glare and a miss. This also keeps the ears and nose in the shade. Ear and nose cancer has risen sharply since the advent of the ball cap. The hat also acts as a hard hat. Target pieces coming down at you from a high-overhead can cut like a razor, which the hat shields you against.

Since cowboys here in the West have taken to wearing the always-free-with-advertising-logos-on-the-peak ball caps, facial cancer has skyrocketed. The brimmed hat, such as the shooting/hunting fedora, is also critical to our technique, especially in the beginning.

This broad-brimmed hat with a snap brim (slightly pulled down in the front), forces the shooter to keep the head up. Remember, that's the way we shoot—head up. The brim on the side keeps sun from shining on the back of the shooting glasses. A flair in your intense gaze at the leading edge of the target is sure to cause a miss. The brim in the back keeps water from running down the back of your neck. This is why the flapped deerstalker is so popular in the British Isles. The flapped deerstalker was made famous to Americans by the early Sherlock Holmes series of films. Basil Rathbone's hawk-like features were a perfect match for the cap with bill in front and behind and ear flaps tied up on the crown. Unfortunately, because of the films, most Americans refuse to wear one. Too bad. It's a great hunting companion. I'm less fond of the regular deerstalker. It gives one the appearance of a mushroom. But, they're popular in the British Isles. They probably know something about the hat that I don't.

So what should you wear? Of course that's up to you. But remember the subtitle of this book includes the lofty epithet "Master Gunner." A Master Gunner, as I see him or her, is someone who acts the part, dresses the part, and shoots the part. You represent the best in our profession of "shootist." Look the part, but make it right for you and the type of hunting you do.

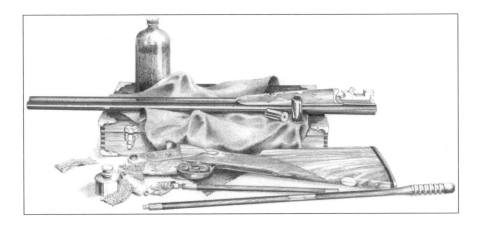

16

CARE, CLEANING, AND MAINTENANCE

Cleaning

As a group, side-by-side shotguns are not robust firearms. They'll even burn your hand in the summer, freeze it in the winter. They'll crack you across your knuckle and the stock will break at the wrist if they are improperly handled. So why do we mess with them? Because when you play by *their* rules, they allow you to hit every target, every time. And you're doing it with a firearm you can carry in the field, all day without fatigue.

I take care of my shotgun right after I care for my dogs when we come out of the field. Here, Steve Roosevelt is putting his gun away after cleaning it. He has already checked the dogs for burrs attached to their coats, in their ears, or between their toes. He checked the pad for cuts and the eyes for any foreign matter. Saline solution comes in handy for washing eyes. So do forceps for removing burrs.

But you have to play by the rules. One of the rules is, take care of your shotgun right after you care for your dog.

Your dog comes first. But, your shotgun gets cared for next. Finally, when the birds are clean and the gear stowed, it's time to sit down and enjoy your favorite beverage and savor the memory of the day, taking care of yourself.

But just what goes into a daily cleaning of the side-by-side?

First, it's just that—your shotgun must be *cleaned* every time you use it. A side-by-side is a trustworthy companion, as long as you treat it gently, keep it spotlessly clean, and keep it well-lubricated. I am going to belabor this point, so that you do not have to tax yourself with time spent cleaning. My point is that if you set up a cleaning kit and a place where you can clean it in a minute or two, it is not a big task. If it's not difficult or time consuming, you'll do it more often. If you do it more often, it will not take as long as the gun will be clean to start. It's like housework, if you put it off several months, it's a real pain—whereas, if you do a little bit daily, it's not much to wipe surfaces clean again.

Side-by-side shotguns are not particularly robust. They thrive on cleanliness, lubrication, and gentle handling. Each one is cleaned and lubricated, every time I use it. With the equipment you see here, I can clean my shotgun in one minute and ten seconds. From top center, the ingredients are: silicone spray, a rag, a snake (useful only for travel), a two-piece Tico Tool (useful in travel, but a bit more bulky), snap caps (not necessary for cleaning, but useful for practice), a one-piece Tico Tool, bore lubricant, rust preventer, a tube of the new fluoropolymer, penetrating, gun grease Tetra Gun, and a homemade disc wrench.

We've already discussed closing the shotgun gently. Be sure you never let the underlugs slam into the bites. This practice gradually wears the underlug and lumps. The underlugs can be replaced, the lumps can't. Damage the lumps of your shotgun and you're facing an expensive repair. Remember to ease the underlugs into place and then push the top lever gently, but firmly, from the gun side. There are a few shotguns which *require* slamming to close. Be sure to refer to the manufacturer's instructions. For those shotguns that need slamming to get the action closed, the manufacturer or importer will tell you so in the owner's manual. Otherwise, treat a side-by-side gently.

With those instructions in mind, I must tell you we have several 12-gauge shotguns in the school with over 200,000 to 250,000 rounds through the barrels. Obviously a little six-and-a-half-pound field gun was never intended for such use. But the fact that they *will*, attests to the sound construction of the school guns—Ugartecheas. I don't sell firearms and I have no connection with the manufacturer except for a sincere respect for a fine product offered at a reasonable price, which will probably last you a lifetime with proper care. There are certainly several other side-by-sides, which are well worth the money (but you'll pay more than you will for a Ugartechea and they won't increase your shooting percentage, so you should realize you are paying for aesthetics), of which, Armas Garbi is one of my favorites.

Keeping your shotgun clean is the other step in its longevity. Closing it gently is the other.

In the school, students and I clean our firearms after every use. This per-use cleaning is easily done. With all the equipment out and ready, cleaning takes one minute and ten seconds. We've timed it and I am not joking.

First, we use a product called a Tico Tool. It looks like a 40-inch, cylindrical polyester mop. The handle is hollow and contains an oiling bob. The people who make it, Silencio from Sparks, Nevada, claim you can clean the barrels in about thirty seconds. That's pretty close, but you'll also want to take the other forty seconds that it takes to clean the *outside* of the firearm as well.

There is no lubricant on the long part of the mop. Push the long part through the bore till it sticks out the muzzle, turn it four or five

It takes about thirty seconds to clean the bores with a Tico Tool. The main body is kind of a fleece fuzz. It is used dry. Simply push the tool through the bore from the breech end, turn it about five times and attach the lubricating bob (sprayed with Rem-Oil) to the eye on the end of the tool, which should be visible at the muzzle. Now, pull the bob back through and you've lubricated the first tube. Do the other and you're done. Understand, this has not removed the plastic fouling, but it has removed most of the ordinary fouling which would cause the barrels to rust.

times, and attach the oiling bob (after spraying it with a spray gun oil), and pull it back through the barrel. Repeat the left barrel and you're clean, *inside the barrels.*

For the outside, I use pure silicone spray. You can find it in a gun store and pay a lot, or you can go to an auto store and buy the same spray silicone, generally for a lot less. You want pure silicone, not silicone mixed with oil or any other components. You certainly do not want any oil. If the shotgun is dry, spray outside of the barrels with silicone and wipe them down with a soft cloth. If the shotgun is to be broken down and placed in a case, replace the forend on the barrels. I also spray and wipe the wooden parts of the shotgun. This makes them very water resistant in the rain. If the shotgun is wet, be sure to wipe thoroughly. Or, better yet, blow off all of the moisture with an air compressor (you can get a small portable one such as those for sporting equipment or, in a pinch, you can use a hairdryer set on the no heat setting).

If your gun has side locks, cock the shotgun first, then remove the side locks according to the manufacturer's instructions. Blow them dry, and then dump the sidelocks into a small container of mineral spirits (paint thinner) or spray with WD-40 (the "WD" stands for "water displacing"). Once the water has separated, then thoroughly dry the pieces with a soft cloth. Finally, re-lube the moving parts with a gentle coating of gun grease. I really like a high-tech gun grease such as Tetra-Lube. Blow out the inside of the shotgun as well, and dry it. Wipe all parts thoroughly. Reinstall the locks in the reverse order in which you removed them.

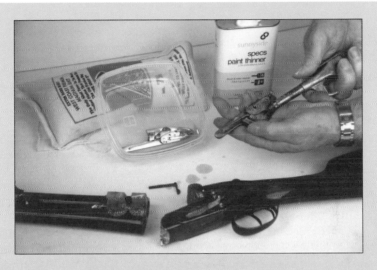

It's a simple matter to remove the sidelocks if they're hand-detachable. Simply turn the lever of the left side out, until half of the screw threads are showing on the other side. Now push on the lever. The right-hand lock will move outward a slight amount. Remove the screw and drop the right lock onto a piece of carpet or a terry-cloth towel. Now push the left-hand lock from the other side and the locks are out. If the locks aren't hand-detachable, sidelocks can still be removed with a screwdriver. You must use special thin-bit screwdrivers, available from Brownell's. Remove the two screws at the upper front of the lock, then remove the main screw using the same method as a hand-detachable. Be careful to place the right-hand screw on the right and the left on the left, so they will return to the cock which they came from. And for goodness sake, cock the locks before you take them out of the shotgun. The firing pins will jump backward past the hammers, and you won't be able to reinstall the locks until you pull the firing pins forward, or recock the lock by hand. Now, I blow the locks dry with my air compressor and drop the locks into a small container with mineral spirits. This is my Garbi. You can see the hand-detachable screw just above the action of body and the chambers.

Be sure to spray the face of the standing breech with silicone and wipe it vigorously. Those black rings around the face are powder residue. They can, in time, etch the face of the standing breech, so you want to be sure to remove them after each use. If you clean after each use, this is a very quick process.

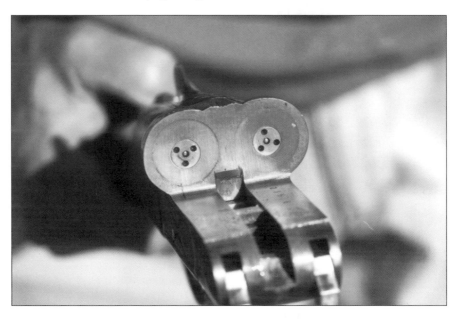

Call it habit, but I always remove the powder residue from the face of the standing breech. Someone once told me that over time the residue can etch into the metal. I simply spray it with some silicone spray and vigorously rub it clean. It becomes very clean.

Release the firing pins by placing a plastic screwdriver handle against the standing breech and, after releasing the safety, pull first the front trigger (right firing pin for a right-handed gun), then the rear (left for a right-handed gun). Hold the screwdriver handle firmly against the face when you pull the appropriate trigger. You can also use a coin instead of a screwdriver handle. We use a coin in the school, because I want the students to feel the power of a firing pin. Be ready though and hold the coin tight. The hit of a pin is strong. Hold it loosely and it will sting your hand or fly away. You'll quickly see why releasing this spring's tension is important, as well as why firing the gun without snap caps can break the firing pin, as it relies on some tension when it release in order not to crack upon its own pressure.

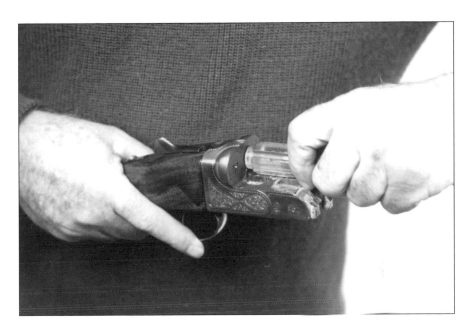

Release the firing pins by pulling first the front (right for a right-handed gun) trigger and then the rear. Catch the firing pin with a plastic handled screwdriver held tightly against the disc, or a coin.

If for some strange reason your gun has a single, inertia trigger (recoil operated), you may have to bump the butt against a padded solid object to get the other firing pin to release.

As for the wiping down, a soft cloth will do, but a silicone rag is better. Better still, spray the silicone on the gun, wood, and metal, and wipe it off with the rag which has also been gently sprayed with silicone. If you keep the same small rag in a Ziploc bag, it'll stay pre-treated. If you're considering refinishing the stock or forend or both, don't use silicone on the wood. It will penetrate the wood and nothing will stick to it, including any refinish. If refinishing any time soon, the sanded stock must first be washed with a product like lacquer thinner or acetone, before the refinishing will stick, including any type of linseed treatment.

I want to get back to the Tico Tool for a moment. A word of caution—the Tico Tool, generally speaking, won't remove plastic fouling left behind by the wad from your shells. With each shot, a little smear of plastic is deposited in your barrel. Look down the bore, just ahead of the forcing cones, and you may see smears or streaks. That's plastic. It's got to come out, but with the regular cleaning described above, this should be only necessary a few times a year, if you live in a very dry climate. Moisture can hide behind the plastic and rust the bore. Where you live, greatly determines how often you remove the plastic. I take it out of the school guns about every thousand rounds. People who are compulsive cleaners may insist on taking it out every time that the shotgun is used. Out here in the arid West, I don't think it's that critical. But if I lived in a humid state, *I'd* take it out every time I used the gun.

You don't have to get the plastic out the way I do it. I use my electric drill. Most people just scrub plastic out with a regular cleaning rod, plastic solvent, and a brass bristle brush. I've got a lot of shotguns to worry about and I don't need to do it but a few times a year for each gun. So the way I do it is to wrap a terry-cloth towel around the barrels and put them in my vise, breech end toward me, and tight enough to hold them in place. Always clean firearms from the breech, if possible (which is always possible with side-by-sides, so you won't wear the critical muzzle end down with the rod). If you must clean from the muzzle end, use a rod with a conical muzzle protector.

I lean a piece of plywood against the muzzle, so I can tell when the brass brush reaches the end of the barrel. If the brush comes out of the muzzle, the rod rotates on the chokes (bad), and the gauze pad comes off (inconvenient). So with my method, I unscrew a handle from a standard cleaning rod and chuck it in my ⅜-inch or ½-inch variable-speed, electric hand drill. This may sound like overkill, but if you have it all set up in a kit, you'll see it is very quick and easier than traditional methods, thus saving you time. Put a brass bristle brush on the business end of the rod and wrap a gauze pad around the bristles. The gauze pad should be saturated with a bore cleaner that specifies it will remove plastic.

First, put the brass brush with the saturated pad into the chambers. NEVER TURN ON THE DRILL WITH THE CLEANING ROD CHUCKED IN IT UNLESS IT IS FIRST PUSHED INTO THE CHAMBER OF THE FIREARM. If the brush-end of the rod isn't supported by the chamber, the rod will whip around and break off with some force, which can be dangerous. With the brush in the breech, start the drill. You don't want the rod to turn very fast, 300 or 400 rpm should be fine.

To remove the plastic residue in the barrels, I chuck a regular metal shotgun rod into my ½-inch drill.

Slowly work the brush down the bore, concentrating on those parts of the barrel where you spotted smears of plastic. You'll see when the brush touches the plywood and you can reverse the direction. Two or three slow passes should do it. But remember to stop the drill before you remove the brass brush to keep the rod from whipping.

Use a fresh gauze pad for each barrel. The gauze holds the cleaning solution against the surface and the brush scours it off. Admittedly, the brushes wear out faster, but there's a lot less labor involved. One of my students uses a full-length bore-cleaning brush and rod, with spray-on cleaner—probably as fast, but not as thorough of a cleaning as my power scrub, but if done a bit more regularly, it may be another fast choice for a deeper cleaning than the daily Tico Tool method. In any event, you need to remove the plastic fowling, to avoid rust. This is the whole point. Whatever your method, make it easy on yourself, or you won't do it often enough.

Well-made side-by-sides will have their screw slots north and south, aligned with the shotgun's long axis. This is a handy feature. Not only does it look good, but every time you look at the firearm, you can easily tell if a screw has come loose. You'll want to straighten out (tighten) the slot. Don't try to do this with just any screwdriver, such as those available in a hardware store. Gun screws have different slots. A screwdriver that slips even once drastically reduces the value of your shotgun. Cased guns will come with turn screws fitted to the gun's slots. Certain manufacturers have slots that are different than others. But if your gun is one of the more popular imported guns, a set of thin-bit screwdrivers can be had from Brownell's in Iowa, which will work great on these guns. They call them Thin-Bit Magna Tips. They're a good buy. Get a magnetic handle to go with them. Be very careful when entering a screw slot. Be sure to rest the firearm on a smooth, padded surface or you can use a vice with padded jaws. Select a tip that fits *exactly into the slot*. Then put on the handle and apply gentle pressure. Return the slot to its normal position. If it won't move, head for your gunsmith.

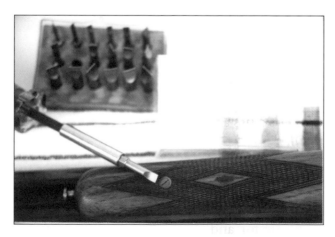

Check to make sure all visible screw heads are north-south. Again, don't attempt to use a common screwdriver unless you grind it to fit. The Magna-Tip Thin-Bit screwdriver blades are nearly a must. Brownell's has them. You may also want to get a small brass-headed hammer. Use this to gently tap striker pins and sear pins back into place if they drift sideways. This, then, is the extent of my gunsmithing.

Trust me—adjusting screw slots, tapping trigger pins back in place with a small brass hammer, and replacing firing pins is the extent of my gunsmithing. Anything more than that, I need to see a professional. Remember, my guns see a lot of use in the school. Replacing firing pins can be done in the field. I always carry a spare set in a small box called a striker box. I can lay my coat down in the field, remove the disk from the face of the standing breech and replace the firing pin, firing pin spring, if needed, and replace the disc. Be sure to cock the firearm before removing the disk. There's a lot more pressure against the firing pin and spring when the gun's uncocked. Make life easy. Cock the gun first.

Have your gunsmith show you this whole procedure before you attempt it the first time. What we are talking about here is learning how to wax your car and change your own oil, not rebuild an engine.

Maintenance

Every six months, the school guns that are in constant use go in for a thorough internal cleaning and inspection by my gunsmith. School guns get a lifetime of ordinary use in a single year, but this is something you will want to monitor based upon your use and your climate. Like car maintenance, your own guns must have an *annual* trip to a competent, side-by-side gunsmith. One of our graduates had a tough learning experience. In spite of my warnings, this guy, who's a real peach, decided to use his local gunsmith for reasons we hear all too often, such as: "Well, he's a real good friend of mine and I've used him for years and he says he works on side-by-sides all the time."

Listen to me one more time before you suffer a "learning experience" as well. Most gunsmiths are not experienced in working on side-by-sides; they see only a couple a year. Like car repairs, you get what you pay for and what you want to pay for is day-to-day experience.

So this graduate used his good friend. It was a relatively new gun, an Arietta. Several weeks later, this student called me and said, "Buz, there's something wrong with my gun. The forcing cones don't look right and the chokes look like they have a ripple in them."

"Well, you better have it sent to Tony," I said referring to my gunsmith, Tony Fanelli at Blue Arms Gunsmithing. He followed my recommendation.

Tony called me several days after the gun arrived, "Buz, this gun is butchered."

I asked him what was wrong.

He told me the forcing cones and the chokes were way off the graduate's specifications.

"But, there's a worse problem. The gun was damaged in shipment." He went on to explain that something had pierced the shipping box in one place and the box had been crushed in another.

"There's a big dent in the barrel and a divot in the stock."

"Can you fix it?"

"Sure," he replied, "I can take the dent out of the barrel and reblue the barrels, but they'll have to be back-bored and new chokes and forcing cones created to the customer's request. That 'smith caused a lot of damage to this gun. Then, of course," he continued, "we've got to fix the stock and refinish it." The shipping company, a well-known name, decided to pay the cost to replace the barrels at their expense, which may take a lot of time to obtain the replacement from the importer/manufacturer. Plus, the stock has to be refinished—which will take some time while we are waiting for the barrels to arrive.

When you ship guns or travel with guns, don't take the cheap way out! When you ship firearms, double pack them. I always start out with a hard case, like an Americase. Oh, sure, they're heavy, so you'll pay more for shipping, but what's your gun worth? I have an Americase. I also use Jon Hall cases that are made in Clay Center, Kansas. They're plastic and all but bomb proof. I have five in the school. One is over twenty-five years old. There are also some newer hard cases on the market from Italy, which are a good value.

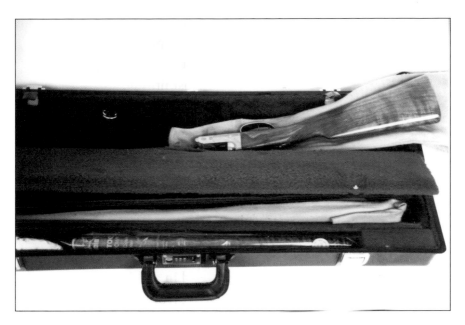

In the school, I've used Jon Hall cases for years. There's a case for each gun and its backup. Can you see the felt sock on the barrels in the foreground? At one time, I bought a bunch of felt, all different colors. My tailor, Sheri, made a dozen sets of color-coordinated gun socks. Mixing barrels with actions, can cause a mechanical disaster. There's a serial number on the barrels, action body, and forend. I still check 'em before I re-case the gun. There are thirty-some-odd shotguns in the school, all identical and looking the same. Placing them in the case has its ritual also. If the butt of the stock goes to the right of the case, then the breech goes in the same direction. Socks also keep the grease off the lining of the case.

Start with a good break-down gun case for shipping or air transport. Wrap your shotgun in paper, or put it in your gun sock and then wrap it in paper. Fill any open places with balled-up paper so the firearm can't move around. My Jon Hall cases will carry two guns with the receivers strapped into place. They're close together. If the straps should somehow loosen, you want to be sure your stocks or receivers can't come together and rub. Here's another tip—I have my gun socks made by my tailor. Pick up several yards of felt in different colors. Each gun will have its receiver in the same colored gun sock as its barrels. Although side-by-sides may look alike, be of the same model, and have sequential serial numbers, they are *not* alike. The barrels and stocks are usually not interchangeable, which also helps you keep them paired-up if you have several guns of similar make.

This is also why I always travel with two shotguns, so I always have a spare. If they are similar, they can be easily confused, which is dangerous if you combine barrels and stocks of different guns. While the color-coded barrels and receivers are a help in identifying the matching parts, your best bet is to check serial numbers. Our shotguns have the full serial number on the receiver and barrels. The forend and stock have the last three digits of the serial number.

We have another code we use when the gun is cased. "If the butt goes to the right of the gun case, then the breech end of the barrels go to the right as well. In the Jon Hall cases, the barrels are on one side of the divided case, the receivers are on the other. That's why there's less of a chance for a mix-up. To be safe, check the serial numbers before assembly.

When I travel by air, I always use a Jon Hall or Americase. The problem is that gun cases *look* like gun cases. So it's up to us to make them *NOT* look like gun cases. When you buy your travel gun case, keep the box it comes in. Carefully take it apart, turn it inside out and put it back together with any writing on the inside. Wisely, the Jon Hall company didn't put any writing on the shipping case. Now get a luggage handle with straps at your local luggage store. Put your shotguns in the case, and put the case back inside the shipping box. Now strap the handle in place at the balance point of the boxed case. Tape the straps in place with duct tape or better yet with the fiberglass-reinforced shipping tape, but keep it on hand as you will need to open it for airport inspections. Wrap some colored cloth tape around the box to reinforce it. Put your name and address on the box. You can use a felt-tipped marker, or if you move about, put your name and address on a three-by-five card and cover it with transparent shipping tape.

Here's an important tip. Get a luggage tag and put it on your gun case inside the box. If you're really paranoid, see if your ticketing agent will put a baggage tag on the gun case that's inside the box. If somehow your case and the box get separated, the case, at least, will end up at your destination. If you do this, remember to keep the gun case check-in receipt in a separate place. Some airports require that you show baggage claim tickets before they'll let you out of the baggage claim area. They'll wonder why you're leaving without one piece of luggage. It's probably not necessary to do all this, but I've traveled hundreds of trips without losing the box or its precious contents with this method. But if you're worried, the practice will give you a certain piece of mind. Even with the added security at airports, I've heard of no instances in which traveling sportsmen were hassled because they were carrying firearms. You just have to be prepared.

When you go to the ticket counter, leave one end of the cardboard box open so the ticket agent can inspect to insure your gun is broken down and empty. Sign and date the declaration and put it in the cardboard box with your case. Now, with the roll of shipping tape you always carry in your carry-on bag, tape the box closed. Get tape that's two-inches wide and you'll need to have something to cut it which is disposable, as they will not allow it on the plane these days or if there is a cutting edge to the tape, you'll need to leave it at the counter and get another one locally for your return trip.

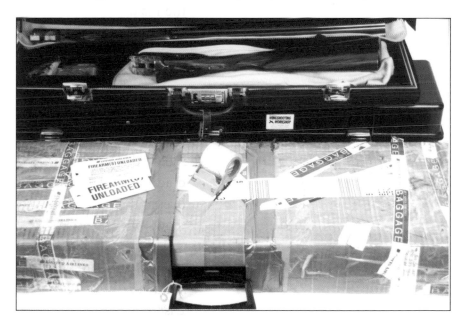

Here's a trick to use when traveling—my Americase is sitting on top of the Jon Hall case. The carton is the original box in which the Americase came.

The cardboard box with your case and guns inside will often come up on the carousel with the other luggage. If it's identified as a gun case, it will arrive on a separate platform with skis, dogs, golf clubs, etc. There are thieves out there who'll look to steal what looks like a gun case, which is where any deception in packaging can help you in insuring its safe arrival. The older and more used the outer box gets, the more wrapped with tape it becomes, the dirtier the box gets, the better.

Caring for your firearms means more than insuring they're spotlessly clean. It also means protecting them from harm or theft while traveling or at home.

Some states are trying to pass legislation that makes you liable if one of your stolen firearms is used in the commission of a crime, a real case of misdirected anger. Nevertheless, you must secure and protect your firearms from theft and fire. That means a gun safe at home. Again, don't cheap out.

Taking care of your guns also means protecting them from theft. To me, this means a fire-proof gun safe, burglar alarms, and a hardened perimeter. Sure I probably won't stop the professional, but I haven't got anything the professional wants. What you really want to stop is the snatch-and-grab kid with a drug habit.

A gun safe is a real investment. One of my graduates is selling large gun safes to building contractors. The gun safe is designed and built into the home or business. Even if the buyer isn't a gun owner, he appreciates a place to keep valuables safe from fire or theft (in a place that doesn't look like a safe). Make no mistake—a professional thief can penetrate any safe. But it takes time; the one thing a thief cannot afford. The more inconvenient you make the theft and more it is hidden from public view, the more likely the bad guy will pass up your home or business in favor of a less protected one.

Again, your best bet is to consult a professional in selecting a safe. Look for a firm that specializes in security. In my case, it's a friend who owns a lock and key establishment. A good locksmith is on the razor's edge from thinking like a thief. They know everything the crook does, but use the knowledge to help rather than hurt you. Listen to them. A good one won't sell you something you don't need. A bad one is worse than a crook. So do your homework. Ask for references. Check them. Talk to the police. Interview various locksmiths. Before long, a pattern will form that indicates your ultimate choice.

In this day and age, it is not paranoid thinking to consider a perimeter of defense for you and your valuables. The first could be good outdoor lighting. Your bushes should be well away from the home so bad guys can't hide in them. Your doors should have good locks. Not the ones you get at discount stores, but the kind a locksmith needs to install. For one high-security lock, you have to appear at the locksmith's and sign a release to get a spare key—this is a good precaution in a day and age where you can buy lock picking tools on eBay. Your name has to be on a list or you won't get the key, no matter what. Be sure anyone you might want to get an extra key, in case of your absence, is on that list as well. If you sell your home, tell the locksmith. In the case of padlocks, buy the best. I once locked the key to the house on the key ring of my Suburban inside the garage. The windows are barred, yet the locks on the doors were store-bought.

I called my locksmith to come pick the locks to get me in. He did. He picked the entry lock in seconds. The double-throw-in-door-lock took minutes to pick. All that was left was my American padlock. Forty five minutes later we were still standing in fresh air. Finally, we resorted to the obvious; we cut off the hasp with a portable cutter. The door still has the same old American padlock, but a new door lock has been installed *and* an American padlock hasp that's hardened. A professional thief can probably get in anyway, but it's going to take time. And the burglar alarm is going to be screaming its guts out and phoning everybody but the National Guard. This is not paranoid to consider in today's day of easy access to most anything.

Here's another tip, while we are on the tangent of home security. Keep a cellular phone in the bedroom. The first thing a burglar does is take the land-line phone off the hook or cut the wire to your house. It keeps you or your alarm system from calling for help. You want to be able to use the cellular phone to call for help. Don't be a hero.

Some alarm systems are on a separate line. Some alarms have their own cell phones so they can't be disconnected, but they may require power. Each installation has its own peculiar set of circumstances. Figure out yours and act accordingly.

The point is, make it difficult to get at you, your family and your firearms. If you are a gun owner in today's age, you are taking a certain risk, which you need to be prepared for any circumstance. If you have very expensive firearms, you may already have an elaborate defense system. In my case, the monetary value of the firearms doesn't warrant the interest of professionals. My guns just aren't worth it. What worries me is the kid or addict who wants to break in, snatch and grab the obvious for a few bucks, and make off with them. Still this is a huge liability, along the lines of identity theft. It's worth considering what we can do to protect against it.

17

ALL GOOD THINGS
MUST END

In Retrospect—A Note of Caution

If you do exactly as I have outlined in this book, you will become a fine shot. If you have fire in the belly, shoot your one hundred targets a week, and practice faithfully, you will become a legendary shot— better than your peers. But, if you succeed, you won't make many friends.

Unfortunately, or fortunately as you may view it, I have made a few friends and probably more enemies who are jealous of my success with the instinctive shooting method developed in the Wing-shooting Workshop. The men and women who have gone before me in this pursuit of instinctive shooting have also made quite a few friends and enemies, many of whom I may have inherited along the way. Someone wise once said, "The power of a man is gauged by the power of his enemies." I am an old man, so I don't care anymore, but it something you need to be prepared to encounter if you are going to shoot outside of the box of common convention—aiming with vertical format guns.

The rules of the game go something like this, "It's okay if you outshoot me, as long as you are playing by the same rules I am—using the same technique and using a similar kind of gun."

"But here you come along using a shotgun that others have been promised is no good." You're shooting a technique that flies in the face of their most sacred cows. Their natural reaction to this instinctive method is that you're cheating—somehow, but they don't know how. Let me tell you a story.

When we first moved to Idaho from the Midwest, I began looking for a place to shoot. It didn't take me long to discover a local gun club. As was my custom, I went to the club and introduced myself. The chill, among trap shooters, was absolute. I thought it strange. The reception was a little warmer with skeet shooters. Because of the nature of instinctive shooting, I was more interested in the skeet range, since they shot a variety of angles not usually available on trap ranges.

This went on for a few months. As usually happened, people asked how I did what I did and as I've already explained, I tried to teach them my technique, if they asked for my help.

Finally, my wife complained, "You're going to have to start charging for these impromptu shooting lessons of yours or get a regular job. We simply can't have you out at the range all the time, not making any money."

I considered starting a school or preparing for a divorce. Arrangements were made with members of the club's board of directors to use the range when the club was normally closed. My school opened for business. Things went along very well. The new school filled quickly. To me, it was just a way of continuing to do what I loved.

Although, at the time, I didn't know as much about how to teach instinctive shooting as I do now, people were still learning to shoot with the technique that I had modified from some of my forebears. Some came just to practice, while other regular club members watched. The grumbling grew, as my students grew in proficiency and number.

Finally, I got a call from one of the board's members asking if I would attend a meeting they were having the following week. When I arrived, I was surprised to see the entire membership in the club house. They first attended to a few matters of regular business. Then, a board member, whom I had never met, got up and announced I was no longer welcome to teach at their range. To say I was flabbergasted was a cruel understatement. Shaken and wondering how what I taught, which was supplementing their regular business, could have concerned them, I asked, "Well, okay, but do you mind if I ask why?" I offered that, "After all, I'm creating new members for you. I'm teaching on a part of the range you don't often use, and we're there when no one else is here."

At this time, the trap shooters were actively trying to tear down the skeet ranges. Skeet targets were flying into the trap fall-out zone and distracting the trap shooters. The skeet shooters didn't like the trap shooters. The sporting clay shooters were starting to arrive on the scene. There was, of course, the regular contingent of hunters, who came out irregularly, usually in preparation for the season. It seemed that none of these various sub-cultures interacted very well.

To answer my question, a board member in a black cowboy hat and boots stood up (I can assure you he was no cowboy) and said, "Idahoans don' want nothin' to do with that damn fool way a shootin' you do, n'r them sissy guns you shoot."

It was devastating. Here I thought I was at the meeting to get applause for helping the club, and instead I got blind-sided and thrown out. At the time, it set me back on my heels. But, of course, as is often the case, it turned out for the best. Had they not evicted me, I would never have developed my own range. It was at The Buz Fawcett Wingshooting Workshop Shooting Grounds that I was able to completely develop and perfect this new/old method, without outside influence. There was always the subconscious outside influence inserted upon me while I was at the gun club. The direct influence came from conflict with the resident skeet shooting professional who frequently criticized, "If you're gonna teach, why don't you teach 'em the *right* way?"

In trying to explain that my method wasn't wrong, it was simply different, I dug my hole even deeper. "Well, if your way is so good, how come more world champions aren't shooting it," he said and, red in the face, stalking off with his over-and-under in hand.

Not long after I found the wonderful and kind Anderson family from whom I rented land, I truly pondered the question, as I continued to read and re-read the methods of Churchill and others who were not so unlike me.

Finally, I started attending sporting clays meets around the region, as a spectator. To my surprise, the swing shooters were the ones who were scoring the 60 to 70 percent scores. Occasionally, I'd run into a shooter who, like myself, simply mounted and shot. They were almost always shooting in the 90 percent bracket. This verified, to me, that I was on the right course, especially given that we were shooting with "the additional handicap of the inferior old-school side-by-side guns." And, there was an elegance and tradition to this method, which was lacking in their own method.

It is said by anthropologists that, "Often the greatest advancements are made in isolated groups." For a while, I isolated myself. Then, it created a strength which I may not have achieved otherwise. Without outside influences, I was free to experiment. I read and re-read about all of the various methods. I studied. I shot. Some would say, I spent some years in the wilderness by myself. What worked, I kept. The faulty, I discarded. Without regard to what others said was right or was wrong.

When you begin to learn this instinctive shooting technique, it may initially feel awkward if you have shot traditional American methods before. If you have never shot before, most say that it feels as natural as throwing a stick. Either way, keep at it. After all, it is the most natural way to shoot. And, probably it is amongst the most traditional way to shoot a shotgun, if you care to take a walk through history. I don't teach this instinctive side-by-side method for historical sake, but because I believe it is the most effective and natural method to becoming a Master Gunner. If I thought that there was a more effective method, I would have stuck with that. But you will make mistakes, miss targets, and in general, you may look like you're on a fool's errand to others. Don't worry. As long as you stay safe, you will learn this method—hopefully, more easily than any other method, which is also part of my success. When other shooters see you trying to learn and, to them, doing everything wrong, they'll rush to help. When you explain that you're simply trying to learn another technique, derogatory comments may begin. If you are the first wind-surfer in the wake of surfboarders, you have to be prepared for a bit of criticism. In the after wake, you will sail away while they stand still.

Brad Z. called me to report an incident. His club owner was watching through the window as the right-handed Brad practiced left-to-right targets. He was standing on, weighting, and locking the right leg, while pivoting to his weak right side (what we call goofy foot).

"Y'r standin' on the wrong leg," the club owner announced as he rushed from the clubhouse.

Politely, and a bit nervously, Brad told the owner that he'd been to the Wingshooting Workshop and was learning to be an instinctive shooter.

"Do they teach ya to stand on the wrong leg?"

Now here's the problem. Brad had been surprised by comments that questioned the skills he'd spent a lot of time and money learning at the Workshop. The club owner had been embarrassed by an answer that responded to his good intentions by surprising *him*. Now you have two individuals, both embarrassed. But at least Brad had the power of the Wingshooting Workshop behind him. At least the owner had heard about the workshop methods.

So if you try this on your own, get to a club when there's no one there. Tell the owner *in advance* what you're about so he's not alarmed. By taking him into your confidence, he'll feel like an insider. Even if he doesn't approve of the technique, at least you're spending money with him at a down-time, and that's good. The best way may be to set up your own trap on private ground where you won't be disturbed. It's not that you have anything to be embarrassed about; it's just that you don't want to be stuck in the box of orthodox thinking. If you are outside of the US, you'll face less resistance, as the Churchill method is more common abroad for side-by-side shooters. It's not that we shoot the Churchill method, but some pieces of our method, such as a more squared stance, will not seem to be as foreign looking on the other side of the pond.

Okay, that's the bad news. The good news is uplifting.

Many graduates of the Workshop report back that the method has been life altering. If what we believe is true, that some 90 percent of the practitioner's brain is coming on line, changes are bound to happen. And happen they do. It's confusing though. The changes seem to be different for each of us.

A graduate, who is a trial lawyer, reported he's now able to shake the prosecution—and their witnesses, and he does it mentally. Our method is not just about the stance, it's about your whole view on the world.

Another told me he had an unusual reaction from his wife. "You've changed," she said. "What happened?" She demanded this *before* he had uttered a word.

One wife commented, "I thought you went to a shooting school, not a seminary."

Still another, who'd wrestled with his father's death for years, heard his father say, "You're all right now, let me go."

Literally, I could fill a chapter with stories like these. Many of them raise the hairs on the nape of my neck. No two tales are alike. The changes reported are mental as well as physical. But one commonality is obvious. This . . . what do you call it . . . method . . . way of life . . . this thing . . . this technique . . . the Predator . . . it changes people.

So how does it affect you? I don't know. But I can give you a few mileposts.

Set for yourself the highest goals. Don't be satisfied with anything less.

Take the high road.

Keep your mouth shut. People are liable to think you're crazy.

Never give up. Remember, this . . . thing . . . whatever it is, we call it, the Predator, is part of you. It's a natural part of you. When you exercise, the exercised part grows. It gets stronger.

For my own part, somewhere along the line, the original directive was, "Lead by example. Not by word."

It's not bad advice. *I've* followed it—perhaps, until now.

APPENDIX 1—THE TEST

A Seven-Point Litany

1. Correct foot position (when possible); focus on the focus-point.
2. Thumb on the safety sets the fit of the shotgun.
3. Heel of the stock in the center of the armpit.
4. Drop the offside hand away to the seam of the trousers.
5. Point the gun-shoulder at the focus-point (call it a gunfighter stance).
6. Now with the offside hand pointing along side of the barrels, and with the elbow locked, roll the hand and arm under the barrels until the pointing finger is in the groove between the barrels.
7. Keeping the stock firmly against the armpit, coil the shotgun straight back until the gun-hand fingers are touching the chest.

APPENDIX 2—GUN CLEANING IN UNDER TWO MINUTES

After the thrill of wingshooting comes the drudgery of cleaning the shotgun. For this purpose most shooters acquire a traditional cleaning kit. Cleaning kits typically include a three-section aluminum cleaning rod and brush of appropriate diameter for the caliber purchased, two tips to hold patches, cloth cleaning patches, a bottle of liquid powder solvent, and a bottle of gun oil. Some kits include a small tube of gun grease, and if it is a shotgun cleaning kit, it usually includes a bore swab. To use one of these kits, merely follow the directions that come with the cleaning kit. It takes about twenty minutes to clean a gun this way and the brush is useful a couple of times a year for deep cleaning.

Shotgun cleaning is not the onerous task it once was, as it can be reduced from twenty minutes to under two minutes. For regular cleaning, you need only make a small kit of your own consisting of: a silicone cloth kept in a small plastic baggie, silicone spray from NAPA auto parts, spray Rem-Oil from Wal-Mart, and a Tico Tool for the bore of your gun.

The Tico Tool looks like a very long, very skinny feather duster. The Tico Tool is merely pushed back and forth through the shotgun's bore, a few times, exactly like a cleaning rod. After pushing back and forth a few times, leaving the rod in the barrel, remove the accessory tip (supplied with the Tico Tool) and spray it lightly with the Rem-Oil. Hook the tip onto the end of the rod. Pull back through the gun. Now you have inside of the barrel cleaned and lightly oiled.

Spray the entire outside of the gun with the silicone spray and use the rag to wipe clean. Particularly scrub the working parts and you can use a toothbrush as needed. The rag is stored in the baggie, so as to remain wet enough to be used to wipe fingerprints off the gun after handling and replaces the traditional oily rag. Silicon cloths are excellent protection against "rust prints."

Apply a couple of drops of Tetra-gun grease to prevent excessive wear on the chopper lumps and the receiver. The firing pins should receive a very light coat as well.

APPENDIX 3—LIST OF RESOURCES

Americase
www.americase.com/store

Armas Garbi Importer to the U.S.
William Larkin Moore & Co., Importer of
Piotti, Rizzini, and Garbi shotguns, and
other fine used guns.
williamlarkinmoore.com/armas-garbi

Case Custom Gunstocks
Gunstocks, stock finishing, checkering,
carving, and repairs.
www.casecustomgunstocks.com

Euro-Chasse Clothing & Accessories
www.eurochasse.com/

The Hunter Collection
Garbi, Piotti, Gamba, Rizzini and fine used
shotguns.
www.hunterguns.com/

Jack Rowe
Importer and service representative for
AYA shotguns.
4213 Oakcrest Ave., Enid, OK 73703
580-233-5942

Kiowa Creek Kennels
Pointers, Labradors, and Bill Tarrant
endorsed gentle dog training.
Gary Ruppel, 42429 Kiowa-Bennet Rd.,
Kiowa, CO 80117
303-621-2196

Morning Mist Kennels
Pointers, retrievers, and gentle dog
training.
4491 E. Franklin Rd., Nampa, ID 83687-
8401
(208) 467-9236

Napa Auto Parts
For silicone spray.
www.napaonline.com

Quilomene San Carlos Vests
One of my students loves these hunting
belts in our big upland countries out west.
www.quilomene.com

Rem-oil
www.remington.com

Russell Moccasin Hunting Boots
www.russellmoccasin.com/

Side-by-side Specialist of Gunsmithing
Tony Fanelli, double guns, 1-208-793-3251

Tetra Gun Grease
Flouropolymer, heavy-duty, gun grease.
www.tetraguncare.com

Ugartechea Importer to the U.S.
www.doubleshotguns.com